THE WORLD OF ORDERIC VITALIS

THE WORLD OF
ORDERIC VITALIS

MARJORIE CHIBNALL

CLARENDON PRESS · OXFORD

Oxford University Press, Walton Street, Oxford OX2 6DP
Oxford New York Toronto
Delhi Bombay Calcutta Madras Karachi
Petaling Jaya Singapore Hong Kong Tokyo
Nairobi Dar es Salaam Cape Town
Melbourne Auckland
and associated companies in
Beirut Berlin Ibadan Nicosia

Oxford is a trade mark of Oxford University Press

Published in the United States
by Oxford University Press, New York

First published 1984
Reprinted 1987

British Library Cataloguing in Publication Data
Chibnall, Marjorie
The world of Orderic Vitalis.
1. Ordericus, Vitalis—Biography
2. Historians—France—Biography
I. Title
907'.2024   BR139.07
ISBN 0-19-821937-7

Printed in Great Britain by
Antony Rowe Ltd,
Chippenham

Preface

This book originated in a suggestion made to me many years ago by Dr Peter Morrison that, whilst working on the edition of Orderic's *Ecclesiastical History*, I might like to have another work in mind, on the world in which Orderic lived. Over the years its shape has changed somewhat, and in its final form it might be called the making of a medieval historian; but I hope it is not too far from the book Dr Morrison first envisaged. Orderic's outlook was moulded by the interests of the people amongst whom he lived, particularly the monks of Saint-Evroult and their patrons, the Anglo-Norman and French knights and magnates; but his intellectual horizons were widened by the books of theology, history, and hagiography that he copied and studied in the library of his monastery. Receptive, but not passive, he has left a marvellous record both of his age and of the importance and variety of historical writing in that age.

It is a pleasure to record my thanks to those who have helped me, particularly to Professor Christopher Holdsworth, who most kindly read an early draft and suggested many improvements. Discussions with my friends in Clare Hall and in the Battle Conferences have been a constant stimulus and corrective. Dr Beryl Smalley, Dr Anna Abulafia, Dr Jonathan Alexander, and Professor Philip Grierson have given me advice and information on particular topics, for which I am very grateful. My work on manuscripts at Alençon was made possible by courtesy of the custodians of the Bibliothèque de la Ville. The final stages of my work were assisted by the generous grant of a Leverhulme Emeritus Fellowship by the Leverhulme Trustees. As always, I owe a great debt to the Press for the support and unobtrusive scholarship of all who have handled the book at every stage towards publication.

Clare Hall, Cambridge   Marjorie Chibnall
December 1983

Contents

List of Maps   viii

PART I   ORDERIC'S LIFE IN ENGLAND
AND NORMANDY

   1.   Family and Boyhood in England,
1075–1085   3
   2.   Normandy, 1085–c.1142   17

PART II   THE MONASTIC WORLD

   3.   The Place of the Monasteries in
Society   45
   4.   Monastic Life   58
   5.   Monastic Studies
     (i)   Liturgy   86
     (ii)   Theology   89
     (iii)   Lives of the Saints   99
     (iv)   Monastic Histories   109

PART III   THE SECULAR WORLD

   6.   Court and Society
     (i)   The Court   117
     (ii)   Lordship and Inheritance   121
     (iii)   Marriage and Canon Law   128
     (iv)   Knighthood and the Peace
Movement   132
   7.   The World Outside
     (i)   Saracens   146
     (ii)   Jews   152
     (iii)   Heretics   161

PART IV   THE HISTORIAN AND HIS WORLD

   8.   The Record of the Past   169
   9.   Contemporary History
     (i)   The Interpretation of Evidence   181
     (ii)   Poetry and History   203
   10.   History and Society   209

Contents

Appendix   The Epilogue to Orderic's *Ecclesiastical History*   221

Genealogical Tables
   I. The family of Giroie   226
  II. The family of Grandmesnil   227
 III. The family of L'Aigle   228

Bibliography of Abbreviated Titles   229

Index   237

List of Maps

  I. Saint-Evroult and its neighbours   19

 II. Abbeys and priories linked by prayer unions with Saint-Evroult   69

III. Places visited by Orderic   222

PART I

ORDERIC'S LIFE IN
ENGLAND AND NORMANDY

1
Family and Boyhood in England,
1075–1085

Orderic Vitalis was born in 'the remote parts of the region of the Mercians' on 16 February 1075, and was baptized in the church of St Eata at Atcham, near Shrewsbury, on the following Holy Saturday.[1] The first ten years of his life were spent in the newly conquered marcher region, the country of his English mother, and spanned the period from the revolt of the earls and Waltheof's execution to the eve of the famous Christmas court at Gloucester in 1085, when plans were laid for taking the Domesday survey. So Domesday Book preserves, besides memories of Shropshire under King Edward, a record of the county as it was when his French father sent him to become a child oblate in the abbey of Saint-Evroult. This Norman monastery, set in another marcher region, was to be his home until his death more than half a century later. There he wrote the *Ecclesiastical History*, in which he recorded his gleanings of the history of the past, his impressions of the varied and changing customs and traditions of the different 'orders' and individuals among whom he lived, and all that we know of his own life. Though his outlook became increasingly Norman as he grew older he always consciously called himself 'Orderic the Englishman',[2] and the memories of his English boyhood were to be an important element in the unique and remarkable book to which he devoted his life.

The Norman Conquest came slightly more slowly to Shropshire than to southern and eastern England. After the English defeat at the battle of Hastings, Edwin, earl of

[1] *The Ecclesiastical History of Orderic Vitalis*, ed. Marjorie Chibnall (Oxford Medieval Texts, 6 vols.), 1968–80, iii. 6–9; vi. 552–3.

[2] He used the name 'Ordricus angligena'; he was christened Ordric, and latinized his name as Ordricus. The letter *e* has been introduced in more modern usage; the common pronunciation, Ordéricus, is not justified.

Mercia, made his peace with King William and was not replaced until after his rebellion and death in 1071. But whenever peace with the Welsh princes was uneasy good fighting
men were welcome in the marches, and even under King
Edward a few Norman knights had been settled in Herefordshire, around Richard's Castle.[3] William fitz Osbern, earl of
Hereford, was planted in the southern march immediately
after the conquest, and began his advance into Gwent with
such ruthless efficiency that he had left his mark clearly on
the region before he met his death in Flanders in 1071.[4]
Some of his vassals and companions may already have been
moving into southern Shropshire in Earl Edgar's lifetime,
for Ralph Mortimer, Hugh l'Asne, and Roger de Lacy were
among those settled there, holding from the king, in 1086;
and when the rebel Edric the Wild and his followers besieged
Shrewsbury in 1069 they found it defended by a Norman
garrison.[5] The establishment of Roger of Montgomery as
earl of Shrewsbury brought in the full flood of Norman
settlement after 1071, with all that this meant in castle,
borough, and church; it was a severe shock, but never
amounted to total dispossession. Some Saxon landholders
adapted themselves to the requirements of Norman fighting;
there was intermarriage with the invaders, and the remodell-
ing of the church respected most of the ancient ecclesiastical
endowments but channelled them to different recipients.
Changes left feelings of injustice and bitterness; but some at
least of the wrongs were ancient wrongs due to the insecurity
of a partly settled frontier region; and there were groups
within which reconciliation was possible, and differences of
language and custom were not an insuperable barrier. A sensi-
tive observer, even a young boy, might become aware of the
contrasts and the mixture of repression and growth, cruelty,
and reconciliation.

[3] Frank Barlow, *Edward the Confessor* (London, 1970), p. 94.

[4] For William fitz Osbern's career in the marches, see *VCH Hereford*, i. 270–4;
W. E. Wightman, 'The palatine earldom of William fitz Osbern in Gloucestershire
and Worcestershire (1066–1071)', *EHR*, lxxvii (1962), 6–17; Orderic, ii. 280–3;
and for the Norman advance into Wales, David Walker, 'The Norman settlement
in Wales', *Anglo-Norman Studies*, i (1979 for 1978), 131–43.

[5] Orderic, ii. 228–9. A detailed analysis and discussion of the Domesday
evidence for Shropshire is given by James Tait, 'Introduction to the Shropshire
Domesday', *VCH Shropshire*, i. 279–308.

The family of Roger of Montgomery had risen to promi-
nence in Normandy during the second quarter of the eleventh
century. Roger II proved his loyalty and military skills during
the early part of Duke William's reign, particularly in the
campaigns against Domfront and Alençon in 1048-9. As
vicomte of the Hiémois he was responsible for the defence of
one of the most vulnerable stretches of frontier in southern
Normandy, bordering on Maine; and the duke rewarded his
service and greatly strengthened his hand in the region by
approving or arranging his marriage with Mabel of Bellême,
heir of a great cross-frontier lordship adjoining the Hiémois.
When the Normans invaded England in September 1066,
Roger was left behind to help the duchess Matilda in the
task of governing Normandy; but if he did not receive the
first spoils of Hastings he was subsequently rewarded, first
with Arundel in Sussex, and then with Shropshire and the
licence to carry the Norman power into central Wales.[6]
Shrewsbury, standing on a hill almost encircled by the river
Severn, was a natural fortress, valued by the Mercian earls,
and here Roger built his castle to command the only ways
into the city not protected by the river. It was to be the
secure base from which he drove his conquest, stage by
stage, castle by castle, through central Wales as far as the
sea. His authority in Shropshire was almost vice-regal; he had
the rare privilege of appointing his own sheriff and gave the
office to his vassal, Warin the Bald, 'small in body but great
in spirit', the chosen husband of his niece Amieria.[7] Apart
from a small area in the south already settled by the Normans
he held virtually the whole of the county in chief of the
king; and before 1086 he had granted fiefs to his leading
vassals, William Pantulf, Corbet and his sons, Picot, and
others. By the time of the Domesday survey thirty-four
knights held lands in the county.

The military element revealed by the survey was prepon-
derantly Norman, although one or two anonymous knights
may have been English, and a few English landholders like

---

[6] For his career and family, see John Le Patourel, *The Norman Empire*
(Oxford, 1976), pp. 17, 63-4; L. Musset, 'L'aristocratie normande', *La noblesse
au moyen âge*, ed. P. Contamine (Paris, 1976), pp. 78-9; J. F. A. Mason, 'Roger
de Montgomery and his sons (1067-1102)', *TRHS*, 5th ser., xiii (1963), 1-28.

[7] Orderic, ii. 262-3.

Toret of Wroxeter, Alward son of Edmund, and Siward lord of Frodesley, weathered the storm as subtenants holding under Norman lords. Their experience of border clashes with the Welsh may have helped them to survive and preserve something of their status. In the town of Shrewsbury itself there was a rapid influx of Frenchmen, as well as destruction of houses on the site where the castle was built; whereas in 1066 there had been 252 burgesses holding messuages in the city, by 1086 the English burgesses complained that 51 dwellings had been destroyed in the castle building, 50 were 'waste' and not paying geld, 39 had been granted to the new abbey of St Peter, and 43 were occupied by French-born burgesses. If the burgesses of Battle may be taken as characteristic, the French immigrants were probably craftsmen or administrative servants attached to the abbey or the Norman households,[8] though the community of Battle grew by new settlement, and at Shrewsbury the French-born burgesses replaced Englishmen. Here, as elsewhere, the mint probably remained in skilled English hands;[9] but there is no chronicle record of the early town, as there is for Battle, and the Domesday survey stands alone for this period.

The third element in early Norman settlement was the church, and here the change was great. Shrewsbury itself was well provided with wealthy churches served by groups of secular clerks; the most important—St Chad's, the royal chapel of St Mary's, and St Alkmund's—all dated from at least the tenth century. There were a number of large minster churches elsewhere in the county, particularly at the hundredal centres, as well as smaller churches with a single priest. But many of the prebends and portions were in the hands of wealthy non-residents, of whom the priest Spirtes had been the most notorious until his disgrace at the end of King Edward's reign, and many were handed on from father to son. There was not a single regular monastery in the county.[10]

---

[8] Eleanor Searle, *Lordship and Community; Battle Abbey and its Banlieu 1066–1538* (Toronto, 1974), pp. 69–88; Cecily Clark, 'Battle *c*.1110; an anthroponymist looks at an Anglo-Norman new town', *Anglo-Norman Studies*, ii (1980 for 1979), 21–41.

[9] Michael Dolley, *The Norman Conquest and the English Coinage* (London, 1966), gives a brief introduction to the history of the mints.

[10] For the Churches of Shropshire see *VCH Shropshire*, ii. 18–83, 114–23.

The Normans, coming from a province where Benedictine monasticism was in full flood, and attempts to reform the clergy by forbidding simony and clerical marriage were just beginning to have some effect, found much to criticize and change. By 1086 the pattern in Shrewsbury, with Norman castle, burgesses, and abbey, was one that was to become familiar during the Norman settlement in south Wales. But, as in the Welsh towns, the Normans lived alongside the earlier inhabitants with their different customs, language, and ancient culture; and the more perceptive recognized the value of both. Chroniclers might condemn the English church in broad general terms; Orderic wrote long afterwards that there was no strict monastic discipline and 'monks differed very little from seculars in their way of life; they wore no habit and took no vows, they indulged in feasting and held private property',[11] but his boyhood memories included clerks who were learned and pious. William of Malmesbury, after castigating the ignorance and loose living of the English clergy in general, added that there were exceptions, and he knew many clerks who had led a simple and holy life.[12] The Normans on their arrival initiated church reform as they understood it in their own duchy. Yet the different pace of ecclesiastical reform in the two countries produced some anomalies, and perhaps also caused crises of conscience for a few Norman clerks who travelled to and fro with their masters.

Among the members of the household that Roger of Montgomery brought with him to Shropshire were three learned clerks, Godebold, Herbert the Grammarian, and Odelerius of Orleans, who served in his chapel and helped with his administration.[13] Like his other chaplains, they were rewarded for their service out of the spoils of the English church. Godebold, the most acquisitive, absorbed almost all the prebends of the wealthy church of St Alkmund; Herbert appears with the title of archdeacon of

[11] Orderic, ii. 246-9.   [12] Malmesbury, *GR*, ii. 305.
[13] J. F. A. Mason, 'The officers and clerks of the Norman earls of Shropshire', *Transactions of the Shropshire Archaeological Society*, lvi (1960), 252-3; M. Chibnall, 'Ecclesiastical patronage and the growth of feudal estates', *Annales de Normandie*, viii (1958), 112-13; R. W. Eyton, *Antiquities of Shropshire* (London, 1854-60), i. 110; ix. 29-30.

Shropshire in the diocese of Chester. Most important to the
historian is Odelerius, for he was the father of Orderic
Vitalis. He received the little church of St Peter in the suburb
of Shrewsbury, the church of Wrockwardine, and land in
Charlton, probably as part of Wrockwardine. Odelerius of
Orleans, son of Constantius, was at that time a man in his
early forties, well-educated, probably in the schools of
France. His name indicates that he was either born or educated at Orleans. He may have been French by birth; but in
the mid-eleventh century, when the Norman schools had not
yet grown in learning and reputation, most Normans went
to schools in France for anything more than the rudiments
of learning.[14] He was still unmarried, either for lack of means
or because the law in Normandy was slowly turning against
the marriage of clerks. Now, in England, he found himself
in possession of a secure income, in a country where the
marriage of priests and other clerks was still lawful. Like his
fellow clerk, Godebold, he took a wife from among the
English; and he became the father of three sons.

The practice of clerical marriage, generally permitted if
not encouraged in western Europe up to the middle of the
eleventh century, was only very slowly being broken down.[15]
Yet clerical celibacy was a central demand in the programme
of reformers at Rome, and gradually, province by province,
canons restricting the marriage of secular priests and clerks
were promulgated in local synods. After Duke William put
the whole weight of his influence on the side of church
reform, by appointing the monk Maurilius as archbishop of
Rouen in 1054, reforming canons were regularly promulgated in the synods of the province.[16] Among them was the
prohibition of the marriage of priests and the hereditary
succession of sons to their fathers' churches, first issued in
1055. In 1064 a council at Lisieux commanded priests who
had married since the first prohibition to put aside their

[14] I have used the term France as many eleventh-century writers did, to
describe the domains of the king of France, in contrast to Normandy.
[15] C. N. L. Brooke, 'Gregorian reform in action: Clerical marriage in England,
1050–1200', *Cambridge Historical Journal*, xii (1956), 1–21.
[16] Raymonde Foreville, 'The synod of the province of Rouen in the eleventh
and twelfth centuries', *Church and Government in the Middle Ages*, ed. Christopher
Brooke and others (Cambridge, 1976), 19–39.

wives, and urged those in minor orders to do the same. The clergy did not take kindly to the prohibition, and when in 1072 Archbishop John of Rouen attempted to impose it on all above the rank of subdeacon, and commanded the unlawfully married clergy to renounce their wives, he was stoned out of the synod.[17] The difficulties encountered by reformers in Normandy were a warning to the practical Lanfranc, after he became archbishop of Canterbury in 1070, to move slowly if he hoped to succeed in England. The council of Winchester in 1076, under his guidance, decreed that no canon should have a wife, but that priests who lived in villages and townships and already had wives were not required to send them away. Those who were not married were to remain celibate, and bishops were not to ordain priests or deacons unless these had first declared that they were unmarried.[18] By this date Odelerius already had a wife, so his marriage was just legal in England, and he was not required to renounce his benefices. Yet he was a man who claimed to have been a close counsellor of monks, and knew and admired them; both his own actions and the reticence of his eldest son Orderic suggest that he was never easy in his conscience about the step he had taken.

This is the most likely explanation of Orderic's negative attitude to his mother. He could not have called himself *angligena* if she had not been English; yet he says nothing whatever about her, whereas his father commanded his respect and admiration.[19] When, later, he wrote of how his father had renounced him when he was ten years old and sent him away to a Norman monastery he twice used the rare word *abdicare*. It was a word he scarcely used elsewhere, though he chose it to describe the renunciation of the world by St Évroul, the patron saint of his Norman abbey;[20] it is very rare in the Vulgate, and is not used for a postulant's turning from the world in the Rule of St Benedict. But it

[17] Orderic, ii. 200–1.

[18] *Councils and Synods*, i. 616–20.

[19] Orderic, iii. 142–51, gives an account of the influence of his father in persuading Roger of Montgomery to found Shrewsbury Abbey, and records how 'when he was turned sixty he took up the yoke of the Lord and bore it to the end of his days'.

[20] Orderic, iii. 268, 'Ad postremum omnibus nudatus sibi se abdicavit . . .'

occurs several times in the works of Bede, which Orderic knew and loved; in particular, Bede used it to tell how King Eadbald renounced his unlawful wife after his conversion to Christianity.[21] Odelerius's act of renunciation may have been similarly inspired; the language of his son suggests that he at least linked the two.

We can do no more than speculate about Orderic's English kindred. It could be argued that his mother may have been the daughter of a priest whose benefices were conferred on her husband; but the only shadow of confirmation for such a theory is Orderic's reference to the abbey of St Peter at Shrewsbury as being founded in his father's *fundus*— a word often used by him in the sense of patrimony. Norman lords frequently married English heiresses and so strengthened their title in English eyes to the lands they occupied. But church lands were already beginning to be differently regarded by Norman churchmen and some magnates, and Roger of Montgomery need not have felt any obligation to respect the hereditary rights enjoyed by English priests in their churches. The identity of Orderic's mother must, therefore, remain an open question. All that is certain is that the first ten years of Orderic's life were spent among English people rather than Normans, and that until he went to Normandy he was linguistically more at home in English and Latin than in French.

He mentions two Saxon priests who were important in his childhood: Ordric, the priest of St Eata's church at Atcham, who baptized him with his own name and stood godfather to him; and Siward, the learned and highly-born priest who served his father's church of St Peter in Shrewsbury, to whom young Orderic was sent at the age of five to learn his letters.[22] Either of these may have been related to his mother, but there is no strong reason for assuming this. Possibly the first few years of his life were spent in or near Charlton, where his father held land; though not in the parish of Atcham it lies within two miles of the little Saxon church on the banks of the broad river Severn where he was baptized.

---

[21] Bede, *Ecclesiastical History*, p. 154.
[22] Orderic, iii. 6–9; vi. 550–7 (below, Appendix), are the passages that describe Orderic's life.

From the time he was five Shrewsbury was his home. Young boys at this time often lived under the close supervision of their teachers; the first master of Guibert of Nogent came to live in the household of Guibert's mother to keep close watch over the education of his charge.[23] So Orderic may have shared the same roof as Siward, the learned priest who taught him; and whether it was the house by St Peter's that belonged to his father or another he does not divulge. Certainly he assisted Siward with the performance of divine service in the church, perhaps acting as an acolyte. He had ample opportunity to learn from him the legends of his race and the traditions of the noble families from which he was sprung. These contacts with some of the best and most learned of the English in his native county helped to foster his lifelong sympathy for the losses they had suffered through the invasion of their land by his father's people.

When he first landed in Normandy he felt as bewildered as Joseph in Egypt, and could not understand the language spoken around him. His father must have known some English or have conversed with his son in Latin. Orderic's Latin as he wrote it later was fluent and colloquial as well as learned; it may have been a spoken language for him as well as his first written language. The few English words and phrases he later introduced into his *History* are from the spoken dialect, not the formal, written Anglo-Saxon language.[24] Evidently he had little or no direct contact with either the Norman garrison at the castle or the French speaking burgesses in the town. But he was alert and observant, and even late in life his writing took some colour from his childhood memories. Some recollections became idealized; physical beauty (*pulchritudo*) was a characteristic he liked to attribute to the highly-born of all races, but it was often emphasized when he wrote of the English. Harold was *pulcherrimus*; Edwin and Morcar were endowed with great beauty; Edwin outshone thousands by his physical beauty, and in one place the whole race is described as most

[23] Guibert of Nogent, *De vita sua*, ed. E.-R. Labande (Paris, 1981), i. 4, 5 (pp. 26–37); trans. John F. Benton, *Self and Society in Medieval France* (New York/Evanston, 1970), pp. 44–9.

[24] The languages used in England after the Norman Conquest are discussed by M. T. Clanchy, *From Memory to Written Record* (London, 1979), pp. 151–74.

beautiful.[25] In this there was perhaps an elegaic element; Norman men were characterized by the same superlative only when, like Richard of Chester who went down with the *White Ship*, they died tragically and young. His pity extended to the Welsh, sometimes brutally enslaved by their Norman conquerors. The slave trade was slow to die out in the region; in 1086 there were many more slaves in Shropshire than in other border counties. Orderic may have seen captives recently enslaved, and had them in mind when he wrote a passionate denunciation of Robert of Rhuddlan's conduct in Wales:

> For fifteen years he harried the Welsh mercilessly; he invaded the lands of men who, when they still enjoyed their original liberty, had owed nothing to the Normans, pursued them through woods and marshes and over steep mountains, and found different ways of enforcing their submission. Some he slaughtered mercilessly on the spot like cattle; others he kept for years in fetters, or forced into a harsh and unlawful slavery. It is not right that Christians should so oppress their brothers, who have been reborn in the faith of Christ by holy baptism.[26]

But if he sometimes idealized the lost freedom and status of some, he remembered too the perils and drawbacks of the province. The dangers of travel even before the conquest are indicated by the obligations of the burgesses of Shrewsbury in King Edward's day to provide guard and escort for the king if he visited the town. Twelve of the leading men were to serve him as guards whenever he slept in the town; if he went hunting the most prominent burgesses who had horses were to accompany him to the county boundary.[27] Radmen, substantial tenants who owed armed escort service, were numerous in Shropshire. The woods too must even then have provided a hiding place for outlaws who had broken the king's peace; after the conquest their numbers were swollen by the dispossessed who gathered in bands and prepared for rebellion. Legends, local at first, grew up around them. Orderic remembered Edric the Wild as an almost legendary figure, whereas he knew nothing of Hereward in the distant Fens. Edric was one of the *silvatici,* the outlaws of the woods who, like the rebels of the north, lived in tents or huts and

---

[25] Orderic, ii. 170, 202, 216, 258; iv. 94.   [26] Orderic, iv. 138–9.
[27] *VCH Shropshire*, i. 309–10.

shunned the soft life of houses.[28] There may have been an echo of the tales about them in his comments, long afterwards, on the Welsh who took to the dense woods like wolves to escape from Flemish settlers, and lived as public enemies, slaying, plundering, and burning.[29] He recalled with a shudder the sinister 'evil road' across Wenlock Edge, which Henry I opened up and made safer during his campaigns in 1102. The English gave it the name of *huvel hegen*; for a whole mile it 'passed through a deep cutting strewn with huge boulders; it was so narrow that two horsemen could barely ride abreast, and was overshadowed on both sides by a thick wood, in which archers used to lie hidden and suddenly send javelins or arrows whistling to take their toll of passers-by'.[30] Perhaps Orderic himself had travelled along it; this was the road he would have taken if his first night's lodging had been in the priory of Wenlock when he set out on the long journey to Normandy.

Henry I, however, widened the road and made it safer for travellers. Orderic's mature judgement made him aware that the Norman conquest had brought reform and reconstruction in time as well as injustice and dispossession. When he wrote in glowing terms of King Henry's fostering of monasteries he may well have had Shropshire in mind: 'In his days every religious order grew and flourished to the glory of the Creator. Monks and clerks bear witness to this, for they cut down dense woods and now give praise in high-roofed monasteries and spiritual palaces built there, chanting to God with peace of mind in the places where formerly robber outlaws used to lurk to perform evil deeds.'[31] The last sentence would certainly not be out of place in a history of the abbey of Haughmond, founded on the wooded slopes of a hill just outside Shrewsbury. If Orderic returned to the county of his birth when, more than thirty years after his departure for Normandy, he revisited England and spent some time in Worcester priory, he would have found it a region more welcoming to monks and safer for travellers.

---

[28] Orderic, ii. 228, 216; for the growth of legends, see Maurice Keen, *The Outlaws of Medieval England* (London, 1961), pp. 28–30.
[29] Orderic, vi. 442–3.   [30] Orderic, vi. 28–9.
[31] Orderic, v. 294–7.

In 1085 it was certainly no place for a child oblate; and indeed, three years earlier when Orderic was seven years old, his father had arranged for his reception in the Norman abbey of Saint-Evroult.[32] The choice was not made at random, though at first sight it may seem surprising. Normans taking part in the English adventure retained a strong attachment to their homeland, and the reputation of the abbey of Saint-Evroult was very high among families settled in the Welsh marches. It is true that the attitude of the house of Montgomery-Bellême had been mixed; a bitter feud arising from incompatible feudal loyalties in a troubled region on the frontiers of Normandy and Maine existed between the sons of Giroie, part founders of the abbey, and the lords of Bellême. Earl Roger's first wife, Mabel of Bellême, had been accused of hostility in the abbey's early days, when resources were scanty, for she frequently descended on the monks with a large retinue of knights and demanded hospitality. But the monks were not alone in their troubles; and her recklessness in riding roughshod over the rights of others stirred up hatred among neighbouring lords and finally led to her murder at Bures-sur-Dive one December night in 1077. Earl Roger then took as his second wife Adelais of Le Puiset, a gentle and pious woman, who encouraged her husband's benefactions. In time he made reparation to Saint-Evroult by granting property and revenues in Normandy and England. The abbey's renown in his household did not, however, depend solely on his favour. One of his vassals, William Pantulf, who came from Noron near Falaise and had received lands in Shropshire and Staffordshire, had regarded the house as his family monastery long before Mabel's death. In 1073 he had given churches and lands at Noron to found a small cell, dependent on the abbey.[33] A few years later he found fresh cause for gratitude, when he came under suspicion of having plotted Mabel's murder, even though he had been in Apulia at the time. He

[32] For the events in this paragraph see Orderic, i. 6–7; ii. 54–7; iii. 134–7, 160–3.

[33] Dependent priories like Noron were given their own endowments and required to maintain full liturgical services in the priory church; but monks were sent out and recalled by the abbot of the mother church, and remained subject to his authority.

fled with his family to Saint-Evroult and took refuge under the protection of Abbot Mainer, until he could persuade his enemies to allow him to clear himself by undergoing the ordeal of hot iron. His dramatic story must have resounded in Earl Roger's Shropshire household, just as it did at Saint-Evroult when Orderic recorded it long afterwards.

In the northern marcher county of Cheshire, at about the same time, a remarkable conversion carried off five young knights from the household of Earl Hugh of Chester to Saint-Evroult. Ruthlessness and insensitivity were qualities necessary for beating down the resolute defence of the princes of North Wales, and Earl Hugh had them in abundance. His huge household had the character of an army, only half held in control. He himself was a great mountain of a man, given over to feasting, hunting, and sexual lust; always to the forefront in battle, and lavish to the point of prodigality. Yet like many rough and worldly men, he liked to have men of religion at hand, and even counted St Anselm among his friends. Serving in Hugh's chapel was a remarkable clerk, Gerold of Avranches, who undertook the formidable task of winning some of the young knights in this wild household to a better way of life. He told them stories of Christian knights such as St George, St Demetrius, St Maurice, and St William of Gellone, who had turned from secular warfare to fight spiritual battles, and inspired five of them to abandon the world. Arnold of Tilleul, Roger of Warenne, Drogo of Neufmarché, and two others travelled to Saint-Evroult, which had been founded by Arnold's kindred, and were received as postulants by Abbot Mainer.[34]

Even if Odelerius did not meet them when they passed through Shropshire, he certainly did so when he visited Saint-Evroult, probably in the course of a pilgrimage to Rome in 1082. The abbey was then at the height of its fame as a centre of religion and learning. Odelerius may have seen two other late converts to monastic life, who had entered the abbey under the patronage of great Norman lords. They were Goisbert, the friend and former physician of Ralph of Tosny, and the learned scholar, later to become the revered master

[34] Orderic, ii. 260-3; iii. 118-21, 216-17, 226-31.

of young Orderic, John of Rheims.[35] It was a community
that stood in sharp contrast to everything in Shropshire.

Earl Roger was just beginning to make some substantial
restoration to the local church by establishing a Cluniac
priory at Wenlock, and endowing it with lands formerly
owned by a decayed nunnery and secular minster.[36] After
his return from Rome, Odelerius used all his powers of
persuasion to induce his lord to embark on a much greater
undertaking: the establishment of a new, independent abbey
at Shrewsbury, where the wooden church of St Peter stood.
That enterprise, initiated in 1083, was sufficiently far
advanced for monks from Sées, a Norman abbey founded
by Roger of Montgomery and Mabel, to be installed by 1087;
later it received both Odelerius himself, as an adult convert
after Earl Roger's death, and his second son, Benedict, as
an oblate.[37] When Odelerius sent Orderic to Normandy he
told him that by sacrificing all family ties he could serve
God more fully, and taste the joys of Paradise after his death.
The sacrifice was a hard one for father and son; both wept
bitterly on parting. But by choosing Saint-Evroult for his
talented son rather than waiting a few years to place him in
a struggling, new community in Shrewsbury, he ensured that
if—in the metaphor of Orderic's favourite parable—he
was to labour in the Lord's vineyard from the first hour of
childhood to the evening of old age to earn his eternal
reward, the vineyard should at least be in fertile ground.

---

[35] Orderic, iii. 124–7, 150–1, 164–5.
[36] *VCH Shropshire*, ii. 38–40.
[37] Orderic, i. 3–4; below, Appendix.

2
Normandy, 1085–*c*.1142

The abbey of Saint-Evroult was founded just before 1050
in a turbulent region on the southern frontier of Normandy.
When Orderic was received there in 1085 the monastic community was large and thriving, and the neighbourhood was
enjoying a rare interval of comparative peace. During the
years of his rule as abbot from 1066 to 1089, Mainer
admitted ninety new monks, including some who were
wealthy and influential and others who were scholars of
standing. A new abbey church, barely begun under his predecessors, was completed by him; and the essential monastic
offices—cloister, chapter-house, dormitory, refectory,
kitchen, and store rooms—were rebuilt during his abbacy.[1]
This was a major undertaking, for the nearest stone quarries
at Le Merlerault were six miles away, and it was difficult to
procure sufficient horses, oxen, and wagons to haul the ashlar
blocks to the site of the abbey. Gifts of cash from some of
the greatest in the land made it possible to meet the cost of
transport and building. Lanfranc gave £44 sterling and two
marks of gold in 1077,[2] and later sent £40 sterling from Kent
by the hand of the monk Roger of Le Sap, whom he knew
and loved as a man learned in letters. This money was used
to build the tower of the church and the dormitory.
Queen Matilda, shortly before her death in 1083, gave 100
Rouen livres for the building of a stone refectory, so that
the monks could all take their meals together. William of
Rots, cantor, dean, and archdeacon of Bayeux, gave £40
sterling.[3] Many of the new monks made substantial gifts when
they renounced the world and received the monastic habit.

---

[1] Mainer's achievements are described in Orderic, ii. 146–53.

[2] At this date the value of a mark of gold, which was based on weight, would
have been approximately £6. 10*s*. sterling.

[3] Later he became abbot of Fécamp; the respect and affection he inspired
appears in the tributes written by Hildebert of Lavardin, Baudry of Bourgueil,
and Athelelm of Fly, among many others, after his death (Orderic, vi. 138–41).

Since the abbey was completely rebuilt in the thirteenth
century, and the site has never been properly excavated, the
size of Mainer's new buildings can only be conjectured.[4]
Probably little, if any, smaller than the later church and
offices, they must have been on a scale to house more than
fifty monks, even when the abbot had sent out communities
to colonize dependent conventual priories at Parnes, Auffay,
Maule, and Noron, in addition to the already existing priory
at Neufmarché.[5] Fifty years before there had been nothing in
this northern fringe of the forest of Ouche except two
dilapidated churches, St Peter's and Notre-Dame-du-Bois, one
on each side of the marshy valley of the Charentonne, to
bear witness to the existence of an earlier Merovingian
monastery. The sarcophagi of noble persons from a vanished
age could be seen in the church of Notre-Dame. St Peter's
was to become the site of a new abbey. A spring, popularly
reputed to have healing powers, had at one time drawn
pilgrims; the cult died out after the invasions and civil wars of
the tenth century, when the valley became depopulated and
the place was given over to herdsmen with their beasts. The
legend of the discovery of a ruined church by a herdsman in
search of his lost bull testifies to the way scrub and woodland
had taken over the site of the former monastery.[6] But with
the foundation of a Norman abbey[7] new settlements began.
A small rural township sprang up at the gate of the abbey;
hamlets were multiplied; clearings were extended. With its
spacious church and splendid ritual, its fine library and thriving monastic school, the abbey became a centre of hospitality
and learning as well as spiritual life. There were serious difficulties in the early years, which Orderic was later to describe;
but nothing in his long life suggests the kind of internal

[4] Attempts at reconstruction have been made by René Gobillot and Jacques
Thirion (*Orderic Vital et l'abbaye de Saint-Evroul* (Société historique et archéologique de l'Orne, Alençon, 1912), pp. 109–14 and plates XI, XII; *Saint-Evroult
et l'abbaye d'Ouche* (Art de Basse Normandie, no. 41), pp. 37–59).

[5] Estimates can be only approximate; we do not know the death rate to off-
set the ninety new professions under Mainer, nor the exact size of the community
when he became abbot. There are no early figures for the small priories; at Auffay
the monks replaced six canons, and except at Noron, which was small, the scale
of the endowment would have supported communities of from six to twelve.

[6] Orderic, i. 12–13; iii. 276–7, 286–7, 328–35.

[7] See below, pp. 20–1.

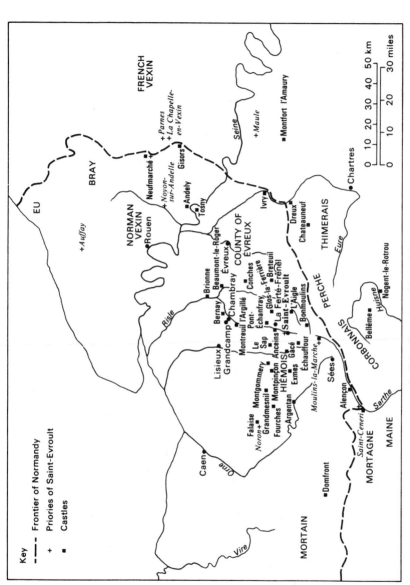

I. Saint-Evroult and its neighbours

dissension or disorder that disturbed some monasteries, even the greatest such as Cluny. There were hardships due to years of famine and war; the main problem came from its position in a troubled frontier zone.

Indeed the abbey, as Orderic wrote on more than one occasion, was situated 'in barren country, surrounded by the most villainous neighbours'.[8] External threats multiplied because the main stems of the two families who had combined to found the monastery failed to keep a firm grip on the region. William Giroie, whose influence had helped to determine the actual site, was one of the seven sons of a Breton lord. This man, named Giroie, had won his inheritance through service under the lords of Bellême, with the consent of Richard II, duke of Normandy. William, the eldest of Giroie's sons to survive the civil wars of Duke William's minority, became the vassal of both William Talvas of Bellême and a lord from Maine, Geoffrey of Mayenne. In his precarious allegiance to two lords engaged in a struggle for power in the valley of the Sarthe, William Giroie served Geoffrey better than he served Talvas; and the latter took savage vengeance by blinding and mutilating him. He turned to religion, entered the abbey of Bec-Hellouin, and made a substantial gift to that house out of his patrimony in the forest of Ouche. Lanfranc and two or three other monks of Bec were sent to the old church of St Peter, and were already trying to restore religious life there when William Giroie decided to found a new, independent abbey rather than a small priory.[9] His motives may have been partly secular and prudent. In the period 1047 to 1050 Duke William was engaged in a struggle to establish his authority along the southern frontiers of Normandy, and was ready to take a new monastic foundation, endowed by Norman lords, under his protection. The Giroie family too stood to gain since the foundation of a great abbey might help to attract settlers and consolidate their power in the region.[10] So the abbey of Bec was compensated with land elsewhere and the monks were sent back to Bec.

[8] Orderic, ii. 148; iii. 118. For the situation of the abbey see Map I.

[9] Orderic, ii. 14–16, 22–39, 58–67, 78–83, 122–5. See also M. Chibnall, *Annales de Normandie*, viii (1958), 103–8. For the families of Giroie and Grandmesnil see below, Tables I and II, pp. 226–7.

[10] At this time, too, the rebel Guy of Brionne was holding out in Brionne and

William Giroie enlisted the help of his sister's sons, Hugh
and Robert of Grandmesnil, in his ambitious enterprise.
The outcome was the formal foundation of Saint-Evroult
in 1050, and its endowment by the families of Giroie and
Grandmesnil. Both were embroiled in frontier feuds, and
both were willing, if the ambitions of the duke of Normandy
seemed to conflict with their own, to put their own interests
first. In particular they wished to establish a hereditary right
to the castles they held, whereas the duke treated the office
of castellan as a charge to be held on his behalf and trans-
mitted with his consent. The frontier castle of Saint-Céneri
on the Sarthe, which was Robert son of Giroie's share of the
family inheritance, was destined to be a bone of contention
for three-quarters of a century. Robert's loyalty was
temporarily secured by a marriage with a kinswoman of the
duke;[11] but a few years later he transferred his allegiance to
the king of France, rebelled against Duke William, and
refused him entry into the castle. He died in mysterious
circumstances, possibly poisoned by his wife, in the course of
the siege that ensued; his sons had to go into exile, their
lands were given to Roger of Montgomery, and the castle
was not recovered by his eldest son Robert until after
Duke William's death, when Robert Curthose proved more
pliable.[12] Various misfortunes, notably the hostility of the
Bellême family, forced the descendants of William Giroie to
go and seek their fortunes in Italy. One of William's sons
became commander of the papal forces, and a grandson made
a prosperous marriage with a Lombard heiress and settled in
Apulia.[13] From time to time they sent gifts back home to

threatening Bec, so that the abbey itself was in a precarious position. See
M. Gibson, *Lanfranc of Bec* (Oxford, 1978), pp. 30–1.

[11] He occasionally appears as a witness to ducal charters about 1055
(Fauroux, nos. 137, 160–2).
[12] For the ducal policy towards castles see J. Yver, 'Les châteaux-forts en
Normandie', *BSAN* liii (1957 for 1955–6), 28–115; for the Giroie family and
Saint-Céneri see Orderic, ii. 26–9, 78–83; iii. 134–5; iv. 154–7. Orderic's account
of the death of Robert son of Giroie is as nearly an accusation of poisoning as he
would allow himself in writing of founders' kin: 'When he was sitting peacefully
at the winter fireside, he noticed that his wife Adelaide, the duke's kinswoman,
had four apples in her hand; playfully he snatched two of them, not knowing they
were poisoned, and ate them in spite of her protests' (Orderic, ii. 80–1).
[13] Orderic, ii. 58–9, 98–9, 126–7.

the family monastery, but they could not protect it against enemies at the gate; and even when the lords of Saint-Cenéri were restored to their inheritance they were some thirty miles from Saint-Evroult, and constantly involved in frontier wars. They could do little more than protect a small castle priory at Saint-Céneri, where they had established monks from Saint-Evroult.[14]

The Grandmesnil was a greater family, and throve in Normandy a little longer, though their share in rebellion at the time of the French invasion in 1057 almost brought ruin on the abbey no less than the family. In the chequered allegiance of Giroie and Grandmesnil the house of Bellême played a major part. With the counts of Mortagne, they dominated a region that was the gateway into Normandy for armies invading from Anjou or France. Lords of many castles and vassals of both the king of France and the duke of Normandy, the lords of Bellême were alternately wooed and threatened by both rulers.[15] Duke William successfully took the initiative after his capture of Alençon and Domfront, when William Talvas of Bellême had been ruined by the rebellion of his son Arnold. For a time the inheritance hung uncertainly between Ivo, bishop of Sées and lord of Bellême, Mabel daughter of Talvas, one or two younger possibly illegitimate sons, and a powerful collateral descendant, Rotrou of Mortagne. Inheritance customs at the time allowed some flexibility of descent within a family, by agreement between lord and kindred. Duke William's choice went to Mabel, and he gave her in marriage to one of his most loyal and powerful vassals, Roger of Montgomery, vicomte of Exmes, later to become earl of Shrewsbury. The exact terms of the arrangement are not known; there may have been a partition with Bishop Ivo, or Roger may have been authorized to hold what he could take. Whatever the legal

[14] The cell was on the site of an earlier Merovingian monastery (Orderic, iv. 156–7); monks from Saint-Evroult had been established there at the time the abbey was refounded (Orderic, ii. 36–7).

[15] For the Bellême family see Orderic, ii. 362–5; J.-F. Lemarignier, *Recherches sur l'hommage en marche et les frontières féodales* (Lille, 1945), pp. 60–7; A. Guillou, *Le Comte d'Anjou et son entourage au xie siècle* (Paris, 1972), i, 69–72; D. Bates, *Normandy before 1066* (London, 1982), pp. 78–81; Kathleen Thompson, 'The Cross-Channel Estates of the Montgommery-Bellême Family c.1050–1112'; unpublished MA dissertation, University of Wales, Cardiff, 1983.

position, Roger and Mabel became the representatives of
Norman power in the region around Sées, acting with full
ducal favour. Their dominance cut off the powerful and
aggressive Grandmesnil from any hope of expansion in that
region. The result was first rebellion, and then reconciliation and compensation elsewhere. Hugh of Grandmesnil was
made castellan of Neufmarché on the Vexin frontier, and
allowed to turn his aggressiveness against the French Vexin;[16]
in due course he accompanied William on the conquest of
England and was richly rewarded with estates there. This
brought fresh endowments to Saint-Evroult; dependent
priories were founded at Neufmarché and at Ware in Hert-
fordshire, which was Hugh's principal place of residence in
England. The donors themselves, however, were no longer so
directly involved in the politics of the Hiémois. After Hugh's
death in 1098 his sons fell out of favour; in time their lands
and even their position as patrons of Saint-Evroult were
taken over by the descendants of the house of Beaumont, the
lords of Meulan and Leicester.[17]

With its chief founders far away, sometimes even in exile,
the abbey was unusually dependent on other neighbours
for its well-being. When Orderic referred to them as
nequissimi or *pessimi* he had in mind the lords of Bellême
in particular. They were turbulent and ambitious. By the
eleventh century the older Carolingian unit of government,
known as the pagus, had disintegrated, and many French
lords had taken advantage of the growing weakness of the
monarchy to establish the power of their families in local
castellanies. In Normandy and Anjou, however, the counts
had established a strong régime, holding the local castellans
in check.[18] The lords of Bellême may have aimed at a similar
independence in their more limited domains. To achieve
semi-independence, they played off one power against

---

[16] Orderic, ii. 130-1, 264-5.

[17] For the accumulation of properties by the house of Beaumont see
Complete Peerage, vii. 521-30. Robert, earl of Leicester, was admitted to the
fraternity of Saint-Evroult with the same privileges at his obit as a monk of the
abbey by Abbot Warin (J. Laporte, 'Services obituaires', *Revue Mabillon*, xlvi
(1956), 182). His son, Robert, renewed the link with the Grandmesnil later in the
twelfth century by his marriage to Pernel of Grandmesnil.

[18] Cf. Bates, *Normandy*, pp. 46-50; and see below, pp. 35, 122.

another, changing their allegiance shrewdly as their interests
dictated. Bellême itself remained an 'advanced bastion of
Normandy, which the dukes never succeeded in fully incor-
porating in their dominions'. Even when paying homage to
the dukes the Bellême lords kept a tight grip on their
numerous castles, and never willingly conceded the duke's
claim to place his own garrisons in them at will. Orderic's
relentless hostility to them had its origins in the brutal treatment the descendants of Giroie had suffered at their hands;
this may at times have warped his judgement of their
motives. But there is independent evidence of the crimes of
some of them. Mabel's excesses must have gone beyond what
was acceptable even in a violent age for some of the knights
dispossessed by her to have burst into her castle one night
and cut off her head as she lay in bed: an act that forced
them into lifelong exile as far away as Jerusalem, where they
served under the Saracens for twenty years before the first
crusade.[19] Even her epitaph described her as 'terrible to her
enemies'; and William of Malmesbury was as appalled as
Orderic by the cruelties of her son, Robert of Bellême.[20]
Like such men as the notorious Thomas of Marle in the
Île de France, Robert ruthlessly brushed aside even the few
half-accepted rules of war, and preferred imprisoning and
torturing his enemies to accepting ransoms for their release.
In or soon after 1077 Robert of Bellême succeeded to some
right in his mother's lands and held them together with his
father under the duke of Normandy. But when, in 1087, he
heard of the death of William the Conqueror as he was riding
to Rouen to confer with him, he took independent action.
The news reached him at the gates of Brionne and immediately, as Orderic graphically related, he wheeled his horse
round and galloped back to catch the king's garrisons off
their guard and turn them out of Alençon, Bellême, and
other castles.[21] Pillaging by his men-at-arms broke out all
through the region.

The other great family contending for influence on this

---

[19] Orderic, iii. 134-9; v. 156-9. When Robert Curthose reached Jerusalem
during the first crusade, Hugh Bunel, who had committed the murder, welcomed
him as his lord and offered him service.

[20] Orderic, v. 234-5; Malmesbury, *GR*, ii. 475-6.

[21] Orderic, iv. 112-15.

stretch of the Norman frontier was that of the lords of
Perche, who steadily extended their power south-westward
through the Corbonnais into Mortagne, and laid claim to
Bellême itself.[22] They were descended from Rotrou I, count
of Perche, and Adeline, daughter of Warin of Bellême,
through whom they had a hereditary claim to Bellême at
least as strong as that of the descendants of Mabel and
Roger of Montgomery. Both Earl Roger and Count Rotrou
had married granddaughters of William of Bellême (who
died *c*.1028), and in spite of the fact that the duke of
Normandy had lent his support to Mabel the conflicting
claims were kept alive for several generations. The two
families were repeatedly involved in fighting, and at times
incurred ecclesiastical censure. Rotrou I was excommunicated for plundering the lands of the church of Chartres,[23]
and he and his descendants had great difficulty in restraining
their unruly vassals in the Corbonnais. But his family never
incurred such widespread censure as the Bellême. Rotrou II
took part in the first crusade, and after his return led more
than one expedition to fight against the Moors in Spain.

This family's ambitions also took in Moulins-la-Marche,
a fortress held by a powerful marcher family under the
dukes of Normandy. After Guitmund, the castellan, betrayed
his lord by handing over the castle to King Henry of France
in 1054, Duke William entrusted it, not to any of Guitmund's
eight sons, but to his daughter's husband, William. This
William of Moulins-la-Marche and his sons after him kept a
firm grip on the fortress, and monks of Saint-Evroult were
invited to establish a castle priory there.[24] The counts of
Perche had to wait until the reign of Stephen to secure
even a temporary grant of the castle, which had ultimately
to be handed over to Henry II.

Orderic regarded the lords of Mortagne and Perche sympathetically, the more so as there was a marriage alliance
between them and his abbey's neighbours and benefactors,
the lords of L'Aigle. Even when Rotrou's son Geoffrey burnt

---

[22] For their position as frontier lords see Lemarignier, *L'Hommage en marche*,
pp. 62–3.
[23] Orderic, ii. 360–1.
[24] Orderic, iii. 132–3.

the nearby township of Échauffour whilst fighting against Robert of Bellême, Orderic could describe him with admiration as a man of distinguished birth, great wealth and armed strength, with many vassals and friends, and above all one who was fortified by the fear of God.[25]

The lords of L'Aigle, who became allied in marriage with the counts of Perche, had the great merit in the eyes of the monks of Saint-Evroult of being founders' kin. William Giroie's wife, Hiltrude, was a sister of Engenulf of L'Aigle. This family had great connections; Engenulf's son, Richer, married Judith, the daughter of Richard Goz, vicomte of the Avranchin; and their son Gilbert took as his wife Juliana, the daughter of Geoffrey II, count of Perche. Engenulf himself fought at Hastings, and the family acquired and retained wealth in England, in spite of occasionally fluctuating in loyalty between the kings of England and France. They gave lands to the abbey of their kinsmen, and were remembered with gratitude. Only when Richer allowed his men to plunder the lands of the abbey, burnt the township of Saint-Evroult, and ill-treated the monks during the civil wars of Stephen's reign, did Orderic allow himself an outburst of bitter condemnation of the brutality.[26]

The echoes of another feud, involving the lords of Breteuil and the Beaumont family, were frequently heard in the abbey, for the fee of Breteuil extended almost to their gates.[27] The particular bone of contention was the great and ancient castle of Ivry, founded by Count Raoul of Ivry and his wife Albereda, which William the Conqueror entrusted to Roger of Beaumont. Robert Curthose, however, gave it to William of Breteuil, the great-grandson of Raoul and Albereda. It was extorted from him soon afterwards by the most ruthless of his vassals, Ascelin Goel, a man who did not hesitate to imprison his own feudal lord in a dungeon to force him to give up the castle; and for half a century the two families struggled for possession, with the Beaumont lords of Meulan keeping their own claim alive in the background. Among the vassals of the fee of Breteuil were the lords of

[25] Orderic, iv. 160–1. For the family of L'Aigle see below, Table III, p. 228.
[26] Orderic, i. 212; vi. 458–61 and *passim*.
[27] Lemarignier, *L'Hommage en marche*, pp. 57–9.

Pont-Échanfray, local knights who were benefactors of the abbey. One of them, Ralph the Red, served for some years in the king's household troops, and contributed much to Orderic's knowledge of that élite military force.[28]

Other frontier lords, whose interests lay further to the east and north, never threatened the abbey directly. But in the reign of Henry I the counts of Évreux founded a priory at Noyon-sur-Andelle as a dependency of Saint-Evroult, so that the struggle of Amaury of Montfort to gain possession of the county of Évreux had a direct relevance to the monks. And their Vexin priories at Neufmarché, Parnes, and La Chapelle left them with no illusions about the belligerence of the lords of the Vexin.

Orderic's pessimistic view of the abbey's neighbours was derived almost as much from the conduct of the lesser, knightly families settled nearby as from that of great lords such as the notorious Bellême. Even when Normandy was in strong hands and enjoyed relative stability, the frontier region was liable to attack from outside; invasion and any weakening of ducal control allowed local feuds to flare up immediately. Local castellans prepared for siege and pillaged the country round about. Pont-Échanfray, traditionally friendly, might be occupied by predatory stipendiary knights; L'Aigle might house bandits.[29] The worst disturbances undoubtedly occurred during the weak rule of Robert Curthose, and again after the death of Henry I in 1135. But at any time a Norman invasion of Maine or Anjou might bring an army within ten or twenty miles of the abbey; and an attack by the king of France and his allies might cause the whole region to flare up. Peace came to be specially cherished by the monks and they counted above all on the dukes, who had taken the abbey into their general protection, to maintain it.

Orderic's first two years as a monk fell in a time of peace. William I's last campaign in Maine had come to an end, and he was occupied with the defence of England and the Vexin frontier. But his peace died with him. Abbot Mainer was one of the many prelates who attended his funeral at Caen, and

[28] M. Chibnall, 'Mercenaries and the *familia regis*', *History*, lxii (1977), 15–23.
[29] Orderic, vi. 458–63, 534–7; for stipendiary knights see below, pp. 55, 120–3, 138, 152.

brought back to the abbey news of a breakdown of order
so severe that even the king's residence at Rouen was
pillaged, and fires were started all over the city of Caen
during the funeral.[30] Life became perilous for the monks and
their men as Robert of Bellême terrorized the region, and the
new duke, Robert Curthose, proved incapable of keeping
order. His readiness to give away ducal rights to his vassals
to secure their allegiance enabled them to maintain their own
garrisons in the ducal castles and wage private war. Both his
younger brothers, William Rufus and Henry, were determined
to secure some part of the Norman inheritance. When Henry,
after a period of wandering in exile, established himself in
the strong fortress of Domfront, his knights were among the
marauders who threatened the lives and property of the
abbey's tenants and vassals.[31] The years of Robert's nominal
rule brought home vividly to the observant young monk
growing up at Saint-Evroult the importance of strong ducal
power. Not only were lives and property constantly in
danger; church reform too was threatened, for its effectiveness had depended on the goodwill and vigilance of the duke.
As Orderic recorded, 'Ecclesiastical order and monastic
discipline were often disturbed by disorders resulting from
the neglect of secular rulers. All who desired to follow a
monastic way of life in Nomandy or on its frontiers in the
time of Duke Robert and King Philip of France learnt this
to their cost.'[32]

Ecclesiastically Saint-Evroult suffered first from a pro-
tracted attack on its privileges by its diocesan, the bishop of
Lisieux;[33] and then for several years from the interference
of the notorious Ranulf Flambard in the affairs of the see.
When Abbot Mainer died in 1089 the community chose as
his successor a learned and eloquent monk, Serlo of Orgères,
who was destined to be promoted only two years later to the
bishopric of Sées. Orderic remembered him with affection
and gratitude; Serlo ruled the community when Orderic was
passing through the years of adolescence, between fourteen

---

[30] Orderic, iv. 100–7.   [31] See below, p. 105.
[32] Orderic, iv. 256–7.
[33] For the early elections and relations between the abbey and the bishop of
Lisieux see J. Yver, 'Autour de l'absence d'avouerie en Normandie', *BSAN*, lvii
(1965), 271–9.

and sixteen. 'I am convinced', Orderic wrote later, 'that
Normandy has produced no more elegant or more eloquent
son than Serlo . . . He was very well read in both secular and
divine learning, and could give an immediate answer to every
problem put to him. He was severe to persistent evil-doers,
but very merciful to anyone who confessed his guilt with
tears, and as tender as a compassionate father to a sick
son.'[34] This, surely, is a record of personal experience. Whatever the troubles of the monks during this period, they were
fortunate in their abbots. After Serlo became bishop of
Sées in 1091 the monks elected as abbot another of their
own brethren, Roger of Le Sap, 'a man of simple life, considerable learning, great uprightness, and gentle manners',
who had been a friend of Lanfranc.[35] At least ninety monks
were admitted during the thirty-three years of his rule, and
in the words of his epitaph:

A man gentle and simple, shining with works of goodness,
He instructed men well, best of all by example.[36]

His successor in 1123, Warin of Les Essarts, was also freely
chosen from inside the community for his merits, and
governed no less ably.[37]

There were, however, difficulties with the bishop. The
practice at Saint-Evroult, which appears to have been normal
in Normandy at that time, was for the abbot elect to seek the
approval of the duke of Normandy. The duke then invested
him with the lands and temporal possessions of his abbey,
and asked the diocesan bishop to bless him as abbot.[38] When
the bishop performed the ceremony the new abbot made
a simple promise of obedience to him. The form of promise
was traditional, and like the ceremonial might vary slightly in

[34] Orderic, vi. 338–9.
[35] Orderic, iv. 254–5.
[36] Orderic, vi. 326–9.
[37] Free election was variously interpreted at different dates. The foundation
charter of Saint-Evroult conceded that the abbot should be elected in accordance
with the Rule, and that election should not be influenced by friendship, kinship,
or money. During Orderic's lifetime this was normally accepted at Saint-Evroult
in the spirit of the earlier church reform in Normandy, as simply excluding hereditary right and simony, but not ducal influence, provided the candidate was
suitable.
[38] Yver, *BSAN* (1965), pp. 271–9.

different regions. But at a time when literacy was penetrating more deeply into society, and written documents often accompanied ceremonies in the transfer of property and authority,[39] it is not surprising that some bishops began to ask for written professions of obedience. Lanfranc as archbishop of Canterbury obtained written professions from two abbots.[40] In Normandy both Odo of Bayeux and Gilbert Maminot of Lisieux sometimes made similar demands of abbots elect. The subject proved to be an emotive one, for there was one ceremony in which written professions had had a place for centuries. This was the reception of new monks, and it went back to the earliest days of the Rule; even a novice who could not write was required to put his mark on his petition for admission and lay it on the altar with his own hand.[41] When in 1088 the abbot elect of Troarn feared that he might be asked for a written profession he consulted Anselm of Bec.[42] Anselm's reply was that a monk's duty was to obey all his superiors, including his diocesan bishop, but this was included in the profession he had made as a novice, which lasted for life; to repeat it was superfluous. He considered that a simple promise of obedience was sufficient.[43] Some went even further in their resistance. Norman monks continued to regard the innovation with suspicion for several decades; the prevailing view was that it was either unnecessary or dangerous, and might become a pretext for oppression by the bishop.

So, when Gilbert Maminot demanded a written profession of obedience from Serlo before consenting to bless him as abbot of Saint-Evroult, Serlo refused to comply. He was never blessed during the two years he governed the abbey. Roger of Le Sap was in the same position until the dispute

---

[39] There is an excellent introduction to the subject in Clanchy, *From Memory to Written Record*. Brian Stock, *The Implications of Literacy* (Princeton, 1983), provides some useful insights into rituals, symbols, and written records.

[40] See Michael Richter, *Canterbury Professions* (Canterbury and York Society, vol. lxvii), 1973), pp. xl, xlvii–lxxvi.

[41] RSB ch. 58.

[42] Anselm, *Opera*, iii. 263–4 (ep. 123).

[43] The whole question was complicated by the theological issue of whether the profession of a monk, often spoken of as a second baptism, was in fact a sacrament not to be repeated. For fuller discussion see M. Chibnall, 'From Bec to Canterbury: Anselm and monastic privilege', *Anselm Studies*, i (1983), 27–30.

was settled in 1099; the bishop continued to press his claims and the abbot, remaining unblessed, never carrried his pastoral staff. These difficulties showed how much the churches of Normandy depended on the effective protection of the duke; there was no suggestion of seeking support from the pope, or even the archbishop of Rouen. Robert Curthose, affable and weak, was content to allow the letters he had written telling the bishop of Lisieux to invest the new abbot with spiritual authority to be held in abeyance; he was no match for the proud and worldy Gilbert Maminot. The dispute was settled only when Robert was away on crusade, and the monks in desperation appealed to William Rufus. Whatever might be said of the king's worldliness and scepticism, he stood on his rights and expected to be obeyed; he ordered the unwilling bishop to be content with the customs enjoyed by his predecessors, and to bless the abbot without delay.[44]

In the more tranquil year that followed the abbey became the scene of a great liturgical ceremony. On the day that Abbot Roger returned home to his monks after being blessed by the bishop the community resolved to prepare for the dedication of the new church, delayed for many years because of the quarrel with the diocesan. There is no record of what restrictions in the performance of the liturgy had resulted from the delay, but the ceremonial must have been slightly muted. The suggestion arose spontaneously, during the normal *colloquium* in the cloister, and was welcomed with enthusiasm by all who were present.[45] On 13 November the three bishops of Lisieux, Évreux, and Sées came to carry out the dedication. The ceremonies lasted for three days and six altars were blessed; Bishop Serlo returned on 31 December to bless a seventh altar in the north transept. Many abbots and other church dignitaries, and many lay magnates attended. It was an occasion for the laity to make fresh gifts; William of Breteuil, Robert of Grandmesnil, Gilbert of L'Aigle, and Ralph of Conches did not fail in their duty to the church their ancestors had honoured. They laid their charters on the altar which was still damp from the holy water sprinked during the ceremony. Orderic made

[44] Orderic, v. 262-3.   [45] Orderic, v. 264-7.

a note of the dedication in the margin of one of the abbey's manuscripts, together with the news of the fall of Jerusalem to the Christians a few months earlier, and the death of Pope Urban II, who had launched the crusade.[46] At twenty-four he was not yet writing history, but he could not allow such memorable events to pass without written commemoration.

In 1101 Gilbert Maminot died, and for the next five years the diocese of Lisieux was exposed to the rapacity of Ranulf Flambard. For all his failings of worldliness, obstinacy, and self-indulgence, Gilbert had been a man of great learning and some medical skill, just and firm as a rule, but merciful, in his administration of his diocese, and with a sense of the dignity of his office that made his consecrations and ordinations great occasions when he could be persuaded to undertake them.[47] At the time of his death Robert Curthose was back in Normandy, and was prepared to leave ecclesiastical affairs to Ranulf Flambard, the exiled bishop of Durham, who had escaped from imprisonment in the tower of London and taken refuge in Normandy. Ranulf procured the bishopric of Lisieux first for his brother Fulcher, barely literate, but at least of canonical age; when Fulcher died only a few months later Ranulf intruded his own son, Thomas, a boy of about twelve. He himself in effect ruled the see 'as a prince in the city'.[48] The scandal shocked reformers, from the canonist, Ivo of Chartres, to Pope Paschal II;[49] but it was not until Henry I had defeated and captured his brother Robert in 1106 that Lisieux was given a suitable bishop. The man chosen was John, formerly archdeacon of Sées and king's chaplain. He was one of the ablest administrators in King Henry's court, and became head of the exchequer in Normandy. In spite of his curial duties he never neglected his see; for thirty-four years he 'exercised his

[46] Orderic, i. 100; Bibl. nat. MS lat. 10062, fo. 123, col. 2.

[47] Orderic, iii. 18–22.

[48] See C. W. David, *Robert Curthose* (Harvard University Press, 1920), pp. 151–3; R. W. Southern, *Medieval Humanism* (Oxford, 1970), pp. 196–8; Orderic, v. 320–3.

[49] Ivo of Chartres, *Epistolae* (Migne, *PL*, clxii), pp. 162–3 (ep. 157). Paschal II accused Robert Curthose of treating the church not as a spouse but as a slave (J. Ramackers, *Papsturkunden in Frankreich*, neue folge ii. Normandie (Göttingen, 1937), no. 4, p. 57).

charge very ably, and did much good to the church and clergy and God's people'.[50] He and King Henry between them gave Normandy, and particularly the diocese of Lisieux, a stability that had not been known for many years. Orderic's formative years were a time of great upheaval and war in the secular world, and disorder in the church. The years of his maturity and independent writing were passed in an abbey that enjoyed the rule of two abbots who were keenly alive to their pastoral duties and were never called upon to take a political stand; the government of church and state in the duchy were in the hands of an able and conscientious curial bishop who worked in harmony with the king, and a king who believed in church reform as long as it was carried out under his supervision. There were frontier wars and rebellions; but an effective royal power was in existence, ready to deal out ruthless justice. All this must be remembered in reading Orderic's account of the events of his day.

His own life was spent principally in choir and cloister; he never gained administrative office, and all his energies went into work in the monastic school and library, and his share in the common liturgical service of the abbey. He was ordained sub-deacon at the age of sixteen, and deacon two years later. Finally, on 21 December 1107, when he was thirty-two, William Bonne-Âme, archbishop of Rouen, ordained him priest with 120 other priests and 244 deacons.[51] Apart from references in his own writings, his work is known only from the appearance of his characteristic handwriting in many manuscripts belonging to Saint-Evroult. Sometimes he copied whole works; sometimes he merely wrote an occasional line or a verse in a commentary, leaving the main body of the work to scribes working under his direction; sometimes he corrected the text and added marginal notes.[52] These activities suggest that for a considerable time he was in charge of the scriptorium, and held the office variously described in customaries as *armarius* or *bibliothecarius*. Since the *armarius* was responsible for supplying the texts

[50] Orderic, vi. 142–5.
[51] Orderic, vi. 554–7.
[52] L. Delisle, 'Notes sur les manuscrits autographes d'Orderic Vital', *Matériaux pour l'édition de Guillaume de Jumièges*, ed. J. Lair (Paris, 1910), pp. 7–27; Orderic, i. 201–3.

for public and private reading by the monks, he may have had some influence in choosing the works to be copied in the scriptorium.[53] Among the books entered in the earliest library catalogue in Orderic's hand is Bede's *History of the English People*,[54] which he himself copied; and among the many lives of saints which came from his pen are the lives of St Guthlac, St Ethelwold, and other English saints; he made no secret of his admiration for the saints of his native land.

His literary talents soon showed themselves. Any pupil of John of Rheims might have tried his hand at verse; and Orderic began writing epitaphs and commemorative verses for the abbey's patrons in his early twenties. It was probably during the rule of Robert Curthose or William Rufus that he produced a satire in verse on the morals of the court,[55] which gave him some material for a similar attack when he came to write his *Ecclesiastical History*. A denunciation of the evils of the times might have been written then, or in Stephen's reign, much later. He could turn his pen to gentler themes: prayers, acts or contribution, a verse litany. Historical writing seems not to have come his way until he was in his thirties, possibly because his master, John of Rheims, had an interest in writing history, and provided all that the abbey required. Orderic began in the first decade of the twelfth century, by writing up the annals of Saint-Evroult, and by interpolating lengthy passages into the history of the Normans written by William of Jumièges.[56] But during the same years he copied and read historical works; and he had opportunities for meeting secular and ecclesiastical magnates, both in his abbey and on occasional journeys elsewhere.

Many gifts to the abbey were made in the chapter-house, where lay men and women were received into the fraternity

[53] B. de Gaiffier, 'L'hagiographe et son public au xie siècle', *Miscellanea Historica in honorem Leonis van der Essen* (Brussels/Paris, 1947), i. 143-4.

[54] There is a facsimile of this page in Delisle, 'Manuscrits autographes', plate 4.

[55] Delisle, 'Manuscrits autographes', pp. 20-1.

[56] E. M. C. van Houts, 'Quelques remarques sur les interpolations attribuées à Orderic Vital dans les *Gesta Normannorum Ducum* de Guillaume de Jumièges', *Revue d'histoire des textes*, viii (1978), 213-22, has expressed doubts about the attribution of the Saint-Evroult interpolations to Orderic. Although Orderic probably used material collected by John of Rheims, I remain convinced that in their final form the interpolations are his (Orderic, i. 29-30). A new edition of the *Gesta Normannorum Ducum* is being prepared by E. M. C. van Houts.

of the house, so that whilst remaining in the world they might enjoy the benefits of the monks' prayers.[57] At Candlemas in 1113 King Henry I himself spent two days in the abbey, looked into the endowments, and promised to grant a new charter of confirmation.[58] Its priories too were meeting grounds for monks and knights on many occasions. Orderic's keen insight into the characters of the patrons of Auffay, and the sharp sense of loss expressed in the epitaph he wrote for the pious Avice of Auffay, are clear indications that he had spent some time in that priory.[59] In 1106 he was certainly in France, at the priory of Maule; and there he witnessed the ceremony of homage when Ansold, lord of Maule, made his son Peter his heir during a meeting of the feudal court.[60]

Maule gave him a window into France; the founders belonged to the great Parisian family of Le Riche and were aspiring French castellans. Wealthy, cultured, and openhanded, they were vassals of the king of France; but the necessity of sometimes fighting against the Normans seems never to have strained their devotion to the monks of Saint-Evroult. Some of their ambitions exactly resembled those of the Norman frontier lords like the Giroie, who struggled to gain hereditary control of the castle of Saint-Cenéri. When Ansold fortified his castle at Maule Orderic sympathized with his action, as he sympathized with Robert of Saint-Cénéri's claims. Many French castellans had done the same with more success than most of the Normans; but by the early twelfth century the French kings were beginning to assert their authority over the castellans of the Île-de-France. In 1120 or a little later Louis VI came to Maule and forced Ansold's son, Peter, to dismantle the fortifications.[61] Through Maule Orderic quickly learned of events in France. Ecclesiastically the priory was in the diocese of Chartres, which was ruled by the great canonist and reformer, Ivo of Chartres. For the most part Orderic saw church reform from a Norman point of view, with the duke at the centre, working hand in hand

---

[57] This is noted in charters printed in Le Prévost, v. 182–95, *passim*. For fraternities see below, pp. 67–70.

[58] Orderic, vi. 174–7.
[60] Orderic, iii. 182–5.

[59] Orderic, iii. 246–61.
[61] Orderic, iii. 206–7.

with the bishops. His contacts with Chartres helped to make him at least dimly aware of the growing strength of the new reforms, focused on the papacy.

One of his journeys opened his eyes to papal reform in action. There is every reason to believe that he was present in 1119 at the council of Rheims, of which he gave a detailed account later.[62] The fact that by then he was seriously at work on history with the encouragement of his abbot may have marked him out for inclusion in the abbot's retinue on that occasion. He may have gone on almost directly from Rheims to pay visits, which he mentioned later without giving dates, to Cambrai and England. At Cambrai, whatever the purpose of his visit, he saw the chronicle of Sigebert of Gembloux in the abbey of St Sepulchre.[63] In England he stayed at Crowland by invitation of Abbot Geoffrey of Orleans, a former monk of Saint-Evroult, who invited him to write the early history of the abbey.[64] There was time for a visit to Thorney, then ruled by another fellow monk, Robert of Prunelai; he may have been there about Christmas time, for he added the name of St Évroul, whose feast fell on 29 December, to the calendar of the abbey.[65] A little later he was at Worcester; what took him to the West Country can only be conjectured. He may have made a detour to visit the abbey at Shrewsbury where his father had died and his brother Benedict had become a monk. Some of his kinsfolk may still have been alive there; his younger brother Everard had been assured of half his father's property, to be held from the abbey.[66] If so Orderic might have broken his journey at Worcester on his way from Shrewsbury to the coast. On the other hand Worcester may have been his main objective, particularly if he had learned at Crowland of the work being done by John of Worcester on the great chronicle of the cathedral priory. He certainly met and talked with his fellow historian, John, about the writing of universal history, much to his profit.[67] About this

---

[62] Orderic, i. 25-6.   [63] Orderic, ii. 188-9.
[64] See below, p. 107.
[65] St John's College, Oxford, MS 17, fo. 21v.   [66] Orderic, iii. 146-7.
[67] Orderic, ii. 188-9; for the Worcester chronicle see Martin Brett, 'John of Worcester and his contemporaries', *The Writing of History in the Middle Ages*, ed. R. H. C. Davis and J. M. Wallace-Hadrill (Oxford, 1981), 101-26.

time his original plan of writing a history of his own abbey, set perhaps in the history of the region, was being broadened into something a great deal more comprehensive. He was already thinking in terms of a universal chronicle of the church, and the chronicles at Cambrai and Worcester showed him how it might be written.[68]

His creative years corresponded almost exactly with the period when his friend and contemporary, Warin of Les Essarts, was abbot of Saint-Evroult. This may have been chance; Roger of Le Sap first gave him the welcome task of writing the history of the house, and there are signs of the widening of his interests and ambitions by 1119, four years before Warin became abbot. But eleven and a half of the thirteen books of the *Ecclesiastical History* were written, or at least put together to incorporate earlier drafts dealing with isolated topics, between 1123 and 1137. The whole work was offered, as convention required, to Father Warin for his correction and approval, shortly before Warin's death. Of any travels he may have undertaken to collect materials during those years he has left almost no information. Only twice did he state that he had witnessed a particular event. He attended the great gathering at Cluny, when Peter the Venerable issued reforming statutes for houses observing Cluniac customs; an occasion he remembered for the inspiring liturgical celebrations, when 1,212 monks chanted and prayed together.[69] And, much more trivially, he mentioned a violent thunderstorm which he had witnessed at Saint-Evroult's property of Le Merlerault, because he wished to record the remarkable fact that only women and female animals were killed by lightning: a puzzling phenomenon which may have reminded him of a similar occurrence at Morville, recorded in the chronicle of John of Worcester.[70] In spite of intermittent rebellions in various parts of Normandy, which disturbed the peace until the rival claims

[68] For the dating of his work on the *Ecclesiastical History* see Orderic, i. 45–8, and the introductions to vols. ii–vi. M. C. Garand, 'Auteurs latins et autographes des xie et xiie siècles', *Scrittura et Civiltà*, v (1981), 101–3 has suggested that he had written the first chapters before 1110.

[69] Orderic, vi. 424–7.

[70] Orderic, vi. 436–9; *The Chronicle of John of Worcester*, ed. J. R. H. Weaver, (Oxford, 1908), pp. 13–14.

of Henry I's nephew, William Clito, ended with William's death in 1128, these were years of relative stability. Intellectual work could continue in the cloister alongside the central liturgical celebrations of monastic life in the choir.

It has been suggested that Orderic wished to write a 'simple history' and was compelled gradually to make some concessions to his brethren, who clamoured for more legends and miracles of saints, suitable for reading in church and cloister.[71] This is very doubtful. Any opposition he had to face seems to have come in the early stages of his work, possibly because of the reluctance of John of Rheims to yield place to a younger scholar; the only fault Orderic could find in his revered master was that he was not wholly guiltless of anger and envy.[72] He himself relished hagiography as much as anyone, and eagerly collected any miracles he could find; but he believed that preserving the record of human history as evidence of God's purpose for man was a duty each generation owed to posterity. Many of his fellow monks shared this view, or at least enjoyed hearing about the deeds of their noble kinsmen. Naturally there were some who thought otherwise; in a community of fifty or more there must have been, if not as many views as monks, at least a wide spectrum of opinion on the proper place of different kinds of study in the life of each individual. Tensions were particularly acute at a time when the debate on the exclusion of the world from the cloister was at its height.[73]

In several places Orderic defended the wide scope of his historical writing. Jerome and Origen had had to defend themselves against their detractors. Later historians took their cue from Jerome in fending off critics, real or antici-

[71] Bernard Guenée, *Histoire et culture historique dans l'occident médiévale* (Paris, 1980), pp. 54-5, citing R. D. Ray, 'Orderic Vitalis and his readers', *Studia Monastica*, xiv (1972), 17-23. Although Ray's article, written when only one volume of the Oxford edition of Orderic's *Ecclesiastical History* had appeared, contains valuable insights, the revised dating proposed in later volumes of this edition indicates that his views may need to be modified. Almost all the lives of saints in Orderic's *History* are incorporated either in the earlier books or in the chronicle originally planned as a separate work; the one exception is the account of the life and miracles of St Évroul, added at a late date to the sixth book as a result of the translation of relics from Rebais in 1131. The content of the last five books is almost exclusively the more general history of Orderic's own times.
[72] Orderic, iii. 170-1.
[73] For further discussion of these topics see below, pp. 82-5.

pated.[74] No doubt some of these critics were real persons; but the defence, and even the terms of it, became in time almost a conventional necessity. Orderic's words in his preface to Book VI might seem at first sight to be a defence against opposition in his own monastery:

> Everyone should daily grow in knowledge of how he ought to live, and follow the noble examples of famous men now dead to the best of his ability . . . So the learned do their work out of good will and reveal past events to future generations ungrudgingly, though sometimes idle and ignorant men attack their achievements with wolfish fangs . . . We find Jerome and Origen and other learned doctors deploring the cavils of their critics . . . Let denigrators, who neither produce anything of their own nor accept the work of others with good will, be silent. Let them learn what they do not know; and if they cannot learn, let them at least suffer their fellows to produce what they think fit.[75]

But William of Malmesbury said much the same in the prologue to Book IV of his *Gesta regum*.[76] He wrote that he had been attacked for trying to write the history of his own time by critics who asserted that it was impossible to avoid suppressing evil deeds or flattering powerful contemporaries, and by idle persons who dismissed as impossible anything they shrank from undertaking themselves. He had, he claimed, given way to such reasoning in the past and put aside his historical writing; but now, at the pressing request of friends, he was returning to his discarded work. Jerome had once refuted his critics, saying, 'Let them read or reject my writings as they please'; and William, too, would press on with work that was intended for serious, not frivolous readers.

No doubt both he and Orderic had real critics who accused them of wasting their time on unsuitable work, or over-estimating their own abilities, and they knew that such views would continue to be expressed in every generation. They replied in similar terms, yet there is no evidence that either could have seen the work of the other. Unless Orderic, writing after the *Gesta regum* was completed, had read Malmesbury's preface, the similarities between their protestations must have arisen from a well-established, familiar

---

[74] See the preface to Jerome's *Vita Malchi*, Migne, *PL*, xxiii. 53.
[75] Orderic, iii. 212-15.
[76] Malmesbury, *GR*, ii. 357-8.

tradition. Half way through their work both paused to justify pressing on to the end, as Jerome had done. Given the amount of historical writing that continued to flow from the pens of both men, neither can have hesitated for very long. Even though Malmesbury, a prolific writer in many disciplines, expressed the view that theology was a more suitable occupation for his mature years,[77] he never wholly abandoned history and wrote the *Historia novella* late in life. And once Abbot Warin had given Orderic his head there was no holding him. He wrote history until age and weariness compelled him to bring his work to a close.

The last years of Orderic's life were clouded, much as his first years in Normandy had been. Henry I's death in December 1135 meant the outbreak of civil wars, of which Orderic was never to see the end. He was able to continue his historical work with unabated vigour for another eighteen months; even when raiders from L'Aigle burnt the little township of Saint-Evroult in May 1136 and the flames almost reached the gate of the abbey he continued writing the thirteenth book of his history.[78] By the spring of 1137 he offered it to Abbot Warin and laid down his pen for many months, perhaps as much as two years. Fighting was flaring up all around the abbey; every year the forces of Geoffrey of Anjou crossed the frontiers in an attempt to conquer Normandy, and after burning and looting trailed back in disorder.[79] But by 1141 Normandy was almost battered into submission. Warin's successor as abbot of Saint-Evroult, Richard of Leicester, spent much of his time in travelling on necessary business. Worn out by a journey to Rome in 1139 to attend the second Lateran Council, he died in England a few months later.[80] Both he and his successor, Ralph, another monk of the abbey, appear to have been capable and respected abbots; but two changes in two years cannot have contributed to orderly life in those troubled times. Nevertheless Orderic had another burst of historical writing; too much of importance was going on to remain unrecorded. Up to the

[77] See Farmer, *Studia Monastica*, 1962, p. 288.
[78] Orderic, vi. 460–3.
[79] Orderic, vi. 454–7, 466–75, 482–7, 514–17, 526–9.
[80] Orderic, vi. 536–9.

summer of 1141 he continued to write down the news that reached him from various parts of the Anglo-Norman realm, and even the kingdom of Jerusalem. When he ended his history for the second time, and added the epilogue describing his own life, disaster seemed to have overwhelmed his world.

Defeated at the battle of Lincoln, Stephen, whom Orderic had accepted as the legitimate king from the moment of his coronation, was languishing in a dungeon. The Normans were everywhere capitulating to the Angevins; and (whatever allegiance may have been felt to Henry I's daughter Matilda) no one who had witnessed year after year the behaviour of the Angevin troops, contemptuously nicknamed 'Guiribecci', could welcome the prospect of Angevin rule. As a last straw John, the aged and respected bishop of Lisieux, died; the see remained vacant and Orderic, remembering the disorders of the previous vacancy, wrote sadly, 'I do not know when or by what kind of a bishop it may be filled'. So, with the world collapsing around his monastery and old age overtaking him, Orderic finally brought his history to an end. Turning to the spiritual peace of the cloister, where from the time of his reception he had been loved and honoured greatly above what he regarded as his deserts, he penned one of the most moving declarations of faith every written.[81]

When he died we do not know; there was unfortunately no one to carry on his history, or to write a letter describing his death as Cuthbert described the death of Bede.[82] The day was probably 13 July, when the obit of a monk named Ordricus is entered in the calendar of the abbey; the year was either 1142 or a later year.[83]

---

[81] Orderic, vi. 550–7; see below, Appendix.
[82] Bede, *Ecclesiastical History*, ed. Colgrave and Mynors, pp. 579–87.
[83] Orderic, i. 113 n. 1.

PART II

THE MONASTIC WORLD

3
The Place of the Monasteries
in Society

When Orderic was received by Abbot Mainer at Saint-Evroult in 1085 all the great Norman abbeys were Benedictine. Each had its own traditions and liturgical customs within the broad framework of the Benedictine rule. Spiritually they were autonomous, and all were still in their prime as houses mostly between thirty and sixty years from their foundation. Securely established, with the first phase of building behind them; well provided with books for liturgical purposes and spiritual reading, they were centres of local and sometimes more than local piety. Recruitment was vigorous; numbers were still rising and donations flowed in steadily. If the greatest were ducal foundations and the duke's general protection encompassed them all, the private foundations were still at the centre of the piety, pride, and ambition of all the greatest Norman families. The legends of their saints blended with legends of the family origins of their patrons and benefactors in their foundation histories. Envisaged by monastic teachers as arks of salvation in a flood of worldly perils, they remained an integral part of the society which brought them into being.

To understand how this came about we must look at the earlier history of the church in Normandy. Just as the first Norman leader, Rollo, by his formal acceptance of baptism in 911, had given an example to his pagan Viking followers, the dukes descended from him led the way in encouraging and protecting the slow revival of religious life after the invasions and wars of the ninth and tenth centuries. At first they did not look only to monks. When in 990 Duke Richard I decided to restore Fécamp, situated beside one of his favourite residences, he placed twelve secular clerks in the church.[1]

[1] Lemarignier, *Exemption*, pp. 29-32.

Collegiate establishments of this kind consisted of priests who could serve the church and provide for the spiritual needs of the community round about; they did not share in a communal life and were not obliged to renounce property or marriage. Often they passed on their prebends to their sons. At Fécamp this establishment was soon superseded; from the first Duke Richard wished to revive monastic life, and he applied almost immediately to Cluny for monks. When negotiations failed because the abbot demanded privileges that the duke would not grant, he turned to William of Volpiano, abbot of Saint-Bénigne de Dijon; and in 1001 monks returned to Fécamp, led by William.[2] From this date the monastic revival never looked back, for William was an abbot of vision and unrivalled practical ability, who undertook the reform of many other houses both in Normandy and elsewhere. According to his biographer he had authority over almost forty monasteries and more than 12,000 monks by the end of his life.[3] And his efforts were supported in Normandy by the ducal family. But besides this, the course of events at Fécamp established a pattern that became typical of church restoration all over the duchy in the first half of the eleventh century.

Initially the magnates left monastic foundations to the dukes, and provided for their own spiritual needs by endowing colleges of secular canons in or near their principal residences.[4] And here their church patronage became closely involved with their status as castellans. Castles played a vital part in the feudal society that was very slowly taking shape in western Europe, but their position in Normandy was very different from that in many parts of France. In the territories directly subject to the French king the lords of great estates often secured hereditary rights both to castles and to the public judicial and financial functions which had once been exercised by Carolingian counts. Their power in their

[2] D. Knowles, *The Monastic Order in England* (Cambridge, 1962), pp. 83–6; L. Musset, 'La contribution de Fécamp à la reconquête monastique de la Basse-Normandie (990–1066)', *L'Abbaye bénédictine de Fécamp* (Fécamp, 1959–60), i. 57–66.

[3] R. Glaber, *Vita S. Guillelmi abbatis, AA SS OSB*, VI. i, 331.

[4] See L. Musset, 'Recherches sur les communautés de clercs séculiers en Normandie au xie siècle', *BSAN*, lv (1961 for 1959), 5–38.

castellanies sometimes even became a threat to public order.[5] In Normandy, on the other hand, the dukes kept a much firmer control of castles and jurisdiction, and also in due course of monastic patronage. In the frontier regions concessions sometimes had to be made; but elsewhere with few exceptions William the Conqueror successfully insisted that the castles were held on his behalf by the castellans he appointed, and must either be garrisoned by his knights or handed over to him on demand. His vassals might believe that the regrant of a castle to an heir implied a family right to hold it as part of their patrimony; but the duke consistently treated as rebellion any refusal to admit his men to a castle at his request. His vassals, however, enjoyed the exercise of many other seignorial rights; and the establishment of secular canons in or near their castles was one aspect of these rights. The collegiate churches were in effect private churches; the lords provided the endowments of the various prebends and nominated their kinsfolk and dependants as canons, much as many lords of manors built village churches and appointed priests until reformers attacked the practice. In this way they provided for religious worship while enlarging their power and patronage.[6]

Founding a monastery, on the other hand, involved a much greater financial sacrifice, as well as a sacrifice of some authority. Nevertheless from the early 1030s monastic reform, initiated by the dukes, gradually spread through the province as the vassals of the duke followed his example. To found a monastery became as much an object of ambition and a sign of status for the Norman magnates as the maintenance of a body of armed vassals and the holding of a castle. 'Every one of the great men of Normandy', wrote Orderic later, 'would have thought himself beneath contempt if he had not made provision out of his estates for clerks and monks to serve in the army of God.'[7] Frequently, where churches served by secular canons already existed, monks were established in them, with the proviso that the canons might either become monks themselves or hold their

[5] For France see in particular J. F. Lemarignier, *Le gouvernement royal aux premiers temps capétiens* (Paris, 1965); for Normandy, Yver, *BSAN* (1957), 42-63; and in general, Frank Barlow, *William Rufus* (London, 1983), pp. 3-7.

[6] Yver, *BSAN* (1965), 189-283.   [7] Orderic, ii. 10-11.

prebends for life; as each canon died a monk replaced him, until the whole community was monastic. Not all the new foundations were in or near castles; some, like Saint-Evroult, were founded in forest churches; but the patrons expected to gain from all of them some advantages that were not purely spiritual. And just as the duke insisted on his ultimate control in castles (however much castellans struggled to establish hereditary rights), so he exercised a general protection over abbeys founded by his vassals. This prevented the kind of exploitation by patrons or 'advocates' that existed in many other parts of western Europe.[8] In Normandy founders renounced all seignorial rights, and often explicitly placed their monastery in the guardianship of the duke. Charters recording the endowment of abbeys by the duke's vassals received his confirmation; in the confirmation of the charter of Saint-Evroult, situated as it was in a frontier region rent by conflicting territorial claims, Duke William even threatened to disinherit anyone who invaded its territory.[9] Church reform, encouraged by the duke, helped to underpin his authority.

At the same time his vassals hoped to receive benefits of many kinds from the monasteries they founded. Though they accepted some degree of ducal supervision, they preferred to avoid any kind of control by the abbot of another religious house. Unless the nucleus of a community was provided by a group of hermits, the first monks in any new foundation had to come from another abbey sufficiently secure and populous to send out a new colony. Cluniac houses remained dependent on their mother house, whose abbot or prior appointed and removed their priors, and discipline could be exercised through the general chapter which met at Cluny from time to time. There were no fully Cluniac houses in Normandy until late in the eleventh century.[10] But Cluny

[8] Yver, *BSAN* (1965), 205-10. Outside Normandy lay 'advocates' often exacted extortionate dues from abbeys in return for protection, so that advocacy had some of the features of a twentieth-century protection racket.

[9] Fauroux, no. 122, p. 289: 'si quis ex adverso veniens . . . nostri hujus privilegii cartulam violare temptaverit, noscat se nostre reum esse majestatis et omne patrimonium suum nostris rebus dominicis asscribi debere'.

[10] B. Golding, 'The coming of the Cluniacs', *Anglo-Norman Studies*, iii (1981 for 1980), 65-6.

or its daughter houses could sometimes be persuaded to provide monks for a new foundation without insisting on sub-
jection; Saint-Bénigne allowed William of Volpiano to bring
monks to establish Fécamp as an autonomous house. As the
Norman abbeys grew larger they were able to spare monks of
their own for new ventures. Humphrey de Vieilles founded
Saint-Pierre at Préaux with monks from Saint-Wandrille;
monks from Saint-Wandrille and Préaux formed the first
community at Grestain, under an abbot brought from Saint-
Serge, Angers. When Lesceline, the wife of William of Arques,
founded Saint-Pierre at Lisieux with monks from La Trinité,
Rouen, she insisted explicitly that the abbey was to be
independent; and a similar stipulation was made by Thurstan
Haldup when he founded Lessay with monks from Bec.[11] So
at a time when abbeys elsewhere were tending to seek mutual
support under the direction of a mother abbey, many of
those in ·Normandy remained independent, looking for
protection to their patron and beyond him to the duke. In
time less wealthy donors, who wished to found houses of
their own but had not the resources to support a large
community, were ready to establish small priories served by
colonies of monks from one of the great Norman abbeys, and
remaining subject to its authority. Bec-Hellouin and Saint-
Evroult amongst others acquired a substantial number of
small dependencies; priors and monks were sent out for
a few years from the mother house and then recalled, so that
their religious observance would not become dulled by too
long isolation in a small community. But this development
belonged to the later eleventh and twelfth centuries.

The wording of charters of endowment stressed the
spiritual benefits hoped for by the patrons. A deed of gift
of a frontier lord, Guitmund of Moulins-la-Marche, granting
property in Normandy to Saint-Père de Chartres, begins:

Our Lord Jesus Christ . . . who taught us what things are necessary
for the good of our souls, admonished us to make gifts for his sake out
of our possessions, so that in time to come we might receive an
hundredfold. He taught us also through his apostle that we should pray
for each other in order to be saved. Impelled by these and other considerations, I, Guitmund, with my wife Emma and our children, in

[11] Laport, *Revue Mabillon* (1941), 57–64.

order to alleviate the heavy burden of our sins and ensure that there shall be no lack of men to pray daily for us, with overflowing heart and eager will make the following gifts to Saint-Père de Chartres.[12] . . .

Whether the wording was enriched with biblical quotations or consisted in a simple statement that gifts were made for the souls of the donors, their ancestors, and perhaps their lords as well, this was usually the only intention openly expressed. Indeed, when William the Conqueror gave an estate and church and five free knights in the Cotentin to Saint-Florent-près-Saumur, he explained that he gave everything as freely as he himself possessed it, retaining no secular claim. 'For when the monks said that alms ought to be given freely he replied, as became a man of prudence, "Though we are Normans, we know well that it should be so, and this, God willing, we will do." '[13] But in fact benefactors looked for far more benefits, both tangible and intangible, from the monasteries they endowed. Both sides knew without formal expression the mutual duties that custom required of them; it was only when privilege was abused that lord or abbot needed to spell out exactly how much might reasonably be expected in return for a free gift. Besides this, monasteries, as great landholders and wealthy charitable bodies, had a role to play in the society of which they formed a part.

The foundation of a monastery might help to confirm patrimonial rights or establish a power centre in a disputed region. When Geoffrey Martel, son of Fulk Nerra of Anjou, and his wife Agnes of Burgundy founded La Trinité, Vendôme, in the early 1030s, Geoffrey's ambition was to secure his position in the county of Vendôme and win political independence from his father.[14] Both Saint-Evroult and St Martin's, Sées, were founded during the struggles for power of the families of Giroie-Grandmesnil and Bellême-Montgomery on the southern frontiers of Normandy, with the duke of Normandy as an interested party determined to resist advance by any lord not prepared to accept Norman vassalage on his terms.[15] Many other families planned their

---

[12] Fauroux, no. 117.   [13] Fauroux, no. 199.
[14] Penelope D. Johnson, *Prayer, Patronage and Power* (New York/London, 1981), pp. 8–23.   [15] See above, pp. 20–3, 48.

pious foundations to further their feudal ambitions. Examples could be found in many parts of Europe; one, Sant'Eufemia in Calabria, was of special interest to Normans, for it was colonized in the early 1060s by monks from Saint-Evroult. When Abbot Robert of Grandmesnil was forced into exile because of the rebellion of his kinsfolk, he withdrew to his friends in southern Italy, taking eleven monks with him. Robert's half-sister, Judith, had married Roger, the youngest son of Tancred of Hauteville; and he, in uneasy subordination to his brother Robert Guiscard, was consolidating power in Calabria. Tension between the brothers was becoming acute. Robert Guiscard welcomed his exiled kinsman from Saint-Evroult, and agreed to found a monastery for the Norman monks in the narrow gap between the gulf of Sant'Eufemia and the gulf of Squillace, dominating the route to the south. It helped to form a neutral zone between the territories controlled by the two brothers, until Roger succeeded in conquering Sicily, and Robert Guiscard was left in undisputed command of southern Calabria. The burial of their mother in the abbey further guaranteed that neither of them would violate its territory.[16]

As monastic reform gathered strength, abbeys were expected by their patrons to fulfil potentially incompatible roles. They were centres of peace, entitled to protection, and so able to attract settlers and bring prosperity to a war-torn region. But they were also stone buildings that might be occupied and held by military forces in time of war. Chroniclers frequently complained that impious rebels had made a fortress in an abbey; this could easily be done by stationing troops in it, and throwing up a few outworks. Abbeys could serve too as temporary bases and sources of supply for household troops on the move, since benefactors and other noble travellers had a traditional claim to hospitality and would normally have travelled with a sizeable household. On one occasion Richer of L'Aigle, journeying peacefully from Normandy to England, had fifty knights with him.[17]

[16] For the political situation see Geoffrey of Malaterra, I. xix–xxix, pp. 18–22; F. Chalandon, *Histoire de la domination normande en Italie et en Sicile* (Paris, 1907), i. 149–53; for the foundation of Sant'Eufemia, Orderic, ii. 100–3.
[17] Orderic, vi. 548–9.

This custom, and the problems it might cause, is probably behind Orderic's strange story of the malice of Mabel of Bellême.[18] He accused her of trying to improverish Saint-Evroult by insisting on staying in the abbey with as many as a hundred knights. When Abbot Thierry asked her why she must come with such worldly pomp to a poor monastery, and warned her to restrain her vanity, she flew into a rage and replied, 'Next time I will bring even more knights with me.' The abbot said, 'Believe me, unless you depart from this wickedness, you will suffer for it.' 'And indeed she did', Orderic concluded, 'for the very next night she fell sick and endured great agony. Hastily she commanded her attendants to take her away.' She recovered, but never went near the abbey again. Nevertheless she admired Abbot Thierry personally, and asked him to take charge of the cell she was trying to found at Sées in honour of St Martin. The story is distorted by the relentless hatred that Orderic, as a monk of Saint-Evroult, felt for the family that had persecuted the patrons of his abbey;[19] but it makes sense in terms of the struggle for power in the region. The illness may have been a trivial one, embellished in the telling. Mabel herself had the character of a Norman Amazon; whether or not she actually fought in battle, she had some share in directing knights and planning campaigns. As she and her husband pressed southwards toward the Norman frontier, she may have wished to use first Saint-Evroult and later Sées itself as a base for her household knights on their campaigns. Admiration for the spiritual qualities of Abbot Thierry was at odds with her practical need for the material resources of the abbey over which he ruled, and her ruthless determination to let nothing stand in the way of her family ambitions. The whole episode illustrates the ambivalent attitude of feudal lords to reformed monasteries, and the dilemmas of the monks.

Other family aspirations were more acceptable. Most benefactors regarded any abbey of their foundation as a place

[18] Orderic, ii. 54–7.

[19] There is an over-enthusiastic panegyric of the Bellême family in Du Motey, *Les Origines de la Normandie et du duché d'Alençon* (Paris, 1920). A reasoned study of their motives and achievements is in Kathleen Thompson's unprinted MA dissertation, 'The Cross-Channel estates of the Montgommery-Bellême family *c*.1050–1112' (University of Wales, Cardiff, 1983).

where they and their closest kindred might claim burial rights. Patrons wished their bodies to lie under the protection of a community that would offer constant intercession for their souls. Monasteries were regarded as both family mausoleums and perpetual chantries on a scale appropriate to the dignity of their founders. The personal link only very slowly gave way to one connected with office. Before the end of the eleventh century Saint-Denis was becoming the traditional burial place of the kings of France, and sometimes received a gift of royal insignia, although Philip I insisted on being buried at Fleury-sur-Loire.[20] But there was no established tradition for the bishops or even the dukes of Normandy. William the Conqueror was buried in his abbey of Saint-Étienne de Caen; Queen Matilda in the sister foundation of La Trinité. Henry I was beginning to think in terms of Rouen as the metropolitan centre of Normandy, and its cathedral church as the place where members of the ducal family should rest. When his daughter Matilda lay seriously ill at Bec-Hellouin in 1134, he angrily opposed her wish to be buried there.[21]

He said it was unworthy that his daughter, an Empress who had twice been crowned in Rome, the capital city of the world, by the hands of the supreme pontiff, should be buried in any monastery, even one of the very purest religious observance; she should be carried to the city of Rouen, the metropolis of Normandy, and buried in the cathedral church beside her ancestors, Rollo and his son William Longsword, who had conquered Normandy by force of arms.

To Robert of Torigny, who described the tussle of wills, Matilda's continued resistance was the measure of her wisdom and virtue: 'She scorned temporal glory in the place of her burial; she knew that it was more propitious for the souls of the departed if their bodies might lie in the place where prayers for them were offered up most frequently and devoutly to God.' Robert here summed up the profound convictions of his fellow countrymen; convictions so strong that Henry I was persuaded by his daughter. Since she

[20] P. E. Schramm, 'Der König von Frankreich, Wahl, Krönung, Erbfolge und Königsidee von Anfang der Kapetinger (987) bis zum Ausgang des Mittelalters', *Zeitschrift der Savigny-Stiftung für Rechtsgeschichte*, Kanonistische Abteilung, XXV, lvi (1936), 290. Suger, *Vita Ludovici*, pp. 84–5, objected that this was against *ius naturale*.
[21] Robert of Torigny, Interpolations, viii. 28 (Marx, pp. 304–5).

recovered his capitulation was not put to the test; but a year later he chose for his own place of burial, not the cathedral church in the ducal city of Rouen or any English church connected with the ceremonial of kingship, but the Cluniac abbey he himself had founded at Reading.[22]

Bishops, too, were only slowly learning to turn the centre of their devotions from their own monasteries to the cathedrals, even when they had devoted their wealth and energy to the building or enlarging of their cathedral church. Odo of Bayeux was said to have intended to be buried in Saint-Vigor at Bayeux, though his death in Sicily defeated his intentions, and his final resting place was in Palermo.[23] When Hugh, bishop of Lisieux, died in 1077 his wish to be buried in the nunnery of Saint-Désir (Notre-Dame-du-Pré) that he and his mother had founded at Lisieux was challenged by the canons of the cathedral. Words spoken on his death bed could have been taken to imply a desire to rest in the cathedral church he had spared no pains to build and enrich. An unseemly wrangle delayed his burial, but the nuns took their case to Duke William himself and carried the day. The bishop was buried in his family monastery, in the presence of his brother, Robert, count of Eu.[24]

So the Benedictine abbeys and priories of eleventh-century Normandy were far more than status symbols to the comital and knightly families who founded them. They gave an added security and stability to their estates, whether inherited or acquired, helped to advance their authority during their lifetime, and provided a last resting place for their bodies and perpetual intercession for their souls after death. Besides this, the monasteries were to a great extent peopled by the children of local landed families, whether younger sons with too small an inheritance to support a family, or older sons with a vocation for monastic life. They acted too as credit institutions, capable of setting up young sons of knightly families for a career in the world. Such men might enter the

---

[22] The burial places chosen by the Norman rulers are discussed by L. Musset, 'Les sépultures des souverains normands: un aspect de l'idéologie du pouvoir', *Annales de Normandie*, xxvii (1977), 350–1.

[23] Abbé Faucon, *Essai historique sur le prieuré de Saint-Vigor-le-Grand* (Caen, 1861), pp. 66–76; Orderic, iv. 116–19.

[24] Orderic, iii. 14–19.

households of greater lords as landless knights receiving wages and food, provided they had a horse and adequate equipment. By such service they hoped to make their fortune and win a reward in land, or a money-fief, or the hand of an heiress. At the worst, if they survived into old age, they might have sufficient resources to purchase from an abbey a corrody entitling them to an annual allowance of food and clothing, or enter the monastic community as lay brethren.[25]

The initial provision of a horse might, however, prove to be beyond the resources of their family. Some abbeys kept and bred horses; others received them as gifts. At a date before 1030 a knight named Gradeloc gave a church to the abbey of Mont Saint-Michel, on condition that whenever he or his sons Ansger and Harvey needed to go to battle they might have the use of two horses for as long as necessary. This proved a burden to the abbey at a time of great disorder, and the obligation to lend horses was relaxed in exchange for eight pounds in cash.[26] Usually abbeys preferred to give horses outright, in return for the gift of some small revenue, or the renunciation of a right in family property destined to be given to the abbey. Billeheld, the wife of Baudry of Bocquencé and her sons Baudry and Robert gave some tithes to Saint-Evroult and confirmed the earlier gifts of their family; on the same day the abbot gave them a war horse. The charter carefully specified that they had not asked for it, but they received it gladly, as Robert wished to train his younger brother Baudry as a knight.[27] Thus the principle that alms should be freely given was upheld; but a younger son was provided for without unduly eroding the family patrimony, much as a younger son in the eighteenth century might be started in life by the purchase of a commission. Over the years the income from the tithe would more than pay for the horse. Sometimes horses were given on the death

[25] See below, p. 79.

[26] The charter is printed by R. Génestal, *Rôle des monastères comme établissements de crédit* (Paris, 1901), pp. 217-18. The charter gives details of a series of complicated transactions, beginning with a loan of four pounds to Gradeloc, which he repaid, and including the right of refuge on the Mount as a last resort in time of war.

[27] Le Prévost, v. 184; the date was early in the abbacy of Roger of Le Sap (1091-1123). The donors were received into the fraternity of the house.

of a knight, perhaps with the intention of storing up resources for another member of the family. In another charter of the time of Abbot Roger of Le Sap (1091–1123) Samson of Cullei made a grant to Saint-Evroult and received a horse which Arnold of Le Tilleul had given; Samson came of a family which held land from the abbey and provided knights for its service.[28]

Peasants no less than knights took advantage of the capital resources of abbeys, and sometimes borrowed from them to provide the necessary equipment for bringing new land under cultivation, and establishing married children on new holdings. Abbeys carried out the functions of rural banks at a time when credit was scarce; and they may well have provided better terms than extortionate secular usurers. At least they frequently made use of the contract known as a *vivum gagum*, by which they held the land that had been pledged only until the produce had paid for the loan with concealed interest, so that the debtor was assured of recovering his land in the end; whereas those who lent illegally at mortgage took all the produce as interest and still demanded full repayment of the original loan from the debtor's diminished resources before restoring the land.[29]

From the first were some contradictions in the position of monasteries, and these became accentuated. For half a century from about 1040 Benedictine monachism carried all before it in Normandy. Its popularity grew with the reform movement; but the reform worked towards withdrawing monks from the world. Colleges of secular canons, fitted for parochial work, were converted into priories for monks just when monks were being encouraged not to undertake parochial duties. Many monastic schools remained open

[28] Le Prévost, v. 193–4; see also M. Chibnall, 'Military service in Normandy before 1066', *Anglo-Norman Studies*, v (1983 for 1982), 70. For other grants of horses to benefactors see J. J. Vernier, *Chartes de l'abbaye de Jumièges* (Rouen/ Paris, 1916), i. 22, 48, 69, 74–5, 80; Orderic, iii. 190–1, 200–1, 204–5.

[29] The transactions in which monasteries were involved are described by Génestal, *Rôle des monastères, passim*. An example of a usurious loan to a poor miller by the steward of William of Breteuil is given by Orderic, iv. 244–5; he had taken the mill as a pledge, and because the loan was not repaid had disinherited the miller by leaving the mill to his own sons. Monasteries, too, sometimes struck hard bargains, but some of their loans were on the principle of the *vivum gagum*, where the capital was gradually repaid out of the produce from the land pledged.

to outside pupils, but increasingly they preferred to teach only their oblates and monks. The clergy attached to a castle chapel provided both chaplain service for the military household and administrative help in writing and keeping records for the greater courts. Castle priories in particular faced a dilemma.[30] However much a lord wished to have monks as his confessors and spiritual mentors, when he turned his castle church into a priory he was forcing duties upon the monks that they were less and less willing to perform. Many priories founded actually in castles moved to more peaceful and less cramped sites some distance from the castles within a generation. This is typical of some of the stresses that in time gave rise to the growth of new religious orders.

[30] For castle priories see D. J. A. Matthew, *The Norman Monasteries and their English Possessions* (Oxford, 1962), pp. 55–7.

4

Monastic Life

Although the Norman abbeys began a new life in the eleventh century many of them were refoundations, and they took over some of the traditions of previous monastic houses. Dom Laporte distinguished three waves of monasticism in the province of Rouen.[1] Very little is known of the fourth-century Gallo-Roman foundations; they disappeared in the Germanic invasions. But in the seventh century a number of spiritual leaders whose influence was to be more lasting settled in the province. The monasteries established by St Wandrille at Fontenelle, St Philbert at Jumièges, St Ouen at Rouen, and St Évroul in the forest of Ouche varied in organization, but all attracted hundreds of postulants. They took some of their discipline from the Rule of St Benedict, whose influence was spreading in Gaul from the seventh century, and added other customs such as those of St Columbanus, which emphasized individual asceticism. St Évroul was said by his first biographer to have recited the monastic hours 'according to the Roman and Gallic customs of St Benedict and the Irish customs of St Columbanus'.[2] St Wandrille, coming from Bobbio, established a mixed cenobitic and eremitic community, settled round a number of small sanctuaries built within a radius of about a mile from the main church. St Philbert's abbey had more corporate life, with two churches only and a dormitory and refectory for the whole community. In the course of the next two centuries all these abbeys attracted gifts from royal and noble patrons. Although some of the estates given in one generation were taken back in the next by heirs who had not renounced their claims, the communities found themselves the lords of

---

[1] J. Laporte, 'Les origines du monachisme dans la province de Rouen', *Revue Mabillon*, xxxi (1941), 1-13, 25-41, 49-68.

[2] M. Chibnall, 'The Merovingian monastery of St. Evroul', *Studies in Church History*, viii (1972), 34.

great estates scattered far beyond the frontiers of the province.

This phase ended with the ninth-century Viking invasions
and the tenth-century wars of succession in France. The
communities were broken up; most of the monks fled into
exile taking only the few most precious books and relics
they were able to carry. A handful of monks and clerks sometimes remained behind for a time to try to keep alive a claim
to estates that had fallen into secular hands; the churches
and conventual buildings were looted and left to crumble
into ruins. When monastic life was restored in the eleventh
century, after tentative beginnings half a century earlier,
the impetus had to come from outside Normandy. There
were active centres of revival in Lotharingia, Burgundy,
and Italy; all these contributed to the new Norman monasticism.

The monks of Jumièges never returned from their priory
of Haspres to which they had fled, and the restoration of
their abbey was tentatively begun with a few monks from
Saint-Cyprien, Poitiers, but these had little influence.
Memories of Saint-Wandrille (Fontenelle) were kept alive
by monks who were given a refuge at Saint-Pierre of Mont
Blandain, in a suburb of Ghent. Surprisingly, it was not from
there that monks returned to Fontenelle, but from another
abbey in Ghent, Saint-Bavon, which had been restored by
Gerard de Brogne.[3] Their leader was the monk Maynard,
a kinsman of the count of Flanders, who had been inspired
by Gerard.[4] He brought with him the ideals that Gerard had
spread among the Lotharingian monasteries. At first the
movement made little progress, but its influence remained
lasting in Normandy. The heart of Gerard's reform was
respect for the basic observance of regular life: poverty,
chastity, obedience to the abbot, observance of fasts. He
saw too that it was essential to resist the spoliation of the
powerful in order to preserve the minimum security necessary
for settled monastic life; but he looked for support to the

[3] J. Laporte has proved that the restoration came from Saint-Bavon, Ghent,
and not from Mont Blandain, as had previously been supposed (*Mont Saint-
Michel*, i. 57–8, 728–9).

[4] See J. Laporte, 'Gerard de Brogne', *Congrès du Millénaire* (Maredsous,
1959), p. 154.

diocesan bishop,[5] and never aimed at complete exemption
or the creation of an ordered hierarchy of monasteries. This
may have contributed to the favour his movement continued
to find in Normandy, where patrons usually liked to found
autonomous abbeys, subject only to the bishop.

Cluniac influence took longer to reach Normandy. When
Duke William of Aquitaine founded the abbey of Cluny in
910 the first essential was to secure complete independence
from all lay control. The abbey was therefore placed directly
under the Holy See; and the community's right to elect its
own abbot in accordance with the Rule of St Benedict was
guaranteed. Cluny would claim proudly to be 'subject to no
prince or prelate'.[6] From the first the abbots were well aware
of the need to secure a sound economic basis to ensure
spiritual independence. They succeeded so well that Cluniac
monks were sought by patrons from far afield, and in time
a network of Cluniac houses spread across Western Europe.
Cluniac reform, whilst sharing with that of Gerard de Brogne
an insistence on strict monastic discipline, went further in its
demand for exemption, and built up a more elaborate liturgy.
The magnificence and solemnity of the ritual in the great
abbey church impressed visiting monks and laymen alike.
Since Cluniac houses wished to exclude control by the
bishops, they looked to each other for support. Unity was
preserved by following the same monastic customs, copied
from house to house; discipline by building up a loose con-
federation of dependent priories, and holding periodic
general chapters where statutes could be issued for all the
priories that fully accepted Cluniac authority. Some houses
reformed by Cluniac monks remained independent at the
wish of patrons; in these the influence of Cluny showed itself
principally in liturgical custom. This is what happened in
Normandy. Cluniac customs were brought first of all in 1001
by William of Volpiano and his monks, who came from
Cluny's daughter house at Saint-Bénigne, and went on to
establish Bernay and many other monasteries.[7] Later in the

[5] For the place of the bishop as spiritual adviser to monks, see RSB, chs. 62, 64.
[6] Orderic, vi. 270-1; Noreen Hunt, *Cluny under Saint Hugh* (London, 1967),
pp. 19-20.
[7] Knowles, *Monastic Order*, pp. 83-5. For William of Volpiano see also
E. Sackur, *Die Cluniacenser* (Halle, 1892), ii. 126-33, 207-13.

century imitation was encouraged by individuals like Robert of Grandmesnil, founder and second abbot of Saint-Evroult, who had spent some time in Cluny as a novice.[8] So Cluniac influence was undeniably very strong in many Norman abbeys; but no house directly subject to Cluny or one of its priories had been founded in Normandy before 1066. There was an echo of the Cluniac exemption clause in the foundation charter of Fécamp, which promised freedom of election 'as at Cluny'.[9] But freedom had different meanings in different places; and in making their elections the abbeys in William the Conqueror's Normandy only very rarely resisted a ducal nominee.

The third centre of revival was Italy, where the eremitical movement partly inspired by St Romuald was strong, and spiritual devotion remained of central importance. William of Volpiano himself was a native of Piedmont, and had learnt to love architecture and intellectual studies as well as the spiritual side of monastic life before he came to Cluny, and thence to Normandy. A man of many talents, he left his mark on all aspects of life in the Norman monasteries. One trace of his influence remains visible to this day in the austere and grandiose architecture of the abbey church at Bernay, which J. Decaens has characterized as 'Ottonian and Lombard' in style.[10] His disciple John of Fécamp, who came from Ravenna to be abbot of Fécamp, has been called the greatest spiritual writer of the epoch before St Bernard, and many of his prayers were included in the Roman missal, where they were wrongly attributed to St Ambrose.[11]

So in Normandy both new foundations and restored monasteries benefited from three strong movements of reform. Although all followed the Rule of St Benedict, there was no uniformity; they might differ in their organization, in spiritual and intellectual interests, and in liturgical customs. Many still treasured traditions that went back to the Columbanian or Gallo-Roman practices of earlier Neustrian monks.

[8] Orderic, ii. 74–5.

[9] Lemarignier, *Exemption*, pp. 34–5.

[10] J. Decaens, 'La datation de l'abbaye de Bernay', *Anglo-Norman Studies*, v (1983 for 1982), 114.

[11] A. Wilmart, *Auteurs spirituels et textes dévots au Moyen Âge latin* (Paris, 1932), 101–25, 126–37.

Their monasticism was eclectic, open at first to various influences; but gradually each house or group of houses developed its own way of life, cherishing its customs while holding more firmly if under attack to the traditions that were common to them all.

Much in their way of life reflected the society of which they formed part. The ideal of poverty was personal, not corporate. Even abbeys that began in a flight from the world by a small group of men prepared to live by the labour of their own hands soon attracted numerous disciples and accepted ample endowments. Most founders regarded the provision of sufficient property to support a sizeable community as the prerequisite for orderly spiritual life; most abbots demanded it before they would agree to send out new colonies of monks. The alternative to economic independence in that turbulent world was apt to be secularization. So abbeys that resisted domination by magnates in their turn became great lords, with all the responsibilities of lordship. They received vows of fealty and held courts for their vassals. Cultivating their fields, collecting their revenues, administering their property, and building their great churches required increased numbers of household servants and dependent peasants, as well as involving monks in secular business.

The property aquired in the eleventh century never exactly corresponded with the lost ancient patrimonies, though many former church lands were restored to monastic ownership. Geographically estates were less widespread, at least up to the time of the Norman conquest of England; they were adapted to new political structures. At first the wealth of the Norman church was concentrated in Normandy. Jumièges, for example, lost its ancient possessions in Cambrésis and Poitou.[12] Many of the lands that the first abbey of Saint-Evroult had held in the Île-de-France passed to the Parisian house of Saint-Germain-des-Prés; while Saint-Evroult itself acquired the estates of the former monastery of Saint-Céneri on the Sarthe, and established a dependent priory there.[13]

[12] L. Musset, 'Les destins de la propriété monastique durant les invasions normandes', *Jumièges*, i. 49–55.

[13] Marie de la Motte-Callas, 'Les possessions territoriales de Saint-Germain-des-Prés', *Revue d'histoire de l'église de France*, xliii (1957), 62–70; Orderic, iii, pp. xvii–xviii.

But from the 1060s its estates were spreading into the French Vexin and across the Channel in England. The prosperity of great abbeys such as these was bound up with that of the duchy; their growing patrimonies chart the expansion of Norman power and ambition. They were not prepared to be dependencies of even the greatest Burgundian abbey; indeed they established dependent priories of their own.

Their possessions also reflect the sources of Norman wealth. When Saint-Evroult was restored about 1050 it received an endowment very different from that of the former Merovingian house.[14] Gifts of great arable estates had become comparatively rare. Between five or ten donations or purchases conveyed substantial demesne and peasant lands in a hamlet or village; gifts of a few ploughlands were more common. But the abbey received over thirty churches, more than half of which explicitly included the priest's land. Gifts of tithe were equally numerous, and these often listed the tithes of market tolls, mills, and money rents alongside agricultural produce.[15] They are an indication of the active commercial life of Normandy, which had penetrated even to the more rural areas, and to the wide circulation of money.[16] At a different level they reflect the first stage of church reform: reformers had condemned the holding of churches and tithes by laymen, but still accepted the transfer of such forms of spiritual property to monasteries.[17] This led to abuses of a different kind; the problem of securing the adequate service of parishes and support for priests remained to be undertaken by later generations.

Little evidence of how properties were administered survives from Normandy at this period. Estates might be directly cultivated by the labour of peasants, or let out either as a whole or piecemeal. Fragmentary evidence from charters and a few early twelfth-century surveys, such as those of the

[14] Descriptions of some of the great estates of the ninth century survive in surveys such as the *Polyptique de l'abbaye de Saint-Rémi de Reims*, ed. M. B. Guérard (Paris, 1853).

[15] Orderic, ii. 32–39; Fauroux, no. 122.

[16] See Bates, *Normandy*, pp. 95–8.

[17] One of the clearest short introductions to the problem of the proprietary church is Knowles, *Monastic Order*, pp. 562–8, 595–600. For monastic possession of tithes see G. Constable, *Monastic Tithes* (Cambridge, 1964), pp. 99–136.

nunnery of La Trinité de Caen, show that crop-sharing or *métayage* was a favoured form of letting.[18] Alternatively lands and rights could be let out to a farmer at a fixed rent: a practice certainly very common in England at the time of the Domesday survey.[19] Unless a farmer was entrusted with the whole administration of a property, bailiffs or provosts had to be appointed to collect rents in cash and corn and give general supervision. Many small dependent priories or provostships served as administrative centres. Monks no less than laymen were employed as over-seers, sometimes to the detriment of their spiritual life. Robert, a Norman monk who obtained the provostship of Argenteuil from Saint-Denis 'because he did not care to lead a life of tranquillity and poverty in the cloister', met his death at the hands of an enraged peasant from whom he was aggressively demanding customary dues.[20] But the estates might be administered successfully for the benefit of monks and laymen alike. Surplus wealth could help to provide the capital necessary to extend cultivation by clearing woodlands and draining marshes. Adequate revenues served to support the community and enabled the monks to carry out what was widely believed to be their allotted work.

Writers in the eleventh and twelfth centuries liked to describe society in terms of 'orders', each with its own function. Knights should be trained to fight, peasants to till the soil, monks to pray and intercede with God for the whole world.[21] At Cluny first of all, but soon in all the reformed Benedictine houses, a steady lengthening of the horarium from the basic requirements laid down in the Rule of St Benedict was taking place.[22] There was now a daily High Mass; and to this were added a second earlier Mass (sometimes

---

[18] Fauroux, no. 232; Paris, Bibliothèque nationale, MS latin 5650, fo. 22v.

[19] For the 'farming' of manors at this date (so called from the payment of a *firma* or fixed rent), see R. Lennard, *Rural England 1086–1135* (Oxford, 1959), ch. vi, especially pp. 153–9.

[20] Robert's disreputable career began when, as simoniacal abbot of Saint-Pierre-sur-Dive he turned the abbey into a fortress and held it against King Henry. After being deposed and exiled he took refuge at Saint-Denis (Orderic, vi. 72–5, 82–3).

[21] See below, p. 117.

[22] *Monastic Constitutions of Lanfranc*, pp. xiv–xviii.

called the Morrow or Chapter Mass), a whole series of extra psalms, prayers, and minor offices. These included the regular recitation of the *Psalmi familiares* for kinsfolk and benefactors, the Office of the Dead, and the Office of All Saints. Various traditions were followed in individual monasteries; as ritual grew in complexity customs began to be written down in detail and passed from house to house for imitation in whole or in part. Even after being recorded in customaries, they were constantly revised. Custom was 'normative as well as descriptive; it applied to what should be done rather than simply to what was done'.[23] This trend was most apparent at Cluny, where at least two collections of the older customs were further revised in the great customaries of Bernard and Ulrich in the second half of the eleventh century.[24] Individual houses differed in what they found it necessary to record. The customs of Cluny and one of its daughter houses, Saint-Bénigne de Dijon, were concerned principally with the liturgy, and described in detail the horarium and calendar of monastic life. Those of Fruttuaria had more to say on organization: on the activities and duties of the monastic officers.[25] Norman houses drew their customs from a variety of sources, reflecting the influences that had shaped each one of them. Fécamp, for instance, owed much to Saint-Bénigne, and in turn left its mark on Mont Saint-Michel, but the late eleventh-century sacramentary of the Mount shows that its liturgy had its own individuality, particularly in the development of its angelology.[26] Bec-Hellouin, perhaps the most independent of all the great abbeys, had strong affinities with Fécamp and Fruttuaria, somewhat less with the Lotharingian houses, and least of all with Cluny.[27] When, after the conquest of England, Norman monks were appointed to

[23] G. Constable, 'Monastic legislation at Cluny in the eleventh and twelfth centuries', *Proceedings of the Fourth International Congress of Medieval Canon Law, Monumenta Iuris Canonici*, Series C: Subsidia, v (Vatican City, 1976), p. 156 (reprinted *Cluniac Studies*, ch. i).

[24] Giles Constable, *Statuta Petri Venerabilis* (*CCM* vi), pp. 29–30.

[25] J. Laporte, *Mont Saint-Michel*, i. 75.

[26] H. Tardif, 'La liturgie de la messe au Mont Saint-Michel' *Mont Saint-Michel*, i. 353–77. The special function of angels as divine messengers is stressed in several places, for instance in an unusual postcommunion for the Annunciation and the feast of St Michael (ibid., p. 366).

[27] Marie Pascal Dickson, *Consuetudines Beccenses* (*CCM* iv), pp. xxxvii–xli.

English offices, they showed a similar freedom of choice in the customs they established in English monasteries. Lanfranc's customs, introduced first at Christ Church, Canterbury, had far more in common with Cluny and some Flemish houses than with his own abbey of Bec.[28] Herbert Losinga wrote to the abbey of Fécamp, where he had made his profession, asking for a copy of their customs to help him in founding the priory of Norwich.[29] Some English customs, going back at least to the tenth-century *Regularis concordia*, were observed at Norwich alongside those of Fécamp;[30] but there was not a trace of the *Regularis concordia* in the customs of Lanfranc.

The increasing length and solemnity of the liturgy led to other changes in the lives of monks. In particular the manual toil, prescribed in the Rule, was no longer seen as necessarily, or even rightly, labour in the fields. The Rule had laid down that since sloth is the enemy of the soul the brethren should be occupied at certain times in manual work, at others in spiritual reading.[31] But defenders of change pointed out that Christ had told Mary that she had chosen the better part; a monk could fulfil the intention of the Rule by devoting part of this time to liturgical prayer, the recitation of psalms, and similar exercises.[32] To this in practice many added the copying and decoration of manuscripts; Orderic considered that he was keeping sloth at bay by writing history.[33] He expressed admiration for the humility of a nobly born monk, St William of Gellone, who had helped with road building, worked in orchard and vineyard, and acted as cook, until his abbot forbade him to perform servile work, and told him to devote himself, as Mary had done, to spiritual

[28] For the sources of Lanfranc's customs see *Monastic Constitutions of Lanfranc*, p. xiii.

[29] *The Life, Letters and Sermons of Bishop Herbert of Losinga*, ed. Goulburn and Symonds (London, 1878), i. 65-6.

[30] J. B. L. Tolhurst, *The Customary of the Cathedral Priory Church of Norwich* (Henry Bradshaw Society, lxxxii, 1948), pp. xiv-xvi.

[31] RSB ch. 48.

[32] *Letters of Peter the Venerable*, ep. 28. viii (i. 70-1). See C. Holdsworth, 'The blessing of work: the Cistercian view', *Studies in Church History*, x. 64-6, for examples of the reply that Martha and Mary should both be accommodated in each individual's way of life.

[33] Orderic, i. 130-1; iii. 4-7, 150-1.

contemplation.[34] Roger of Warenne, one of the most highly born monks at Saint-Evroult, was similarly praised for insisting on greasing the shoes and washing the slippers of the brethren.[35] Since field work had been abandoned the shoes were no longer very dirty, but the act was symbolic of humility.

This new interpretation of manual work was shared by founders and benefactors. Some wealthy laymen gave revenues to support a particular monk to pray daily on their behalf.[36] There was a great flowering of confraternities, in which laymen and clerks alike could participate in the benefits of monastic intercession. Every house kept records of its benefactors, and of their families and friends, who were to be commemorated on the anniversary of their death. Names were entered in necrologies kept in the chapter-house, and in commemoration books preserved in the church.[37] Orderic recorded details of some of the customs at Saint-Evroult. Osbern, abbot from 1061 to 1066, established a general anniversary on 26 June for the mothers and fathers, brothers and sisters of all the monks.[38] The names were inscribed on a long roll when they took the habit, followed by the names of their kinsfolk. The roll was kept by the altar in the church, and the anniversary was observed with a ringing of bells for the Office of the Dead. The roll was then untied and laid on the altar, and prayers were offered, first for the dead, then for the living parents and benefactors, and all the faithful. The Morrow Mass was solemnly sung by the abbot.[39] On the same day the almoner assembled in the convent as many poor persons as there were monks, and the cellarer provided each one with his portion of bread and drink and a main course in the guest-house; after the chapter all the monks washed the feet of the poor as they did on Maundy Thursday.

A network of prayer unions spread across Western Europe,

[34] Orderic, iii. 222-5.

[35] Orderic, iii. 230-1.

[36] Ansold of Maule gave revenues to Jumièges for this purpose (J. J. Vernier, *Chartes de l'abbaye de Jumièges* i. 80).

[37] See Laporte, *Revue Mabillon* (1956), pp. 141-88; G. Constable, 'The *Liber Memorialis* of Remiremont', *Speculum*, xlvii (1972), 261-77.

[38] Orderic, ii. 114-15.

[39] Sometimes also called the Morning or Chapter Mass, this was celebrated usually before the meeting of the chapter.

linking together monastic houses and assuring monks and
nuns of the prayers of their brethren from the moment of
their death. As the name of each new house or individual
was added to the commemoration book, details of the
offices to be performed were noted. Obituary rolls, carried
from house to house, contained the names of those who had
died recently.[40] Obligations steadily increased; an early list
from the abbey of Jumièges contained a list of seventeen
monasteries. A much longer list from Saint-Evroult, with
additions up to the late twelfth century, recorded over
eighty. Mont Saint-Michel had twenty-three spiritual fraternities in Normandy alone.[41] The burden of intercession was
in time to become intolerable and lead to collective commemoration; but in Orderic's lifetime it was still a treasured,
if arduous, part of monastic life and duty. To many, both
inside and outside the monasteries, it represented the
justification of monasticism.

Laymen no less than monks were admitted to fraternities,
sometimes as individuals, sometimes as families, or even in
groups described as brotherhoods.[42] Saint-Evroult's commemorative book noted that a fraternity, commonly known
as a *frarria*, had been established in the nearby village of
Grandcamp; when a member died the group offered three
shillings, and the monks commemorated him as if he had
been one of their own household. At Chambrais, adjacent to
Grandcamp, a *frarria bacalariorum* was formed on the same
lines; when a member died the monks promised to grant
him their customary absolution. This must surely have been
an association of household knights, probably young men of
the type of 'jeunes' described by Duby.[43] The lords of
Ferrières-Saint-Hilaire held both Grandcamp and Chambrais;
the latter had an ancient castle, and later became the

[40] L. Delisle, *Rouleaux des Morts* (Société de l'histoire de France, Paris,
1866).

[41] M. Le Pesant, *Mont Saint-Michel*, i. 745; Laporte, *Revue Mabillon* (1956),
pp. 141–88. See Map II.

[42] The corporate need for intercession was met in towns as burgess wealth
increased through the establishment of religious gilds by traders and craftsmen.
Usually these were attached to parish or other town churches; Saint-Evroult, in its
forest setting, attracted no such urban fraternities.

[43] Laporte, *Revue Mabillon* (1956), p. 181. For the 'jeunes' see below,
pp. 123, 152.

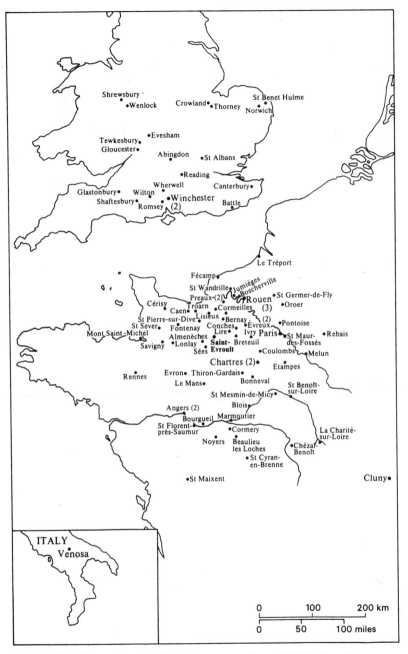

II. Abbeys and priories linked by prayer unions with Saint-Evroult

caput of the honour.[44] The whole region, with its ancient
iron-works and castles, must have resounded with the turmoil
of knights in their mailed hauberks; and their constant danger
in battle was a warning of the need for spiritual insurance.
Dying knights were often carried to the abbey or its dependent churches in the hope that unction and absolution might
not come too late. Many monks considered that it was a
natural extension of their duty of intercession to admit pious
lay men and women, whose work lay outside the monasteries,
to some of the spiritual benefits of their prayers. So friends
and benefactors were received in the abbey's chapter-house
for the ceremony of admission, and might on other occasions
be allowed to share in worship in the monastic church, or
seek spiritual guidance from the monks in their own cloister.[45]
Whilst this was accepted as normal and even mutually beneficial it followed that the monastic enclosure was not
rigorous. Abbeys were struggling to be at the same time a
refuge from the world for those in search of spiritual perfection and a centre of evangelization. But a way of life designed
to 'monasticize' lay society might easily result in diluting,
if not actually corrupting, monastic zeal.

The monastic ideal represented the lives of monks as
a heroic struggle. The language of temporal warfare had been
borrowed to describe spiritual warfare from the earliest days
of the Christian Church:[46] St Benedict, St Augustine, and
many others had carried on the tradition of St Paul. Orderic
grew up with the ideal from childhood. When he described
his father's eloquent plea to Roger of Montgomery to found
an abbey at Shrewsbury he used words that may have been
as much imagined as remembered; but they catch the spirit
of his father's purpose, and probably embody some of his
own hard experience:

Consider what duties are performed in monasteries obedient to a rule
by those trained in the service of God. Countless benefits are obtained
there every day, and Christ's garrisons strive manfully against the devil.

[44] See A. Le Prévost, *Mémoires et notes pour servir à l'histoire de la départe-
ment de l'Eure*, ed. L. Delisle and L. Passy (Évreux, 1862-9), ii. 81-102.

[45] Orderic, iii. 164-7, 206-7.

[46] RSB Prologue; cf. C. Holdsworth, *Studies in Church History*, xx (1983),
76-7.

Assuredly the harder the struggle of the spiritual warrior the more glorious will be his victory, and the more precious his trophies in the courts of Heaven. Who can describe all the vigils of monks, their hymns and psalms, their prayers and alms, and their daily offerings of Masses with copious tears? . . . Their lot is a harsh life, mean clothing, scanty food and drink, and renunciation of their own wills for the love of the Lord Jesus.[47]

When Orderic as an old man wrote down the brief record of his early life he recalled his father's promise to him that if he became a monk he would share the joys of paradise with the Holy Innocents after his death.[48] This, surely, is a true record of his father's words; and it brings to mind an illustration in the eleventh-century Sacramentary of Mont Saint-Michel: the miniature for the feast of the Holy Innocents. Instead of the usual narrative scene, the initial D encircles a female figure, representing the Church, who holds in one hand the palm of martyrdom and in the other the crown of everlasting life. Behind her, depicted as busts because of the lack of space, is a group of Innocents. Shown not as babes, but as men with long hair, they represent the first martyrs of the Church. The iconography has something in common with the pictures of the saints in heaven in the All Saints miniature in the same Sacramentary.[49] Even though these untonsured figures are not monks, the illustration shows vividly how the significance of the feast of the Innocents could appear to contemporaries well versed in the liturgy. To many, indeed, the life of a monk represented the sacrifice of self for the love of Christ: a kind of martyrdom. The idea was expressed by Rupert of Deutz among others, in a language even more emphatic than Orderic's:

We who are called monks are reckoned among the martyrs, if we live up to our profession. Martyrs endured grievous, though sometimes brief, tortures; we, for our part, suffer daily. Claustral seclusion, constraint by a rule, mean clothing, submission to another, the burden of silence, constant fasting, repeated flagellation, the weariness of

[47] Orderic, iii. 144-5.

[48] Orderic, vi. 552-3.

[49] J. J. G. Alexander, *Norman Illumination at Mont Saint-Michel* (Oxford, 1970), pp. 135-6 and plate 31e.

vigils, rising from sleep to daily offices, above all the shame of confession, the bitterness of penance, public rebukes or chastisement before our brethren, continual attention to prayers, vigilance in reading: all these torment the flesh.[50]

To Orderic, the image of the Holy Innocents must have had a dual significance, since it implied also purity from the corruption of the world, and so was specially appropriate to the children of the cloister, the child oblates.

Naturally there was often a conflict between such ideals and the actual motives and expectations of the men and women from many walks of life who made profession as religious. Sermons, manuals of advice to novices, meditations, the everyday spiritual discourses of such a man as St Anselm, all tell the same story of the problems involved in adapting to the hard and tedious details of everyday life, particularly after the enthusiasm and high hopes of an adult conversion. Anselm warned that the honeymoon delights of first conversion would give way to doubts and temptations; but for those who persevered there would be a third period of secure joy. He drew an analogy with the experience of earthly marriage.[51] Hugh of Barzelle's meditation on the verse, 'Behold, how good and how pleasant it is for brethren to dwell together in unity', began by describing the imperfections of the bad brethren who failed to find it good and pleasant. They renounced the world in word and dress only, were negligent in all their duties, and in consequence experienced all the torments of hell in their own souls.[52] Ailred of Rievaulx drew on his own experience as a novice master when he wrote the *Speculum caritatis* and depicted the perplexity of the newcomer who contrasted the spiritual rapture he had experienced before his conversion with the aridity of the hard life he found during his early months in a strict cloister.[53] The shock of adaptation could be equally great in Benedictine and Cistercian houses, and might be experienced by any new recruit, whether he entered the

[50] Cited, J. Leclercq, *Analecta Monastica* iv (*Studia Anselmiana*, xli (1957)), 114–15; see also idem, *La vie parfaite* (Paris/Turnhout, 1948), pp. 125–60.

[51] *Memorials of St. Anselm*, p. 307.

[52] John Morson, 'The *De cohabitatione fratrum* of Hugh of Barzelle', *Analecta Monastica* iv (*Studia Anselmiana*, 1957), 119–40, especially 128–31.

[53] Migne, *PL*, cxcv, 559–62.

abbey as a child, buoyed up by the promises of parents, or as a convert in later life.

Norman Benedictine monasteries opened their doors to individuals representing every shade of religious intention. Among the fully professed monks the two main groups were the *nutriti,* the children of the cloister, and the *conversi,* who took the monastic habit as grown men and ranged from learned secular clerks to illiterate or semi-literate laymen. Sometimes the two groups were at odds with one another. The *nutriti* claimed to be better because they had never committed wrong in the world, or been soiled by the mire of secular life; the *conversi* boasted that they had the experience of affairs necessary to rule the monastery and to provide the essentials of life for the whole community, besides having greater virtue when they overcame greater temptations. To such bickerings Anselm of Bec had a ready answer: the *nutriti* might be compared to the angels, the *conversi* to the saints in heaven. If St Michael were to say to St Peter, 'You denied the Lord', Peter could reply, 'True, but you never had to suffer even a single blow for the Lord's sake'; but the angels and saints live together in harmony, and do not say such things.[54]

Child oblates were numerous in almost all the great abbeys in the eleventh century. The Rule of St Benedict had made provision for the admission of children, and described the ceremony. The child was to hold a written petition, and during the offertory of the Mass an altar-cloth was to be wrapped round his hand.[55] Originally the act of the parents was binding; there was no question of choice when the oblate came to make his mature profession. Opposition built up slowly; in the well-publicized case of Godeschalk, professed as a child at Fulda under Raban Maur, the Council of Mainz of 829 was persuaded to release him from his vows, on the grounds that no one could be made a monk against his will. But Raban continued to argue that the parents had the right to place a child in a monastery; and this traditional view persisted.[56] By the eleventh century the principle had been

[54] *Memorials of St. Anselm*, pp. 68-9. Cf. C. Harper-Bill, 'The piety of the Anglo-Norman knightly class', *Anglo-Norman Studies*, ii (1980 for 1979), 63-77.
[55] RSB ch. 59.
[56] H. Leclercq, 'Oblat', *Dictionnaire d'archéologie chrétienne et de liturgie*, xii. 1857-77.

accepted that an oblate had the right to withdraw on
reaching mature years. But the practical difficulties of doing
so were very great, since any property rights he might have
possessed had been renounced on admission to the monastery,
and few had the resolution of Godeschalk. Ultimately the
tide of opinion, supported perhaps by social changes which
made the upbringing of children outside court and cloister
a more practical possibility, turned against child oblation;
the practice was drying up by the end of the twelfth
century,[57] though it persisted longer for girls than for boys.[58]
To Orderic it was normal and even praiseworthy; among his
fellow monks were many who had entered the abbey in
childhood as he did, and had devoted their lives willingly to
the work of the community.[59]

There were some limitations to the work they were
qualified, perhaps even permitted to do. A statute of Peter
the Venerable, specifying that boy scholars should not be
excluded from monastic offices when they grew up shows
that the earlier practice in some Cluniac houses at least had
been to exclude them.[60] It seems likely that Saint-Evroult,
which had come under the influence of Cluny, was one of
these abbeys during Orderic's lifetime. Orderic speaks of how
he wrote history to avoid idleness, 'since it is not my lot to
direct others'.[61] Whatever may have been true of priors and
other obedientiaries, among the early abbots only one had
been a child of the cloister. This was the first abbot, Thierry
of Mathonville, who was brought from Jumièges where
he had been professed and educated, and whose difficulties
in practical administration were so great that they must have
given the monks a warning of the dangers involved in the
election of such men. As spiritual guide, teacher, and father
to his monks, Thierry excelled; he had made an admirable
claustral prior at Jumièges, but he had neither the head nor

[57] *Monastic Constitutions of Lanfranc*, pp. xviii–xix.
[58] In the fourteenth century the earl of Oxford was still exercising a hereditary right to present a young girl as an oblate nun in Holy Trinity, Caen (*Charters
and Custumals of the Abbey of Holy Trinity Caen*, ed. M. Chibnall (British
Academy: Records of Social and Economic History, new ser. v), London 1982,
p. xliii).
[59] Orderic, ii. 84–7, 126–9.
[60] *Statutes of Peter the Venerable*, no. 66, p. 97.
[61] Orderic, i. 130–1.

the heart for secular business, and was so sharply criticized by some of his monks (in particular by his prior, Robert of Grandmesnil) that he first withdrew for long periods of meditation to a chapel attached to the abbey, and finally obtained permission to leave on a pilgrimage for Jerusalem.[62] Robert of Grandmesnil, nobly born and educated in secular schools as well as in the court, where he had been a squire of Duke William for five years before his conversion, followed Thierry in office.[63] Osbern, intruded by the duke against the wishes of the monks after Robert was forced into exile, was nevertheless a reforming churchman: a well-educated secular clerk from the Pays de Caux, he had been a canon of Lisieux before becoming a monk at La Trinité-du-Mont, Rouen.[64] The next four abbots, Mainer of Échauffour, Serlo of Orgères, Roger of Le Sap, and Warin of Les Essarts, were all local men educated in secular schools nearby, who had made their professions as grown men.[65] Richard of Leicester, elected in 1137, had been a canon of Leicester for sixteen years before his conversion.[66] Less is known of the conventual priors and priors of dependent cells; but this group included such learned men as Geoffrey of Orleans, Goisbert the doctor of Chartres, and John of Rheims, all of whom had studied in schools of liberal arts before their conversion.[67]

Not one of the child oblates whose careers are described by Orderic held administrative office. Their skills were employed in choir and scriptorium. William Gregory, the son of Guy Bollein, was an able reader and chanter and a distinguished scribe, who spent over fifty years immersed in studies. Reginald Benedict, the son of Arnold of Échauffour, was thoroughly versed in reading and singing, and studied the Bible. A number of others—Bernard, Gilbert, Goscelin, Ralph, William, Herbert of Montreuil—were described as talented boys in the school of Abbot Thierry, and excellent copyists. There is no indication that any of them held administrative office. They might travel on behalf of the

[62] Orderic, ii. 16-19, 42-53, 66-73.
[63] Orderic, ii. 40-1, 74-5.
[64] Orderic, ii. 90-7, 106-9.
[65] Orderic, ii. 74-5, 144-7; iii. 118-19, 240-1.
[66] Orderic, vi. 488-9.
[67] Orderic, ii. 346-7; i. 20.

monastery; Orderic himself went to Rheims and Cluny and England. Reginald Benedict, who had wealthy kinsmen in southern Italy, twice went there in search of benefactions.[68] But more often even the fund raisers were found among men of the court, who had entered the abbey as *conversi*. The exclusion of the children of the cloister from office was by no means general in other abbeys; for example an oblate monk, who had been the obedientiary in charge of the garden at Jumièges, was made abbot of Saint-Pierre-sur-Dive,[69] and there is some evidence that William of Malmesbury might, had he wished, have become abbot of Malmesbury.[70] Guibert of Nogent was in a slightly different position; although primised to the church at birth he was educated outside a monastery, took his vows by his own wish at Saint-Germer de Fly at the remarkably early age of twelve, and rose to be abbot of Nogent; his career illustrates the possibilities open in regions where the education of boys was spreading outside the cloister.[71] Increasingly, too, aptitude was allowed to override custom, even in houses that had been more restrictive. But by the mid-twelfth century the whole question was becoming academic, as the practice of child oblation slowly withered away.

The adult converts included a wide range of laymen and secular clerks. Writing of the abbey of Bec, Orderic adapted his metaphors to the different types of converts in that abbey. William, son of Giroie, Hugh, count of Meulan, and other distinguished knights joined the army of Christ; Lanfranc and Anselm and other learned scholars came here to Christ's school.[72] Both army and school referred in a sense to 'the whole community at its work of worship in the choir';[73] but the different talents and training of these men were emphasized. The lay converts came mostly from knightly or noble families, like the reformer Gerard de Brogne, or Herluin, founder of Bec, or Anselm. Some, like Richard of

[68] Orderic, ii. 126-9.
[69] Orderic, v. 212-13.
[70] Malmesbury, *Historia Novella*, p. xii.
[71] Guibert, *De vita sua*, especially I.3, 15 (Benson, pp. 16, 42, 76-8; Labande, pp. x, 18-19, 110-11).
[72] Orderic, ii. 12, 18-20, 250, and *passim*.
[73] R. W. Southern, *Renaissance and Renewal*, p. 115.

Heudicourt, a noble knight from the Vexin who entered Saint-Evroult,[74] and possibly Herluin himself, turned from the world as mature men whose conversion followed a narrow escape from death in battle. One story at least attributed Herluin's conversion to his realization during a disastrous battle of the imminent danger of death; he vowed that if he escaped alive he would never fight again, save for God alone.[75] Richard of Heudicourt, who had served as a household knight under Hugh of Grandmesnil, took his vows when he lay in danger of death from a serious wound, and lived to serve the abbey for seven years. Anselm, on the other hand, reached his decision after long and serious spiritual consideration.[76] Motives were mixed, and the men whose careers are known rarely fit into accepted stereotypes. Robert of Grandmesnil, an educated man of noble family who deliberately renounced a training in arms, appears as a man of worldly ability and strong religious feeling tempered by ambition, who responded to the splendid ritual of Cluny (which was later to repel Amadeus of Savoy)[77] and wished to see some of it copied at Saint-Evroult. Others were converted while young knights in the prime of life, like the five young nobles in the court of Hugh, earl of Chester, who were carried away by the preaching of the court chaplain, Gerold of Avranches, and the stories of warrior saints he told to capture their imagination.[78] But, particularly in the early days of the monastery, they also included simple, unlettered laymen, like Durand the gardener at Saint-Evroult.[79] And there was always room for monks *ad succurrendum*: benefactors who took the habit at the end of their life, and died as full members of the community.

The clerical, like the lay, converts came from a wide

[74] Orderic, ii. 132.

[75] Orderic, ii. 12; but there are other versions of Herluin's motives (A. A. Porée, *Histoire de l'abbaye du Bec* (Évreux, 1901), i. 32-3).

[76] Southern, *St. Anselm*, pp. 27-30.

[77] Amadeus vacillated for a time between Cluny and Cîteaux, but was finally overcome with remorse for his hesitation in the midst of a sumptuous Mass, and left Cluny to return to Cîteaux (M. Anselme Dimier, 'Un témoin tardif peu connu du conflit entre cisterciens et clunisiens', *Petrus Venerabilis*, ed. G. Constable and J. Kritzeck, *Studia Anselmiana*, xl (1956), 81-94).

[78] Above, p. 15.

[79] Orderic, ii. 20-1.

spectrum of talents, learning, and background. Riculf and Roger, old country priests who had only the bare rudiments of letters necessary for carrying out their duties, were among the first monks in the refounded abbey of Saint-Evroult.[80] A number of priests were persuaded to make their profession when they or their lords gave the churches and tithes which they held to an abbey. This led to some unfortunate conversions; men utterly unfit for the ordered life of a community and too old to change found the discipline insupportable. Adelard, a priest of Le Sap, who came from a prosperous family at Friardel near Orbec, gave his church to Saint-Evroult during a serious illness, and took the habit there, only to regret his decision when he recovered. Abbot Thierry allowed him to go freely, since he would not obey the Rule, and he returned to secular life for fifteen years. He resumed the habit during a second repentance on his death bed, as a monk *ad succurrendum*.[81] Another priest named Ansered, a man of lax morals, was an even more unpromising recruit. He too took the habit in the same abbey when criticially ill, but on recovery seemed more likely to corrupt the brethren than be reformed by them. He returned to the world to consort with common women and be murdered by a jealous rival.[82] One of Guibert of Nogent's recollections of the monks of Saint-Germer concerned a priest whose worldliness, according to him, consisted in nothing worse than love of riding, but who died suddenly on a journey, unshriven and guilty of keeping for himself a gift of two shillings which should have gone to the community.[83]

But many were learned and pious men, educated in the schools of liberal arts or in more modest local schools, and widely read in Scripture; their conversions came from conviction and were lasting. Whilst clerical celibacy was only very slowly being accepted for the secular clergy, many were sons of priests. Others, like John of Rheims, came from the families of humble craftsmen and owed their advancement to patrons. Monastic writers might describe religious houses

---

[80] Orderic, ii. 20-1.
[81] Orderic, ii. 46-7.
[82] Orderic, ii. 44-7.
[83] Guibert, *De vita sua*, I.22 (Benson, pp. 104-5; Labande, pp. 176-9).

as citadels; but in practice their enclosure walls had more in common with the walls of living cells than the stone walls of castle keeps. Every kind of influence passed in and out through them, by a continual process of osmosis.

A certain number of laymen lived in or near any monastery, and acted as servants or *famuli*.[84] Inside the monastery they assisted the obedientiaries, helping in infirmary, guesthouse, and storehouses; outside they accompanied monks on their travels and carried letters.[85] On great festivals some of them had ceremonial duties, such as carrying banners in processions or distributing and collecting staffs for the Rogation procession. Only gradually were efforts made to exclude them from the liturgy; but they were never a part of the full monastic community. They belonged to the household. Lay brothers were in a more intermediate position. The term describing them, *conversi*, was often ambiguous, because of changes taking place in recruitment and training. At first the *conversi* were all those, already described, who took the habit as adults; gradually the term became restricted to those who were illiterate and had not yet taken orders. These men were monks and might become full choir monks. But in time a tendency appeared, in Cluniac houses at least where the changes in custom are most fully documented, for the *conversi* to form a separate group within the monastic community; they sat apart from the other monks in choir and refectory, and sometimes performed only the lowlier offices. They were coming to resemble the lay brothers of the Cistercian and other new orders.

In addition to the professed religious, many Benedictine houses took in a variety of individuals who might be loosely attached to the monastery without making any formal profession. They were most numerous and most diverse up to the end of the eleventh century, when alternative forms of religious life were less securely established. Most important were the hermits, though many of these in time became monks. The examples of St Anthony and the desert Fathers,

---

[84] On *famuli* and *conversi* see G. Constable, ' "Famuli" and "conversi" at Cluny', *Revue bénédictine*, lxxxiii (1973), 326–50, reprinted in *Cluniac Studies*, ch. v; and references there cited.

[85] Cf. Orderic, ii. 94; iii. 242, 338.

of St Benedict and St Columbanus, ensured that eremitism would always have a place even in the heart of cenobitic life.[86] Hermits vowed to lifelong seclusion won widespread respect and admiration, both for their piety and for the many services of counsel and healing (not to mention banking) they provided for the communities around them.[87] Many lived in cells near enough to monasteries for them to receive the sacraments from the monks' church; in England the great abbeys of Crowland, Durham, Westminster, Worcester, Sherborne, and St Albans all had their solitaries.[88] Similarly, many Norman abbeys made provision for dependent religious. Some of these were pious women, like Eva, widow of William Crispin, and Basilia, widow of Gerard de Gournay, who received the veil from the abbot of Bec and lived under the protection of the abbey; Anselm called them his 'dearest mothers'.[89] The island cell of Tombelaine provided a retreat for learned ascetics from the Mont Saint-Michel, but these—like Robert of Tombelaine—were usually monks of the abbey.[90]

Normandy was powerfully influenced by reformers from Italy, where the eremitical movement was flourishing. Besides this, memories of St Columbanus were cherished in the older, recently refounded abbeys such as Saint-Wandrille in particular; and the multiple sanctuaries of the Merovingian houses, even in their ruined state, were an invitation to some form of solitary life or private devotion.[91] St Wandrille himself had built a number of churches within a radius of about a mile from the central church of St Peter; anchorites had lived in groups at sanctuaries dedicated in the names of St Saturnin, St Amande, St Pancras and Our Lady. At Saint-Evroult, where the original community had been established

[86] See J. Leclercq, 'Pierre le Vénerable et l'érémitisme clunisien', *Studia Anselmiana*, xl (1956), 99-120.

[87] For some of the miscellaneous services performed by hermits see H. Mayr-Harting, 'Functions of a twelfth-century recluse', *History*, lx (1975), 337-52; Edward J. Kealey, *Medieval Medicus* (Baltimore/London, 1981), pp. 53-6, 89, 92.

[88] R. M. Clay, *The Hermits and Anchorites of England* (London, 1914), p. 77; Knowles, *Monastic Order*, pp. 170, 188-9.

[89] Anselm, *Opera*, iii. 255-6, ep. 118; Porée, *Histoire de l'abbaye du Bec*, i. 182-4.

[90] Jacques Dubois, *Mont Saint-Michel*, pp. 674-6.

[91] Laporte, *Revue Mabillon*, xxxi (1941), 25-41.

with several sanctuaries, the founder himself had been in the habit of retiring to one of the more distant chapels for private meditation.[92] This chapel survived to be restored and re-dedicated with the new monastery. It stood, surrounded by an orchard, at the foot of a wooded hill near the source of a stream, and provided a retreat for monks needing a more solitary life. One of these was Ralph, son of Giroie, nicknamed 'Ill-tonsured'. A member of the founder's family, he had been both a knight and a student of the liberal arts and medicine in the schools of France and Italy, before deciding to become a monk at Marmoutier. His abbot allowed him to come to Saint-Evroult to help his nephew, Robert of Grandmesnil. In time he contracted leprosy and withdrew to the chapel with one monk as his companion. The chapel also afforded temporary refuge for two other members of the same family, Judith and Emma, who were Robert of Grandmesnil's half-sisters.[93] It was not uncommon for pious women to settle in a small cell outside an abbey, receiving the veil from the abbot and taking part in the major liturgical ceremonies in the church, as Eva and Basilia had done at Bec. In times of war and pillage the veil might provide temporary protection, without any vows being taken.[94] When the Grandmesnil family fell into disgrace and some members had to escape into exile the two young women may have fled to the chapel for reasons of caution rather than religion. By some they were believed to have taken the veil; but they did not consider themselves bound, and later followed their kinsmen to Italy, where they married well. Judith's husband was none other than Roger, later count of Sicily.

It may be through an accident of selection that we hear no more of pious recluses attached to Saint-Evroult; the later books of Orderic's history are less concerned with the internal life of the monastery. Such recluses remained an element in the life of many Benedictine houses. Mostly retreat was either for temporary refreshment or for the closing

[92] M. Chibnall, 'Merovingian monastery', *Studies in Church History*, viii. 31–40.

[93] Orderic, ii. 74–9, 102–5.

[94] Cf. the letter of Lanfranc advising on this problem (*Letters of Lanfranc*, ed. Clover and Gibson, pp. 166–7, ep. 53).

years of life; and these seem to have been the forms most favoured by abbots, especially in Cluniac houses. Peter the Venerable, for one, expressed his views sympathetically but firmly in a letter to his monk, Peter of Poitiers, contrasting his correspondent's solitary mountain retreat with his own struggles in the duties of daily life.[95] The solitary monk could survey, from his mountain top, all the kingdoms of the world beneath his feet; the struggling abbot was daily kicked and trampled underfoot by his enemies. He did not write, he hastened to explain, out of envy, but out of admiration for the spiritual peace which could be a means of recuperation. But let the retreat be temporary, like that of Moses on Sinai or Jesus in the desert, or on the occasion when he dismissed the crowds and went up on to a mountain to pray. In another place he wrote in praise of the withdrawal of a veteran monk, Gerard, to end his days in solitary prayer in a mountain retreat. Gerard, to him, was a model of perfection.[96] But for much of a monk's life he believed that it was best to preserve internal solitude even in the midst of external cares. It was to be a constant theme with believers in cenobitism: 'Build your refuge in the depths of your own heart; make your hermitage there.'

Inevitably as abbeys attempted to bring within their walls all sorts and conditions of men who, for reasons both of religion and of worldly prudence, were drawn to monastic life, strains of many kinds appeared. In some parts of the Church the crisis was acute by the early twelfth century; but the great Norman houses, in common with Cluny itself and many others, were still able both to face their critics boldly and to look at new forms of religious devotion with sympathy. Theirs was an assured and confident Benedictinism. The Rule, they believed, was not to be observed rigidly like the law of Moses; its essentials were to be followed in charity and humility, but it contained some regulations that should be adapted to the changing needs of men in later ages and different regions. Clothing suitable for the Mediterranean would be inadequate in Scotland; countries without olive trees might be forced to use animal fats for cooking. Towards

[95] *Letters of Peter the Venerable*, i. 179-89, ep. 58.
[96] *De miraculis*, I. 8 (Migne, *PL*, clxxxix, 862-71).

the end of the eleventh century, when a number of new foundations began to adopt the Augustinian 'rule' as their spiritual code, and there was a proliferation of Augustinian houses, these were not regarded as rivals by the established Benedictines. Anselm of Bec had the reputation of being a friend and counsellor to Augustinian canons. Even the breaking away of individual monks in search of a more ascetic way of life and a stricter interpretation of the Benedictine Rule seemed at first no more than overemphasis of the more eremitic side of monasticism. As the movement gathered momentum it led to earnest debates in chapter and cloister, and to consultation with spiritual leaders, both abbots and bishops. But discussion usually remained reasoned and charitable. It would be wrong to see the first decades of the twelfth century as an inevitable preliminary to the polemics that came later. Both Orderic himself and his contemporary, William of Malmesbury, who wrote about the new monastic movements, viewed them with sympathy, and believed that they offered an acceptable (though to them slightly less desirable) way of life.[97]

In the forests of Burgundy and on the frontiers of Maine and Brittany the eremitical movement was most active. Under the leadership of Robert of Molesme, Alberic, and Stephen Harding at Cîteaux, of Bernard of Tiron, Vitalis of Savigny, and Robert of Arbrissel elsewhere, groups of hermits gradually formed new monastic communities of stricter observance. They looked critically at the Benedictine Rule, cut away the liturgical accretions, renounced the ownership of tithes and churches, and restored manual labour in the fields to support themselves. They wore habits of undyed wool and insisted on a strict diet without any of the minor indulgences that had crept in when monasticism spread from the mediterranean lands to the more rigorous northern climates. As a result monks all over Normandy, northern France and England, began to look carefully at their own interpretation of the Rule.[98] The monks of Coulombs appealed

[97] Malmesbury, *GR*, ii. 383-4; Orderic, iv. 310-35.
[98] Knowles, *Monastic Order*, pp. 197-202; Jean Becquet, 'L'érémitisme clérical et laic dans l'ouest de la France', *L'eremitismo in Occidente nei secoli XI et XII* (Milan, 1965), pp. 182-202.

to Ivo of Chartres for advice, and his answer was reasoned
and reassuring. In reply to those who tried to persuade
monks to leave their monasteries because they had acquired
and were holding tithes, he wrote:

Let these subtle investigators . . . . tell me whether it is more salutary
for monks to remain as cenobites showing their superiors obedience
which is better than sacrifice and living on the tithes and oblations of
the faithful, which the Church by the law of charity can give to monasteries just as well as to hospitals and the sick and pilgrims; or to
become Sarabites in order to live in isolated places as a law unto themselves, receiving their sustenance from the goods of the poor by the
hands of robbers or from the usury of traders . . . I have written to you
thus, my brethren, so that you may not be alarmed by the thunder of
vain accusation, nor moved from your purpose, but may shape your
lives according to the statutes of the Fathers of old, and hold firmly to
the obedience that you owe to your superiors, and the stability which
you vowed to your monastery . . . In so saying I do not reject the life
of anchorites—of those, that is, who after being instructed in regular
discipline in monasteries go with permission into seclusion, for to
them solitude is a paradise and the city a prison, and they leave either
to pursue an active life supporting themselves by the labour of their
hands, or to refresh their minds in the bliss of contemplation . . . and,
forgetting all that they have left behind, never look back. For the
depths of woods and the summits of mountains do not make a man
blessed unless he has in himself solitude of mind, peace of soul, quiet-
ness of conscience, and a heart uplifted; without these, sloth, idle ques-
tionings, vainglory, and perilous storms of temptations are invariably
the companions of solitude.[99]

In many Benedictine houses similarly reassuring replies
were given. Details of the Rule were intended to be modified according to changing needs. Lanfranc had earlier gone
to the heart of the question when he wrote in the Preface to
his monastic constitutions:

What we have to consider with the greatest care is that what is necessary for the soul's salvation should be safeguarded in every way: faith,
that is, and contempt of the world, together with charity, chastity,
humility, patience, obedience; penance for faults committed and
a humble confession of them; frequent prayers; silence in fitting
measure; and many other things of this kind. Where these are preserved
it may truly be said that the Rule of St. Benedict and the monastic
life are kept, whatever variety there may be in matters which have been
differently ordered in different monasteries.[1]

[99] Ivo of Chartres, *Epistolae* (Migne, *PL*, clxii, 198-202, ep. 192).
[1] *Monastic Constitutions of Lanfranc*, pp. 1-2.

It was the spirit and intention of the Rule that was important.

Later writers, especially Cluniacs, justified at greater
length individual modifications of the letter of the Rule.
The earliest comprehensive summing-up of the traditional
position was given in Peter the Venerable's celebrated Letter
28, addressed to St Bernard, but intended for wider circulation.[2] Peter's letter belongs to some extent to the literature
of polemic; but he must have drawn on arguments put forward in individual cloisters and brought them together in
more cogent form. There can be no doubt that Saint-
Evroult was one of the houses closely in touch with Cluny
at the time, though it is uncertain whether, when Orderic
wrote his treatise on the new monastic orders, he made
direct use of Peter's letter, or whether he expressed widely
held views and common experience. But his treatise was no
polemic; it was a work of balanced and reasoned reassurance
—a firm statement and justification of the old ideals,
intended to strengthen the purpose of monks who had made
their profession in traditional houses such as his own. It was
copied and read in other Norman abbeys; and was a major
source for Robert of Torigny's treatise on the same subject.[3]

[2] *Letters of Peter the Venerable*, i. 52-101.
[3] *Chronique de Robert de Torigni*, ed. L. Delisle (Rouen/Paris, 1872-3),
ii. 184 ff.

5

Monastic Studies

(i) *Liturgy*

We cannot draw a hard line between study and prayer in medieval monasteries. As Richard Southern has pointed out, 'The traditional idea of a school had been an organized community providing instruction in its functions to beginners and practice and rehearsal for its more advanced members. The *scola* of a monastery or cathedral was originally the whole community at its work of worship in the choir.'[1] There was formal teaching in the rudiments of letters for the oblate children; and illiterate or semi-literate *conversi* were given whatever instruction was necessary to enable them to participate in the life and at least a part of the worship of the community.[2] Priscian had a place in most monastic libraries, and even the most learned monks might bear their share of basic teaching. Anselm admitted to difficulty in teaching elementary declensions to children, and urged a young monk of Bec who was visiting Canterbury to take advantage of the skilled guidance available there, and read more widely in such authors as Vergil whom he had not read with Anselm.[3] But though these authors were thought suitable for a young monk seeking mastery of the Latin language, the ultimate purpose was to achieve understanding of the word of God, and to worship him worthily. It was a lifelong enterprise. When Abbot Roger of Saint-Evroult retired from office in extreme old age, he 'passed his days in his chamber, devoting himself to psalms and prayers and devout colloquies. He had with him a priest, well qualified to be his chaplain and companion, from whom he heard the Mass and the canonical offices in

---

[1] 'The schools of Paris and the school of Chartres', *Renaissance and Renewal*, p. 115.
[2] For a fuller treatment of the school of Saint-Evroult see Orderic, i. 15–23.
[3] Anselm, *Opera*, iii. 180–1, ep. 64.

the chapel of St Martin, and with whom he used to converse, asking and answering questions about the obscure symbolism of the Scriptures, and discussing choice passages of commentaries.'[4] So the whole liturgy was a part of the work of the *scola.*

The development of the liturgy had caused many monastic leaders to reconsider and revise their monastic customaries, particularly in the eleventh and early twelfth centuries.[5] Although Gregory VII was anxious to promote a wider use of the earlier Roman liturgy as part of the unification of the Western church, he recognized the existence of a great variety of local influences, both Gallic and Germanic, and these remained strong. Even within a single region the local variations were countless. Among the monasteries the older Benedictine houses, and particularly those influenced by Cluny, were strongly conservative; the accustomed ritual, with all its symbolic meanings, was to be preserved against the attempts at simplification of the newer orders. This did not mean stagnation. Peter the Venerable was in favour of some rationalization of detail, as long as this could be carried through peacefully.[6] Saint-Evroult was among the houses in which liturgy evolved broadly in accordance with established traditions.[7]

These developments often had an intellectual side; the liturgy needed to be explained to participants, and understood by them. The need was common to both monks and seculars; John of Avranches, archbishop of Rouen from 1067 to 1079, wrote an important treatise, *De officiis ecclesiasticis.*[8] But the works of the Carolingian scholars remained popular. The *De officiis* of Amalarius was copied for many monastic libraries,[9] even though it was out of date, since many rites

---

[4] Orderic, vi. 326-7.

[5] For a perceptive approach to liturgical changes see Chrysogonus Waddell, 'The reform of the liturgy from a renaissance perspective', *Renaissance and Renewal*, pp. 88-109, which includes a critical short bibliography of this vast subject.

[6] *Statuta Petri Venerabilis*, no. 61, pp. 91-3.

[7] See above, pp. 64-8.

[8] R. Delamare, *Le 'De officiis ecclesiasticis' de Jean d'Avranches* (Paris, 1923).

[9] G. Northier, *Les Bibliothèques médiévales des abbayes bénédictines de Normandie* (Paris, 1971), Appendix II, under Amalaire de Metz, lists copies at Fécamp, Bec, Mont Saint-Michel, Saint-Evroult, and Jumièges.

had been expanded or modified, and his characteristic method of heaping illustration on illustration without much system made his work turgid and hard to understand. It invited critical treatment rather than mere copying. When William of Malmesbury wrote his 'abbreviation' of Amalarius he professed to do so at the request of a friend, Robert, who found the original daunting. Robert appears to have been a secular clerk, not a monk; but monks had the same difficulties. William's 'abbreviation' was in fact a reinterpretation, appropriate to the twelfth century.[10] He omitted much, but enlarged both on the historical background to the ceremonial and on some figurative explanations; he described some different liturgical practices. The influence of the *ordo Romanus* is evident in his more explicit reference to its practice in discussing the reservation of the Host. But contemporary ideas about society also influenced his comments, particularly his account of the symbolic washing of the walls and floor of the church in Holy Week. Amalarius had written:

The walls of the house are called the church, because they contain the church, but they are not the church. The floor of the church signifies those who hear the masters. The washing of the house, which nominally is called the church, is a symbol of the washing of the feet of the brethren; the washing of the feet of the brethren is a symbol of the remission of sins.

In William's version this becomes:

The wood and stones are not the church; the church is the souls of the faithful. The altar can signify the priests and clergy who serve it; the walls the powerful laymen by whom the people are protected; the floor the humble populace. For every type of Christian man ought to be cleansed through penitence in readiness for holy resurrection. And this is done on the day of the Lord's Supper, because on that day he washed the feet of his disciples. In imitation of this we wash our feet and those of the poor.[11]

By the time William 'abbreviated' Amalarius this ritual, somewhat augmented by the explicit inclusion of the altar, could

---

[10] William's treatise has been published by R. Pfaff, 'The "Abbreviatio Amalarii" of William of Malmesbury', *RTAM*, xlvii (1980), 77–113; xlviii (1981), 128–71.

[11] *RTAM* (1980), p. 92.

be explained quite simply in terms of the three 'orders' in the church, which were then a commonplace of social thinking.[12] His whole treatise is typical of the thoughtful, questioning evolution of liturgical practice and study, within a traditional framework.

(ii) *Theology*

Monasticism, as Jean Leclercq has written, had its own theology, which was different from that of the schools.[13] It was meditative, relying more on illumination than on dialectical reasoning. It was aimed primarily at a different audience, an audience of monks, whose spiritual needs were somewhat different from those of lay folk. Yet once the broad lines of distinction have been drawn, it becomes apparent that there was much variety in study and teaching; individual abbeys had their own characteristics, depending partly on the nature of their recruitment and partly on their library resources. In the secular schools too the studies favoured and methods used at any time were determined as much by the teaching of individual masters as by earlier traditions. Laon, for instance, had had a great school in the ninth century,[14] and was a resort of many students attracted by the teaching of Anselm of Laon and his brother Ralph from the last decade of the eleventh century until the early 1130s. During Anselm's lifetime it was unrivalled as a centre for the study of theology.[15] He was a traditional, not a speculative, theologian; but his teaching was lucid, and he and his brother led the way in fostering the systematic study of the 'sacred page', and in reappraising and supplementing

[12] See below, p. 117.

[13] J. Leclercq, 'The renewal of theology', *Renaissance and Renewal*, pp. 71–2.

[14] E. Jeauneau, 'Les écoles de Laon et d'Auxerre au xie siècle', *Settimane di studio del centro italiano di studi sull'alto medioevo,* xix (1971), 496–509.

[15] On the schools of Laon and the writings of Anselm of Laon see D. E. Luscombe, *The School of Peter Abelard* (Cambridge, 1969), pp. 173–82; B. Smalley, *The Study of the Bible in the Middle Ages* (Oxford, 1952), pp. 49–51; O. Lottin, *Psychologie et morale aux xiie et xiiie siècles* (6 vols. Louvain/Gembloux, 1942–60), v. 9–188. Some new interpretations are suggested by V. I. J. Flint, 'The "School of Laon": a reconsideration', *RTAM*, xliii (1976), 89–110; Southern, *Renaissance and Renewal*, pp. 115–17. Both Flint and Southern stress that it is more accurate to speak of schools *at* Laon than schools *of* Laon at this period.

traditional teaching, even if they never founded a school of theology. Moreover, the pupils who flocked to Laon were secular clerks, seeking a career either as parish priests or as court chaplains with the hope of rising to high office in the church. And at a time when study and renewed interest in pastoral care were among the many offshoots of the reform movement, there was constant interchange of men, books, and ideas between monastic and secular schools. Scholars disenchanted with the world entered monasteries as converts and taught there; these men were an important channel of communication between different centres. Hermits lived on the fringes of both worlds.[16] And monks willingly gave pastoral advice to lay benefactors who frequented their cloisters, and discussed matters of common interest with the parish clergy in neighbouring churches.

The study of the 'sacred page' had always played an important part in the daily life of Benedictine monks. The Rule prescribed that 'the brethren must be occupied at stated hours in manual labour, and again at other hours in sacred reading'.[17] But the horarium suggested was sufficiently flexible for a new emphasis to be given to liturgical development. As daily offices grew in length, more and more time was spent in the choir; the chanting of psalms and reading aloud of lessons and appropriate passages from lives of the saints gradually encroached on both private sacred reading and manual labour, and came to be interpreted as an acceptable form of both activities, at least for some parts of the day. But even at Cluny, where for a time the ideal of an unending round of prayer and praise to be raised to God by day and night came nearest to realization, not all the monks took part in all the offices.[18] The movement of sacred reading into the choir did not stifle it in the cloister; indeed it provided a stimulus. Copying manuscripts, reading the Bible, interpreting and rewriting liturgical treatises, collecting lives of the saints, became more necessary than ever to provide homilies and readings, and ensure that the lengthy ceremonial was

[16] Cf. Gibson, *Lanfranc*, pp. 20-2.
[17] RSB ch. 48.
[18] Noreen Hunt, *Cluny under Saint Hugh*, pp. 114-17; see also B. H. Rosenwein, 'Feudal war and monastic peace', *Viator*, ii (1971), 137 ff.

understood by all the participants. Besides the books for the offices, suitable works were required for public readings in cloister and chapter-house; and in accordance with the Rule books were issued to all the monks for Lenten reading and meditation.[19] Libraries had to provide for all these needs, and scriptoria were active.

Bible study was central in all monasteries. Holy writ, in the words of John of Fécamp, illuminated the dark night of this life.[20] The Bible was approached in its entirety, in the tradition of the early Fathers. Not all abbeys could boast copies of all its books, but as many as possible were among the first volumes to be procured. The most widely read of the works of Gregory the Great, Jerome, and Augustine followed; these included a number of scriptural commentaries. Some houses had commentaries by Origen, Cassiodorus, or Isidore of Seville. Among the most popular of later commentators was Bede; he made use of a wide selection of the works of the early Fathers, and presented traditional interpretations in simple language. Saint-Evroult possessed his commentaries on the Song of Songs, the gospels of Mark and Luke, the Acts of the Apostles, the book of Tobit, and the Apocalypse. But monastic studies did not stop at the Fathers; Carolingian scholars were represented, notably by Raban on Matthew and Haimo of Auxerre on the Pauline epistles. New works continued to be added as they were produced. Saint-Evroult acquired a commentary on Matthew attributed to Anselm of Laon.[21] St Bernard's sermons on the Song of Songs, begun in Orderic's lifetime and written between 1135 and 1153, achieved almost instant circulation among the black monks no less than the

[19] RSB ch. 48, 'In these days of Lent let them each receive a book from the *bibliotheca*, which they shall read through consecutively.' *Bibliotheca* often denoted the Scriptures, and since the Bible had been arranged by Cassiodorus in nine volumes the original meaning of this chapter may have been that each monk should receive a volume of the Bible (Anscari Mundo, *Revue bénédictine*, lx (1950), 65-92). But by the eleventh century this chapter was normally interpreted as meaning any book from the library. For public readings in chapter and cloister see B. de Gaiffier, 'L'hagiographe et son public', pp. 143-4.

[20] John of Fécamp, *Confessio theologica*, cited B. Smalley, 'Some Gospel commentaries of the early twelfth century', *RTAM*, xlv (1978), 148 n. 6.

[21] See the library catalogues edited by G. Northier, *Les Bibliothèques des abbayes bénédictines de Normandie*.

Cistercians.[22] Mont Saint-Michel had more than twenty-five commentaries on books of the Old Testament (including at least five on the psalter), and about twenty on the New Testament, in addition to glossed texts of some parts of the Bible.[23] And by the mid-twelfth century the abbey of Lire could boast possession of commentaries on all the books of the Bible, including some of the most recent by Gilbert, bishop of Poitiers. Besides copying, many monks were, like St Bernard, producing treatises or commentaries of their own, as well as homilies, 'sentences',[24] and gospel harmonies. Monastic piety, founded on faith, did not exclude erudition.

One of the problems faced by eleventh-century monks in their study of the Bible was the sheer bulk of commentaries available. The earlier Carolingian commentaries, such as that of Raban Maur, had tended to become more and more voluminous and less systematic.[25] Verses were cited from every part of the Bible to illustrate the unity of Scripture; long quotations from the Fathers were collected in increasing numbers, often at second or third hand. In addition to the longer treatises, textual glosses (relevant citations inserted in the margins or between the lines of the Bible) proliferated without being standardized.[26] Cloister-bred monks might have an intimate, meditative knowledge of the sacred text, though few had the training necessary to reduce the wealth of citation and comment to any kind of order. But in the secular schools, particularly those attached to cathedrals, a more intensive study of the old liberal arts of logic and rhetoric was sharpening minds to investigate, systematize, and expound. The growing number of adult conversions led to increased cross-fertilization between monastic and cathedral schools, and amongst other things brought about a great advance in the study of theology.

[22] For the date see J. Leclercq, 'La date du ler sermon sur le Cantique des cantiques', *Saint Bernard mystique* (Paris, 1948), pp. 480–3.

[23] J. Laporte, 'Une bibliothèque vivante', *Mont Saint-Michel*, ii. 248.

[24] There were short, reasoned expositions of points in Christian doctrine.

[25] Smalley, *Study of the Bible*, pp. 37–40.

[26] For the development of a standard gloss in the twelfth century see B. Smalley, 'Gilbertus Universalis, bishop of London (1128–34) and the problem of the *Glossa ordinaria*', *RTAM*, vii (1935), 235–62; and for further bibliographical notes, *Oxford Dictionary of the Christian Church*, 2nd edn., p. 572 (*Glossa ordinaria*).

Among the pupils of Fulbert, bishop of Chartres from 1006 to 1028, were Angelramnus, later abbot of Saint-Riquier, and Olbertus, who became abbot of Gembloux.[27] Liège helped to train Maurilius, who taught at Halberstadt before becoming a monk at Fécamp.[28] The most famous example of early migration was Lanfranc, and his work shows how changes in method were penetrating the various schools. Trained in northern Italy, he taught in Normandy, possibly at Mont Saint-Michel, before becoming a monk at Bec and bringing fame to its monastic school. There he gave his attention, amongst other things, to exegesis, and produced commentaries on two fundamental texts: the psalter and the Pauline epistles. His commentary on the psalter has survived only in fragments, and appears to have been mainly traditional; that on the Pauline epistles showed how the techniques of grammar, dialectic, and rhetoric could be used, together with a rigorous selection of quotations, to set out glosses logically and clearly. The theology was traditional and patristic; the method new and enlightening. His work was used in the schools at Laon and Paris as well as at Bec, and was an acknowledged influence on Peter Lombard,[29] whose *Sentences*, completed in 1152, became a standard text-book in the schools.

The majority of monastic exegetes worked primarily for their own communities or friends, and their writings circulated less widely. Study of this formative period in exegesis is still handicapped by the lack of editions of the immense literature of monastic piety; indeed many of the works are anonymous or wrongly attributed. Robert of Tombelaine's commentary on the Song of Songs achieved exceptionally wide circulation because it was wrongly attributed to Gregory the Great.[30] But whatever the intended audience, much monastic endeavour was directed, like that of Lanfranc,

[27] F. Behrends, *The Letters and Poems of Fulbert of Chartres* (Oxford, 1976), p. xxxv.

[28] M. de Bouard, 'Notes et hypothèses sur Maurille moine de Fécamp', *Fécamp*, i. 81-2.

[29] Gibson, *Lanfranc*, pp. 50-61; M. T. Gibson, 'Lanfranc's *Commentary on the Pauline Epistles*', *Journal of Theological Studies*, N.S. xxii (1971), 86-112.

[30] P. Quivy and J. Thiron, 'Robert de Tombelaine et son commentaire sur le Cantique des Cantiques', *Mont Saint-Michel*, ii. 347-56.

to providing more manageable and relevant aids to the study
of the Bible and the liturgy to replace the voluminous and
unsystematic Carolingian commentaries and treatises. The
need to shorten and clarify was felt so acutely that some
works of original scholarship were concealed under the title
of 'abbreviation'. William of Malmesbury described his
commentary on Lamentations as an abbreviation of the
commentary of Paschasius Radbertus; but like his 'abbreviation' of the *De officiis* of Amalarius it contained long
passages of independent comment, specially adapted to
the needs of his own day.[31] He had, he said, previously
amused himself with history, but he found it more fitting in
middle age to devote himself to work of a different kind,
whose purpose was to turn our minds away from the world
and enkindle them for God. Almost any monk of a scholarly
bent, whose duties lay particularly in the library and scriptorium of his monastery, might be tempted to turn his
attention at some time to the study of the Bible, whether he
claimed originality for his work or not. Peter the Deacon,
in Monte Cassino, represented the opposite extreme from
William of Malmesbury, for he tried to claim originality for
exegetical treatises which were the product of wholesale
borrowing from other works.[32] Guibert of Nogent kept
a middle course, and stated frankly what he was doing. Much
monastic theology was then focused on the historical and
allegorical interpretations of the Bible; his interest in exegesis
was particularly in the ethical or tropological sense of Scripture, which he found more appropriate than allegory to an
age when, he said, the faith was known to all, and the need
was to improve morals.[33] So he pointed the way towards
a new trend, whilst making use of much traditional material
in his commentaries.

At Saint-Evroult too there was an individual slant to the
study of the Bible, within the broad framework of monastic

[31] H. Farmer, 'William of Malmesbury's Commentary on Lamentations',
Studia monastica, iv (1962), 283–311; for his commentary on Amalrius see Pfaff,
RTAM (1980–1).
[32] Paul Meyvaert, 'The exegetical treatises of Peter the Deacon', *Sacris Erudiri*,
xiv (1963), 130–48; reprinted, *Benedict, Gregory, Bede and Others* (London,
1977), ch. xiii.
[33] Migne, *PL*, clvi. 337–40; see Smalley, *Study of the Bible*, p. 244.

needs and interests. One of the cathedral schools with which
the abbey had close contact was that of Rheims. St Bruno,
later to be the founder of the Chartreuse, was a master there
for many years before he withdrew from the world about
1082. He had a reputation for skill in both human and divine
learning, and was remembered for his expositions of the
psalter and the Pauline epistles.[34] Some of his pupils, including Robert of Langres and the future Pope Innncent II,
rose to high office in the Church; others came to share his
spirituality and, like him, turned to monastic life. One who
preceded him into the cloister was John of Rheims, who
secured the means to make his profession at Saint-Evroult
about 1078. His independent writings did not, as far as the
library catalogues indicate, include any works of exegesis;
but he wrote a verse Life of Christ, and another of the Virgin
Mary. Besides this he compiled *florilegia* from a wide range
of sources, classical no less than patristic, which provided
exempla for his monastic pupils to use in their sermons and
treatises.[35] Both William of Merlerault and Warin of Sées may
have profited from his teaching in preparing their homilies
and *Sentences*. Whether Orderic Vitalis was directed to the
books he studied and helped to copy by John of Rheims, or
found them through his own researches, his intellectual
growth was certainly shaped by the master he revered.

The most interesting work of exegesis surviving from the
library at Saint-Evroult is the commentary on St Matthew's
gospel, attributed to Anselm of Laon.[36] Orderic himself
copied a considerable part of it and added occasional correc-
tions and marginal notes to the remainder. Although the
attribution to Anselm has been rejected by most modern
scholars because of the inclusion of some post-Anselmian
glosses, there is no reason to doubt that it came from the
Laon milieu, and embodied a good deal of Anselm's instruction.[37] Its interest derives partly from its content, partly from

[34] Bernard Bligny, *L'Église et les ordres religieux dans le royaume de Bourgogne
aux xie et xiie siècles* (Paris, 1960), pp. 257-60; A. Wilmart, 'La Chronique des premiers Chartreux', *Revue Mabillon*, xvi (1926), 119-20.   [35] Orderic, i. 20-3.
[36] This is MS Alençon 26. See B. Smalley, *RTAM*, xlv (1978), 161-2. A facsimile of the one page is given in L. Delisle 'Manuscrits autographes', pl. 7.
[37] V. Flint, *RTAM* (1976), p. 91, seems to regard it as the work of Anselm
himself, though this view was rejected by B. Smalley and O. Lottin.

the fact that it marks a new trend towards a study of
the gospels in the secular schools. Traditionally far more
attention had been given in these schools to the Psalms
and the Epistles of St Paul, whereas monastic study took
in the whole Bible. When Burgundius of Pisa decided to
translate the homilies of St John Chrysostom on St John's
gospel, a little after 1151, he explained that he had undertaken the task because he could find no commentary except
that of Augustine.[38] But Burgundius had not looked far
enough; Rupert of Deutz had made one about 1115, which,
like so many monastic writings, had never circulated
widely.[39] The gospels had been far more closely studied
in eleventh-century monasteries than was often realized;
they formed some of the earliest reading for the monks. Not
only commentaries on the gospels, but also copies of
Augustine's *De concordia evangelistarum* were widely available. This became a standard work for all who wished to
harmonize the different gospels. Monastic devotion, with
its regular cycle of homilies on the life of Christ based on
the lectionary, called for such aids.

Reform during the eleventh century created a widespread
need outside the monasteries for aids to the study of the
Bible, and bore fruit in the secular schools. One consequence
was the production of new commentaries on the gospels;
these both made use of earlier monastic learning and were
themselves quickly borrowed and sometimes expanded in the
monasteries. The commentary on Matthew contained in
Alençon MS 26 was described in the opening rubric as an
exposition on the Gospel of St Matthew compiled from
various authors by the philosopher, Anselm of Laon. But
even if the main commentary was the work of Anselm, there
were some additions from later glosses as well as a little
unusual material relating to St Martial of Limoges; and this
could have been added in Saint-Evroult just as easily as at
Laon. Early in the eleventh century Adhémar of Chabannes
had championed the apostilicity of St Martial, a third-century

[38] Peter Classen, *Burgundio von Pisa* (*Sitzungsberichte der Heidelberger
Akademie der Wissenschaften*, phil. hist. Klasse (1974) iv), pp. 52, 84.

[39] Ibid., p. 84 n. 3. The Commentary of Rupert of Deutz has been edited by
R. Haacke, *Corpus Christianorum, Continuatio Mediaevalis*, ix (1969).

bishop of Limoges, with a thoroughness that extended to producing a forged *Life of St. Martial* (attributed to Aurelian), and had even won papal recognition for the unhistorical claim. The Pseudo-Aurelian's *Life* was known and accepted as genuine at Saint-Evroult; Orderic included an abbreviation of it in the second book of his *Ecclesiastical History*.[40] So when Alençon MS 26 identifies St Martial with one of the seventy disciples, or says of the unnamed child whom Jesus set in the midst of his disciples to teach them humility, 'Many say that this child was St. Martial of Limoges',[41] we cannot be sure whether the identification was made at Laon, or whether Orderic was following the common practice of slipping a little extra information that he happened to have into a text he was copying. The work of librarians and scribes was rarely purely mechanical in the early twelfth century, and Alençon MS 26 is an example both of the lively interest in bible study at Saint-Evroult, and of the abbey's contacts with other schools.[42]

Orderic's own chief interests did not run to independent exegesis. His particular Midas gift was to turn all he touched into history; and he turned his meditations on the New Testament and his study of the commentaries he helped to copy towards producing a history of the Church. His studies turned in the direction of gospel harmonies, and Augustine's *De concordantia evangelistarum*, which reconciled the different accounts in the four gospels, gave him the foundation of a *Life of Christ*. This consisted of an interweaving of the texts of the gospels, in chronological sequence, with some explanations of the meanings of individual names from Jerome and Isidore, and interpretations of particular events and parables taken from Bede, Augustine, and other commentators. It provided the first part of his History.[43] There is nothing quite like it elsewhere; the lost verse life of Christ by John of Rheims may perhaps have pointed the way. But

[40] Orderic, i. 190; L. Duchesne, 'Saint Martial de Limoges', *Annales du Midi* iv (1892), 289-330.

[41] Alençon MS 26, fo. 185.

[42] On the later use of this commentary see B. Smalley, 'The gospels in the Paris schools in the late twelfth and thirteenth centuries', *Franciscan Studies*, xl (1980), 325-6.

[43] Orderic, i. 48-51, 134-49.

if it is a unique example of the way in which one particular
monk used his prayerful study and meditation, it is also a
natural product of a monastic school. Monasteries were,
indeed, the most favourable seeding grounds for the best-
known later gospel harmonies, such as the *Unum ex quatuor*
of Clement of Lanthony, who died about 1190.[44]

The second outcome of the reform movement was the
compilation of numerous *Sentences*. Authorities were
collected and arranged according to subjects, many of which
were concerned with the moral problems of everyday
life and with the sacraments, most probably with the needs
of the pastoral clergy in mind. It is no longer certain that
the *Sentences* once said to be products of the 'school of
Anselm of Laon' should be attributed to pupils of Anselm;
but they were certainly being compiled in the cathedral
schools of northern France, including Laon, in the early
twelfth century.[45] They might be compared with the
Sentences produced in monasteries for the different needs
of abbots and other monastic superiors. Inside the monasteries, abbots were required to instruct their monks. At
Saint-Evroult Abbot Thierry adapted his colloquies to
the intellectual capacities of his different monks; Abbot
Warin was praised for the eloquence and lucidity with which
he expounded holy writ.[46] Any monk with learning and
spiritual insight would find himself a welcome guest in
other houses. One of the monks of Saint-Evroult who compiled *Sentences* was Warin of Sées;[47] when in 1131 he
accompanied his abbot to Rebais on a delicate mission to
persuade the monks there to part with some of the relics
of St Évroul he used his talents to good purpose. During
a week's stay at Rebais he delighted his hosts by the learning
and insight with which he expounded Scripture for them

[44] On the influence of Clement of Lantony see B. Smalley, 'Which William of
Nottingham?', *Medieval and Renaissance Studies*, iii (1954), 200–38; reprinted
Studies in Medieval Thought and Learning (London, 1981), pp. 249–87.

[45] The previously accepted view has been questioned by Flint, *RTAM* (1976),
94–109.

[46] Orderic, ii. 18–21; iii. 344–7. Abbot Isaac of L'Étoile was said to accompany his monks when they went into the fields to work, and to gather them
round him for pastoral instruction whenever they paused from their labours
(B. de Gaiffier, 'L'hagiographe et son public', p. 149).

[47] Orderic, i. 22. The Sentences attributed to him are now Alençon MS 16.

in the cloister, and so no doubt contributed to the success of the difficult undertaking.[48]

Outside the monasteries, too, learning was spreading among the parochial clergy of Normandy. Walchelin, the priest of Saint-Aubin de Bonneval in the diocese of Lisieux, who had a vision of souls undergoing purgatorial torments, had been educated in the schools of France, and was able to relate his vision to the sacramental and penitential teaching familiar to him.[49] The old priests who were caught up against their will in the riots that broke out during the 1119 synod of Rouen may have been sufficiently resistant to reform to be unwilling to give up their concubines; but they were learned and conscientious enough to spend their time together quietly discussing confession and other topics relating to their pastoral work, or reciting their offices as they were bound to do.[50] These and others like them were the friends of monks. The study of the Bible produced discussion and interchange of ideas at many levels.

This was a formative time in the development of various types of medieval theology; and one thing that is certain is the cross-fertilization of secular and monastic studies. Whether the writings of monks became influential in the schools, like Lanfranc's commentaries or Clement of Lanthony's *Harmony*, or remained little known outside the monasteries where they were written, like Rupert of Deutz's *Commentary on St. John* or Orderic's *Life of Christ*, they were products of an active communication between different types of school. Teachers moved from cathedral to cloister; books moved both ways, and discussion was constant. If clerks and monks ultimately adapted their studies to different ends, they drew upon common traditions and recognized that they had much to learn from one another.

(iii) *Lives of the Saints*

After the Bible and aids to bible studies, the most prominent place in the library of any great abbey was given to lives

---

[48] Orderic, iii. 340-1.
[49] Orderic, iv. 236-51. The vision is discussed by Brian Stock, *The Implications of Literacy*, pp. 495-9; his interpretation is a somewhat personal one.
[50] Orderic, vi. 290-5.

of the saints. They were essential in the liturgical offices and
greatly valued as reading material in cloister, refectory, and
chapter. Every saint's day in the calendar of any abbey
called for suitable readings from the life or passion of the
saint for use at Matins and Vespers; a great feast, like that of
St Martin, required all twelve lessons to be taken from the
legend of the saint, and further extracts were read every day
during the octave.[51] Musically gifted monks vied with one
another to compose melodious antiphons and responsories
to do honour to the saints and enhance the devotions of the
faithful.[52] While the apostles and early martyrs and confessors had their Masses and other offices described in every
Sanctorale, others depended for their inclusion on local or
regional cults, connections with other monasteries, or the
acquisition, sometimes of relics, sometimes of a written
Life. In abbeys where the librarian had the responsibility
for building up the library of his house and assigning the
books to be read publicly each week he may have had some
influence in bringing the lives of previously little-known
saints to the notice of his fellow monks, and so preparing
the way for their formal commemoration.[53]

The task of composition and copying did not end with
the provision of a single *Life* for any saint. Some legends
were expanded, and as tastes in hagiography changed others
were revised to appeal to hearers with different expectations.
Only the most venerated texts remained untouched for
centuries. In the eighth and ninth centuries many lives of
revered abbots and prelates had been written in a straightforward, commemorative style. They were the record of the
holy living of men remembered by their communities for
their practical virtues and compassionate understanding
rather than for any miraculous powers. By the eleventh

[51] B. de Gaiffier, 'L'hagiographe et son public', pp. 137–41.
[52] B. de Gaiffier, 'L'hagiographe et son public', p. 139, cites the case of the
celebration of the feast of St Vincent at Saint-Bertin, where the solemnity of the
feast was increased from 3 to 12 lessons after the abbey acquired the *Responsoria
S. Vincentii*, to give the young monks the opportunity of hearing such melodious responsories. Musical composition was important at Saint-Evroult (below,
pp. 101–2).
[53] This was certainly the custom at Farfa (B. Albers, *Consuetudines monas-
ticae*, i. *Consuetudines Farfenses* (Stuttgart, 1900), 167).

century the demand was much more for dramatic lives of miracle working men of God.[54]

There was always a specially close relationship between an abbey and its patron saint or saints. Charters recorded grants as gifts to the saints as much as to the monastery. 'I, Alfred the Giant . . . give to God and St. Vigor and his monks . . .';[55] 'Let all the faithful know that I, Osbern, for the salvation of my soul, give to St Peter and St Ouen . . .',[56] are typical formulas. The abbey's temporal possessions were the patrimony of the saint. Andrew of Fleury recorded that haymakers in a meadow that had recently been given to Fleury (Saint-Bénoit-sur-Loire) met St Benedict in person, visiting his property.[57] When danger threatened, the protection of the saint was invoked; some of the most common accounts of miracles described the supernatural punishment of robbers of shrines and despoilers of monastic lands. St Cuthbert was a particularly formidable defender of the lands of Durham priory. But the patron saint was far more than an avenger; he was an intercessor and a participant in the continuing prayers of the community, gratefully commemorated in the liturgy.

Saint-Evroult was among the refounded abbeys that had lost the bodies of their first patrons. The relics had been carried away into France during the wars of the tenth century; most of the bones found a resting place in the abbey of Rebais, and no fragments were immediately retrieved or miraculously 'discovered'. But the saint, who had founded the Merovingian abbey and been its first abbot, was constantly invoked as protector and intercessor, and much care was given to his commemoration. A copy of his *Life* was brought from Jumièges by the first monks who made up the new community,[58] and this provided the readings for the church offices. It was not in fact the earliest and most authentic life, which may not have been known in Normandy

---

[54] Cf. Southern, *Saint Anselm*, pp. 320–5.
[55] Fauroux, no. 195.
[56] Fauroux, no. 193.
[57] *Vita Gauzlini*, ed. R. H. Bautier and G. Labory (Paris, 1969), pp. 68–71.
[58] Orderic, iii. 363; published by Mabillon, *AA SS OSB*, i. 354–60. This was probably the *Life* shown to Hugh and Robert of Grandmesnil when they were choosing a site for the abbey they wished to found (Orderic, ii. 16–17).

then; but it was adapted to liturgical needs and was of the heroic type popular at the time. When Robert of Grandmesnil became abbot in 1059 he elaborated the choral offices.[59] At his request Arnulf, precentor of Chartres, who was a pupil of Bishop Fulbert, composed an office according to the secular rite, and had it sung to two young monks, Hubert and Ralph, sent from Saint-Evroult. They memorized it and taught it to their companions. A little later, under Abbot Osbern, the office was completed for the requirements of monastic devotion by the monk Guitmund, a talented musician who composed some of the sweetest melodies in the troper and antiphonary of the abbey. He added nine antiphons and three responsories, and Reginald the Bald added seven antiphons and one more responsory. In the course of time a number of hymns were composed by various monks in honour of the saint. It was natural that an abbey with the interest in musical studies that characterized Saint-Evroult should express its devotion to its patron in this way. The work of the historians did not come until later; at first the existing legend was found adequate. There may have been some demand for a verse life; such lives were popular because easier to memorize,[60] and the need was met by John of Rheims. He wrote a verse life of St Évroul and dedicated it to his friend, Ralph d'Escures, who later became archbishop of Canterbury.[61]

When Orderic wrote his first account of the foundation of his abbey he did not include a life of its patron saint. The demand was then for a detailed history of the endowment. But some years later a dramatic event in the life of the monks called for full commemoration in writing. Abbot Warin made a serious attempt to recover some of the saint's relics from Rebais. He succeeded so well that a few bones were triumphantly brought back to the abbey, and solemnly placed in the church in the presence of a great crowd of pilgrims in May 1132. Orderic rose to the occasion by writing a long

---

[59] Orderic, ii. 108-9.

[60] The customs of Hirsau laid down that if the book prescribed had been mislaid the reader should recite what he could from memory (M. Heargott, *Vetus disciplina monastica*, Paris, 1726, p. 465).

[61] Orderic, iii. 168-71. John's verse *Life* is now lost.

narrative of St Évroul's life and cult, and the migration of his relics.[62]

He made use of such written records as he could find, and of oral sources. Unfortunately the *Life of St. Évroul* treasured in his abbey was not the earliest version of the saint's life. The original *Life* was the work of an anonymous monk who probably wrote not long after Évroul's death *c*.706. He gave a straightforward account, moving in its simplicity, of a holy hermit who had founded a religious community in which Columbanian, Benedictine, and other customs were observed.[63] By the eleventh century popular taste demanded more than this, and a second *Life* was produced. It was based on the first, but added material about the saint's early life (possibly culled from the lives of other saints), some short moral homilies, and a few traditional miracles. It omitted almost all the information about monastic organization and custom, and confused the chronology by interpolating names of Évroul's supposed contemporaries, in the mistaken belief that he had died, not in the reign of Childebert III, but over a hundred years earlier, in that of Childebert II. Although Orderic was puzzled by his inability to discover anything about the monastery during this long gap, he accepted the *Life* that was known and used in his abbey. There is no evidence that he ever saw the original version, though there were copies in England, including one at St Augustine's, Canterbury, during his lifetime.[64] Saint-Evroult certainly obtained a copy before the end of the twelfth century, and a third version, a conflation of the other two, was made;[65] but the only known manuscript was written after Orderic's death, in a style that is not his.

The *Life* that he knew was the second version, dating probably from the eleventh century, which presented the saint's life as a heroic struggle. The first *Life* had given an account of how Évroul, a wealthy nobleman from the Bessin

[62] Orderic, iii. 264-343.

[63] For the various versions of the *Life* of St Évroul see Orderic, iii. 363-4; the first *Life* is printed in Orderic, i. 204-11.

[64] Oxford, Bodleian Library, MS Fell 2.

[65] Printed by L. Hommey, *Bulletin de la Société historique et archéologique de l'Orne*, vi (1887), 273-92.

brought up in the Frankish court, decided to abandon the world, and set out with three companions to live a hermit's life in the forest of Ouche. After wandering through its dark depths for a long time they came suddenly upon a clearing, where there was a spring of water. 'Surely', concluded the narrator, 'we must believe that an angel of the Lord led them to the spot'. The second version dramatized this simple statement: Évroul prays eloquently to God, and as he ends his prayer an angel appears to lead the way to a pool and spring. The later hagiographer's imagination is at work in a similar way at every point in the story. When, after the establishment of a monastic community, a beggar is given the last loaf of the brethren, he plants his staff in the ground and a spring wells up—the famous 'fountain of St Évroul', which acquired the reputation of a healing well. A repentant usurer who brings a load of food that same evening vanishes with such speed that the reader can be left in no doubt of supernatural intervention. Whereas the first biographer described in simple terms the apparent death and later revival of two men during a pestilence, barely hinting at a miracle, his successor introduced all the details—prayers, prostration in the dust, calling on the name of the deceased—that accompanied traditional miracles of raising the dead. Orderic copied long extracts from this version, to which he added many dramatic details, enhancing the miraculous elements at every point in the story.

Some of the oral traditions that Orderic also wove into the enlarged *Life* that he wrote suggest an appeal to popular piety. He included stories of the kind suitable for telling to the pilgrims who flocked to the saint's shrine after his relics were brought home. The miracle of the healing spring which bubbled up when a strange visitor to the abbey struck the ground with his staff was enlarged upon; the same miracle was depicted on a capital in the priory church of Saint-Georges de Boscherville, which was colonized by monks from Saint-Evroult. Popular stories of the demon who disturbed the monks and was roasted by the saint in the village bread oven at Échauffour, and of the bull of Bocquence, who led a herdsman to the forgotten ruins of the first abbey in the depths of the forest, made their first appearance in writing.

This is not the scientific hagiography of the Bollandists; it is hagiography produced in a monastery eager for miracles, for retailing to simple, uneducated country folk. Orderic's version was a strange compound of conventional hagiography, popular legend, and oral tradition, of which part—but only part—was historically sound. His account became more authentic when he tried to add something from his own day to the miracles of the abbey's patron saint. This, too, is characteristic of his age; the miracles that often follow the *Lives* of saints include much accurate observation and authentic social detail intermingled with the marvellous elements.[66]

Orderic described two miracles in particular with something nearer to the directness of the first biographer of St Évroul. One took place in 1092, when Henry Beauclerc was striking out from his base at Domfront into the lands of his brother, Robert Curthose, and one of the men of Saint-Evroult, named Ruald, was captured and taken to Domfront by one of Henry's knights.[67] Ruald told Orderic how, after praying to St Évroul to lead him, he had been able to walk out of the fortress through a door which was imperfectly secured, and to cross a courtyard full of soldiers who seemed not to see him. He had eluded pursuit by hiding in the fields, and peasants ploughing there had assured his pursuers, even when offered a reward for information, that they had not seen anyone. 'I believe', wrote Orderic of the inobservant knights in the castle court, 'that they were prevented from seeing him by the saint's power'.[68] But he did no more than hint hopefully at a miracle, in what appears to be a story of negligent guards and peasants refusing to betray a fugitive. His second miracle is even more homely: an account of how a reformed robber and his son were able to bring a gift of white bread safe and dry to the abbey one

[66] A conspicuous example is the *Miracula Sancti Benedicti*; see R. H. Bautier, 'La place de l'abbaye de Fleury-sur-Loire dans l'historiographie française du ixe au xiie siècle', *Études ligériennes d'histoire et d'archéologie médiévales*, ed. René Louis (Auxerre, 1975), pp. 25-33.

[67] Orderic, iv. 258-61.

[68] Christopher Holdsworth has drawn my attention to a similar miraculous escape from captivity by one of St Bernard's brothers, described in the *Vita prima S. Bernardi*, I. 11-12 (Migne, *PL*, clxxxv, 233-4).

Christmas, through deep snow and a swollen river which was running bank high.[69] He might well lament the lack of miracles in his own day;[70] those he found were modest when set beside the highly coloured and circumstantial narratives of popular hagiographers, particularly those associated with relics that were at a pilgrim centre.

If a church given to an abbey was a cult centre, or had acquired an important relic, a search began for a suitable life of the saint. To this, or an abbreviation of it, might be added the miracles reported more recently from the shrine. This was all the more urgent if several churches claimed to possess the body of the same saint. When the church of Parnes in the French Vexin was given to Saint-Evroult to become the seat of a priory, it was already a centre of pilgrimage to the reputed shrine of St Judoc.[71] The claim was disputed by the monks of Saint-Josse-sur-Mer, who cherished their own relics; but Saint-Evroult defended its case resolutely. One of its monks, William of Merlerault, recorded a 'discovery' of the relics during the siege of Gomerfontaine about 1050, to explain their migration to Parnes, and also made a collection of miracles reported from the tomb. Orderic produced a workmanlike 'Life and Miracles' by abbreviating two earlier *Lives* and William of Merlerault's work. Similarly, when William Pantulf brought a tooth of St Nicholas back from southern Italy, and gave it to the little priory he had founded at Noron, Orderic abbreviated John of Bari's account of the translation of St Nicholas from Myra to Bari in 1087, with one or two slight, but significant modifications,[72] and added

[69] Orderic, iii. 342-5.

[70] Orderic, iii. 8-9.

[71] For the lives and miracles of St Judoc see Orderic, ii. 156-68, 366-7. My identification (following J. Trier) of the abbey of Fleury with Fleury-en-Vexin should be corrected to Fleury-sur-Loire; the suggestion of A. Vidier, *L'historiographie à Saint-Benoît-sur-Loire et les Miracles de Saint Benoît* (Paris, 1965), pp. 96-7, that Isembard of Fleury, author of one life of St Judoc, was probably the *bibiliothecarius* of Saint-Benoît-sur-Loire is now generally accepted.

[72] His most significant addition is the statement that the Norman mariners decided to bring back the relics from Myra because of their love of the saint and their desire to enhance the greatness of their *patria* of Bari; John of Bari said simply that they did not wish to be anticipated by the Venetians. Orderic gave the Norman tradition, which saw the translation of the relics to Bari as part of the establishment of Norman dominance in Apulia (M. Chibnall, 'The translation of the relics of St. Nicholas and Norman historical tradition', *Le relazioni*

a few miracles that had come to his knowledge from the abbey of Venosa, which also claimed to possess a relic.[73]

Abbreviating earlier saints' lives and adding later miracles was a common practice when circumstances required the commemoration of an established saint. But hagiography shaded into biography; writers were always aware that the lives of holy abbots or prelates, or even remarkable laymen, might be the first version of the life of a new saint. Sometimes such lives were written with the intention of fostering a cult. Orderic was invited to write something of this kind for an English abbey.

Many abbeys in England were struggling to defend their claims to property threatened by lay invaders or through insecurity of tenure; when necessary they did so with forged histories. Some, including Ely, Ramsey, and St Augustine's, Canterbury, who all used the services of Goscelin of St Bertin, had recourse to skilled forgers.[74] In some the difficulties arose through loss of records. When Crowland lost all its early charters in a serious fire the abbot was the learned Geoffrey of Orleans, a former monk of Saint-Evroult. It was doubtless at his suggestion that Orderic was invited to visit Crowland and write the history of its foundation and an account of the death of Earl Waltheof, whose body rested in the abbey. Miracles were reported at his tomb. During the weeks Orderic spent there he was also requested to abbreviate and clarify the *Life of St Guthlac*, hermit of Crowland, written by Felix (wrongly believed to be bishop of the East Angles). Felix's version was lengthy and somewhat obscure in style. Orderic did this willingly and brought back a copy to Normandy because, as he wrote,

I firmly believe that the holy deeds of the Angles and Saxons of England could be no less edifying to northern Christians than the deeds of Greeks and Egyptians, which devoted scholars have fully recorded in lengthy narratives that are widely read and give much pleasure. Moreover, I believe that, little as these things are known

religiose e chiesastico-giurisdizionali (Congresso internazionale sulle relazioni fra le due sponde adriatiche, i. Rome, 1979), pp. 38–41).

[73] Orderic, iv. 54–75.
[74] For the work of Goscelin see Antonia Gransden, *Historical Writing in England c.550–c.1307* (London, 1974), pp. 107–11.

amongst our own countrymen, they must prove all the more pleasing and full of grace to men of ardent charity who lament their past sins from the bottom of their hearts.[75]

After abbreviating the life of Guthlac and reconstructing the early history of the abbey from information given him by the monks, he turned his attention to Waltheof, the English earl who had forfeited the favour of William the Conqueror in 1075. Waltheof had been accused of complicity in the conspiracy of the earls of Hereford and Norfolk, and executed at the king's command. His body was taken to Crowland for burial, and some years later the monks claimed that it remained incorrupt, and that the head had been found to be joined to the body. The tomb rapidly became a centre of pilgrimage for Waltheof's English compatriots. One Norman monk, who ridiculed the pilgrims and denounced Waltheof as a false traitor who deserved his fate, was struck dead. Abbot Geoffrey, wise enough to be above partisan feeling, approved the cult of Waltheof, and described a vision in which he had seen the earl welcomed into the company of St Guthlac and St Bartholomew. No more suitable hagiographer could have been found than the abbot's English-born fellow monk from Saint-Evroult. Orderic faithfully recorded all that he was told, including Waltheof's pious end and the story that, although his executioners refused to allow him time to recite the Lord's prayer, his severed head had completed the last petition. This, like the traditional tales Orderic had added to the *Life of St Évroul*, may have been intended to appeal to popular piety. But although Crowland continued to observe the feast of the *decollatio* on 31 August the cult did not spread.[76] William of Malmesbury, on this subject more cautious than Orderic, expressed a hope that the story of Waltheof's martyrdom was not contrary to truth.[77] No doubt political feeling was at work both for and against the cult, and in spite of the efforts of the monks of Crowland it remained local. But it illustrates the way in which the

[75] Orderic, ii. 324–5. For his work on Crowland and Waltheof see Orderic, ii. pp. xxiv–xxix, 310–51.

[76] D. H. Farmer, *The Oxford Dictionary of Saints* (Oxford, 1978), pp. 395–6.

[77] Malmesbury, *GP*, p. 321. A recent intepretation of the conspiracy unfavourable to Waltheof is given by W. E. Kapelle, *The Norman Conquest of the North* (London, 1979), pp. 134–7.

lives of saints, central in both the liturgy and monastic daily life, were also on the fringes of history.

(iv) *Monastic Histories*

Historical writing, as a means of preserving the traditions of a community, was almost a natural growth in eleventh-century monasteries. Many early monastic historians began with a series of lives of the first abbots, or with an account of the lay patrons' motives in founding the house. There is no reason to doubt the importance of a genuine wish to inform: to preserve the memory of acts of piety from oblivion. Monks in abbeys that were refoundations of earlier Merovingian houses were particularly conscious of what had been irretrievably lost when books had been destroyed during the period of Viking invasions, or when their predecessors had been negligent in keeping records. They felt that they were saving precious traditions for future generations by writing down the recollections of the old men they questioned and the notable events that occurred in their own day.

But the desire for a truthful record was sometimes overridden by more pragmatic considerations: the wish to promote the cult of a holy abbot, the need to prove the authenticity of relics, or the determination to secure claims to property and privilege. At best such considerations might lead to selective presentation of genuine evidence, at worst to the acceptance of unreliable testimony or to deliberate forgery. Orderic plainly hoped that the holiness of Abbot Thierry of Saint-Evroult might in time be recognized; but Thierry died in distant Cyprus on a pilgrimage to Jerusalem, and so no local Norman cult could be built up. His biographer merely recorded the life of a gentle, greatly loved abbot who had been an exemplary monk, and noted hopefully that many were cured of fevers and other disorders at his tomb; he did not stretch the evidence.[78] Similarly Andrew of Fleury's *Life* of Abbot Gauzlin of Fleury gave for the most part a straightforward account of how the abbot had acquired new possessions and recovered secularized property.[79]

[78] Orderic, ii. 68–72; iii. 334–7.
[79] *Vita Gauzlini*, ed. Bautier and Labory (Paris, 1969) pp. 40–51.

Some of the descriptions of 'discoveries' of relics are more dubious, though they might be based on genuine historical research. When the survivors of war and invasion had been forced to abandon their ruined monasteries in the tenth century, some relics were hidden on the spot, but most were carried away into exile. It was not easy to recover them from the new shrines where they had been given refuge and venerated for many years. New communities of monks in the restored Norman monasteries could not easily reconcile themselves to the loss. The movement of relics was often regarded as an expression of the wishes of the saints themselves. Their departure was held to be a sign of displeasure, because the guardians of their shrines were either unworthy or unable to protect them.[80] When Normandy was overrun by pagan invaders most of the saints departed, and the province was denuded of relics. Patrons of new churches sometimes overcame the difficulty by invoking as patron saints the founders of the Christian church, such as St Peter or St Stephen, rather than the local saint associated with a particular church. Others favoured dedications in the name of the Trinity or the archangel Michael, who could not reasonably be expected to have left any relics. But many restored abbeys still hoped either to retrieve or to 'discover' their lost treasures. The quest, undertaken in the interests of individual monasteries, was not without a more general intention: a wish to show that the Norman people had outgrown their pagan past. By demonstrating that the saints were no longer unwilling to leave their refuges in Picardy or the regions of Beauvais and Orleans the monks could prove the strength of the revived church in Normandy.[81]

Even if many relics could not be brought back, careful investigation might prove that some were in their original

---

[80] Stock miracle stories include accounts of reliquaries that suddenly became too heavy to move, or violators of shrines who were struck dead. The legend of St Nicholas made much of his unwillingness to leave Myra, even when the Emperor Basil attempted to secure relics; his translation by the Normans to Bari in 1087 was believed by some to set the seal on Norman ascendancy in southern Italy. See B. Leib, *Rome, Kiev et Byzance à la fin du xie siècle* (Paris, 1924), pp. 54–5; Orderic, iv. 353–4.

[81] See L. Musset, 'L'exode des reliques du diocèse de Sens au temps des invasions normandes', *Bulletin de la Société historique et archéologique de l'Orne'* (1970), pp. 3–22.

resting places. The discovery of the body of St Wulfram at Saint-Wandrille was a triumph of historical research. Two of the abbey's saints, Wandrille and Ansbert, were known to have remained in Ghent, where they had been taken for safety. But research in records revealed that the *Miracles of St Wandrille* written at Saint-Bertin mentioned only two saints. This gave grounds for hope that Wulfram was not with his companions in exile. So in 1027 excavations began in the restored abbey of Saint-Wandrille; and there, according to the *Historia inventionis Sancti Wulframni*, three tombs were revealed. Two, attributable to St Wandrille and St Ansbert, were empty; the third contained a body immediately identified as that of St Wulfram. The anonymous author of the *Historia inventionis* recorded the discovery with sufficient circumstantial evidence to convince contemporary monks and even some modern historians of the authenticity of the relics, though some have remained sceptical.[82] In this hazardous field of research, extending into archaeology and history, one of the dangers was that over-zealous apologists might destroy reliable evidence with the best intentions, and render the task of future historians almost impossible.[83]

The duty to preserve the 'patrimony' of the saints intact was an incentive to any monastery to defend property and privilege, and the early histories of Fécamp show how forgery might ultimately creep in. The first history of the foundation, written in the eleventh century, gives a relatively simple account of the foundation of a Merovingian monastery by St Vaninge, its destruction by the Northmen, the beginnings of rebuilding under William Longsword, and finally the consecration of the new church under Richard I in 1090. The anonymous author explored early sources: the Passion of

[82] See *Historia inventionis cum miraculis Fontanellae factis, AA SS* March III, 148-50. Various interpretations of the evidence are critically discussed by R. C. van Caenegem, 'The sources of Flemish history in the *Liber Floridus*', in *Liber Floridus Colloquium* (Ghent, 1973), pp. 78-80; he adds the comment that 'Medieval monks had a knack of finding a relic where they hoped and wanted to find it. This even happened with relics of saints who had never existed.'

[83] Peter the Deacon was one of those who so confused the evidence relating to the relics of St Benedict that he added to the difficulties of a particularly difficult investigation (Paul Meyvaert, 'Peter the Deacon and the Tomb of St. Benedict', *Revue bénédictine*, lxv (1955), 3-70).

St Leudegard, the history of Dudo of Saint-Quentin. His purpose seems to have been to inform and commemorate.[84] But by the end of the eleventh century the abbey was involved in a struggle for exemption from the authority of the archbishop of Rouen. Interpolations were made in early diplomas, and these were reinforced by a new history, the *Liber de Revelatione*, designed to show that the house had been exempt from all episcopal jurisdiction and made directly subject to the pope in the time of the first abbot, William of Volpiano.[85] The earlier history was used, but extended for another 26 years, reaching a final climax with Abbot William's journey to Rome in 1016 to obtain a bull of privilege from Benedict VIII. The privileges, based on the written forgeries, were described in detail. The way was prepared by an ambitious narrative, going back before the first foundation, to demonstrate that God had deliberately marked out Fécamp as a place of special sanctity from the earliest times.[86] It is here that the legend of Count Ansegisus and the miraculous white stag, which led the count's huntsmen to the divinely appointed site, appears for the first time. This may partly have been a response to popular demand: a number of monasteries claimed to have been founded at places miraculously designated.[87] But it also helped to enhance the whole picture of special privilege that the chronicler wished to paint.

Not all the chronicles defending privileges depended on forgery. There are many examples, particularly in twelfth-century England, of a wish to preserve a record of how claims were defended at law; and though forged records might be used, many were genuine. Chronicles from Glastonbury, Abingdon, and Battle are notable examples: such records were important whenever it was uncertain whether title deeds were more likely to be accepted as legal proof than oral testimony.[88] The writer of the Battle chronicle gave

[84] Lemarignier, *Exemption*, pp. 255–8.   [85] Migne, *PL*, cli. 701–22.
[86] See Lemarignier, *Exemption*, pp. 34–43, 259–63; David Douglas, 'The first ducal charter for Fécamp', *Fécamp*, i. 45–56.
[87] Cf. P. Johnson, 'Pious legends and historical realities: the foundations of La Trinité de Vendôme, Bonport and Holyrood', *Revue bénédictine*, xci (1981), 184–93.
[88] See Adam of Domerham, *De rebus gestis Glastoniensibus*, ed. T. Hearne

a detailed account, for the benefit of future monks, of the exact legal procedures by which the abbey's advocates had defended its property rights. The Abingdon chronicle included details of disputes spun out through three reigns, and claims upheld in many courts.

So both piety and prudence encouraged the writing of local chronicles for the edification of other monks. Piety ensured that benefactors and abbots would be remembered by those with a duty to pray for them; prudence demanded that the property to support the work of prayer should not be frittered away through ignorance or negligence. Some of these works—notably the lives of early abbots—were intended for reading aloud in cloister or refectory. Others were more suitable for quiet study by monks who had administrative duties, and needed to know how to defend the rights of their house.[89] They are among the products of monastic scriptoria that were intended for a monastic audience; indeed they might claim to be a necessary part of monastic life as it developed in all the great Benedictine houses during this period. No abbey of standing could afford to be without them.

Once it was accepted that the manual work prescribed in the Rule could be carried out in choir and scriptorium, all such activities as participation in the liturgy with its burden of commemoration, bible study, the composition and copying of the lives of saints and abbots, even the recording of the house's early history and possessions, fell into the normal pattern of monastic life. They needed no further justification within the community itself, even if at times they fostered a spirit that went beyond gratitude and pious devotion to become narrow and litigious defence of privilege. But books of all kinds were given or lent to monasteries, and the love of learning did not always exactly correspond with the longing for God. Monastic studies gave, inadvertently, the best historical training available in the late eleventh century. But to go on to write universal history, or even the whole

(Oxford, 1727), ii. 304-15; *Chronicon monasterii de Abingdon*, ed. J. Stevenson (RS, 1858); *The Chronicle of Battle Abbey*, ed. E. Searle (Oxford Medieval Texts 1980). The introduction to the Battle chronicle gives a full discussion of the legal importance of the chronicle.

[89] E. Searle, *Chronicle of Battle Abbey*, pp. 5-7.

history of the Church, called for justification. So too did any appeal to a wider audience outside the cloister. It was not self-evident that a monk's duty extended to evangelization in any sense other than persuading lay men and women to abandon the world for a better way of life in the cloister; many reformers were vigorously opposed to such activities. But it was at all times a short step towards including the writing of history in the tasks proper for a monk; even without deep thought it was possible to cite Jerome, Bede, and many others in justification. And on the wider issues the Church as a whole was committed to eradicating, or at least tempering, the pagan and brutal elements in society; and throughout the whole of Orderic's lifetime monks were in the forefront of the reform movement. So, though justification might be called for, it was not difficult to justify any attempt by a cloistered monk to go beyond the instruction of his own brethren, and record the events of the past in such a way that they might have some influence for good on the secular world outside.

PART III

THE SECULAR WORLD

6
Court and Society

(i) *The Court*

Medieval ecclesiastical writers, reflecting on the place of
human beings in society, saw them in terms of their functions. They sometimes chose a metaphor of the body, with
its eyes, arms, and other members carrying out the tasks for
which God had fitted them. Alternatively, and more commonly up to the twelfth century, they thought of them as
making up two or more 'orders', with appropriate and
divinely ordained duties. The typically Carolingian division
was twofold, into clerks and laymen, and this persisted in
the language of chroniclers long after more subtle divisions
were introduced and widely accepted.[1] In time various
alternatives were offered; it was possible to find even a four-
fold division for theological purposes, into pastoral,
monastic, clerical, and lay.[2] More common, and more important in social theory, was the division into knights, clergy,
and peasants: those who fought, those who prayed, and those
who tilled the fields.[3] This theory grew with the development
of the knights (*milites*) as a professional class of mounted
fighting men, whose skills in war could be justified as a social
necessity, acceptable even in a Christian society. This marked
them off from the unarmed poor, who toiled in the fields
and were entitled to protection. For the turbulence and
violence of society was something with which both churchmen and secular rulers had to come to terms, and which they
endeavoured to curb and direct towards order, justice, and
the maintenance of peace.

[1] For medieval theories of society see Georges Duby, 'The origins of a system
of social classification', and 'The origins of knighthood', in *The Chivalrous Society*,
pp. 88-93, 158-70; *idem, Les trois ordres* (Paris, 1978), trans. Arthur Gold-
hammer, *The Three Orders* (Chicago, 1980); some of the social implications of
Duby's study are, however, not applicable to Normandy.

[2] Paris, Bibliothèque nationale, MS lat. 6503, fo. 62.

[3] Cf. above, pp. 64, 88-9.

'The Normans', wrote Orderic on more than one occasion, 'are a turbulent people, and unless they are restrained by a strong hand they tear each other to pieces.'[4] This was a conventional characterization, most appropriate for the early days when the men of the north had been Viking raiders, but Orderic introduced it almost automatically whenever he described a time of weak ducal authority. No doubt he felt it to be true no less than conventional, living as he did in a frontier zone particularly exposed to local outbreaks of war. Yet nothing he wrote of the Manceaux, or the French in the Vexin and Île de France, or the Flemings, left any grounds for imagining that they were a whit less bellicose, and he had worse to say of the Angevins.[5] Society was not basically anarchic; there were important elements of stability; strong hands often made themselves felt. But it was organized for war; and when war, whether private or between principalities, broke out, the consequences could be devastating for the unfortunate population caught in the fighting. No one had any long-term interest in prolonging disorder, and peace movements, finding expression in the proclamation of the Truce of God and Peace of God, gathered strength during the eleventh century. They had a lasting influence in shaping customary no less than canon law. Although in origin they were moral and ecclesiastical, their effectiveness depended in the long run on secular rulers being willing and able to enforce them. In Normandy the main initiative, from the moment that Duke William established his authority after his victory over rebels at Val-ès-Dunes in 1047, came from the duke, working together with the Norman bishops.[6] The conquest of England, where the king's peace had developed independently as an important element in preserving order and justice, reinforced the practical authority of the king, even in his government of the duchy of Normandy. In France at first more was accomplished by the great monasteries such as Cluny; but by the end of the eleventh century the king was

[4] Orderic, iii. 98–9; iv. 82–3; v. 24–5; vi. 456–7.

[5] Orderic, vi. 466–7, 470–5.

[6] On the peace movement see P. Contamine, *La guerre au Moyen Age* (Paris, 1980), ch. x; H. E. J. Cowdrey, 'The Peace and Truce of God in the eleventh century', *Past and Present*, xlvi (1970), 42–67; M. de Bouard, 'Sur les origines de la Trêve de Dieu en Normandie', *Annales de Normandie*, ix (1959), 169–89.

becoming more fully master at least of his own royal demesne, and in time the peace of the church was absorbed within the king's peace. Orderic's narrative unconsciously reveals the different conditions prevailing in Normandy and France. But his main concern, in spite of the French priories of his abbey, was with Normandy; and consciously he looked to the duke, aided by his vassals, to maintain order, whilst deriving his moral judgements from the teaching of the church. From time to time this produced tension in his account of events, and implausiblity in his interpretation of motives.

Just as the external life of a monastic community centred on church and cloister, that of a baronial community centred on court and hall. Business of various kinds was transacted by the vassals and dependants of any lord, assembled round him, usually at the caput or chief seat of one of his honours. Disputes were settled, at first by some informal or arbitrary process, later by more formal judicial proceedings; vassals did homage to their lords. The court was also a centre of knightly training and, when conditions were favourable, of knightly culture. Traces of the activities of earlier baronial courts can be seen in the wording of charters, when men of an honour witnessed a gift,[7] or judgement was pronounced, or agreement reached. When in 1086 Robert of Bellême persuaded Picot of Sai and Drogo of Commeaux to make a friendly compromise over a disputed dowry, the concord was ratified in his court at Bellême, in the presence of more than forty knights.[8] Chronicles may be more explicit. Gilbert Crispin's *Life of Herluin*, based on oral tradition, begins with an account of Herluin's life as a knight in the court of Gilbert of Brionne. It shows him attending the court regularly, sitting at his lord's table, giving counsel, daily practising his skill in arms.[9] Orderic gives an even fuller and more vivid description of the unruly court of Earl Hugh of Chester, where welfare, feasting, and hunting were the principal occupations of the army of knights and squires who swarmed there, but some

[7] For example Fauroux, no. 191.

[8] Round, *Calendar of Documents preserved in France*, no. 654.

[9] *Vita Herlewini*, in *Gilbert Crispin, Abbot of Westminster*, ed. J. Armitage Robinson (Cambridge, 1911), pp. 87-90; see also C. Harper-Bill, 'Herluin, abbot of Bec, and his biographer', *Studies in Church History*, xv (1978), 15-26.

ideals of justice and devotion were kept alive by the earl's chaplains.[10] And he knew at first hand the more cultured court of the lords of Maule in the Île de France; he described the ceremony when, in 1106, Ansold, lord of Maule, made his son Peter his heir, and the boy received the homage of his knights, while Joslin of Mareil acted as herald, calling out the names and keeping the record.[11]

The courts of which most is known are, naturally, those of kings and counts, particularly in the twelfth century. Walter Map's description of the court of Henry I, though written in the reign of Henry's grandson and tinged with nostalgia for an older, better way of life, is full of authentic detail. It was a centre where the king's barons met to transact business and receive his bounty, and where the permanent members of the household troops, many of them young knights, received fixed grants. 'Every youth on this side of the Alps', wrote Walter, 'whom the king heard of as desiring the renown of a good start in life, he enrolled in his household, and any who had a smaller yearly allowance than 100 shillings received that sum by the hand of his messenger; and whenever it happened that he was sent for by the king he received at his coming a shilling for every day after he left his residence.'[12] Indeed Henry was prepared to enrol mature knights from many lands no less than young aspirants in his household troops. The Welsh *Chronicle of the Princes* tells how, when Cadwgan was driven out of his lands in 1109, Henry invited him to come to his court, and paid him two shillings a day.[13] In 1118 Lambert, the uncle of Lambert of Wattrelos, transferred his allegiance to King Henry, with a number of his friends, and was honourably received in the king's household troops.[14] There were many others; and Walter Map has described how elaborate arrangements were made well in advance for the provision of supplies to the populous court that travelled with the king:

[10] See above, p. 15.

[11] Orderic, iii. 184–5.

[12] Walter Map, *De nugis curialium*, trans. M. R. James, revised C. N. L. Brooke and R. A. B. Mynors (Oxford Medieval Texts, 1983), p. 471.

[13] *Brut y Tywysogyon* (Red Book of Hergest version), ed. Thomas Jones (Cardiff, 1955), p. 71.

[14] *Annales cameracenses, MGH SS*, xvi. 512.

He arranged with great precision, and publicly gave notice of, the days of his travelling and of his stay, with the number of days and the names of the vills, so that everyone might know . . . the course of his living, month by month . . . Everything was managed as befitted a king and with proper control. Hence there was eager sailing from the parts beyond sea to his court, of merchants with wares and luxuries for sale, and likewise from all parts of England.[15]

Of the order of business he wrote:

Those who were ripe in age or wisdom were always in the court with the king before dinner, and the herald's voice cited them to meet those who desired an audience for their business; after noon and the siesta, those were admitted who devoted themselves to sports; and this king's court was in the forenoon a school of virtues and of wisdom, and in the afternoon one of hilarity and decent mirth.[16]

This was the world of the court, even at its best far removed from the world of the cloister.

(ii) *Lordship and Inheritance*

Bishops and abbots had their place at court, as had household chaplains; and ecclesiastical rites played their part in its ceremonial. But however much monastic writers might endeavour to read a Christian ethic into the actions of knights and magnates, the ambitions of these men were rooted in social customs and moral codes that were predominantly secular in origin. Kingship, marriage, and knighthood were only very slowly brought under the influence and legislation of the church. The consecration of kingship had advanced furthest in visible cermonial,[17] and therefore in popular acceptance; but in establishing order in society the king acted as a lord accepted by his vassals no

[15] Walter Map, pp. 471-3.
[16] Walter Map, p. 439.
[17] On the coronation rituals the work of P. E. Schramm, *Zeitschrift der Savigny-Stiftung für Rechtsgeschichte*, liv, kan.abt. xxiii (Weimar, 1934), summarized in his *History of the English Coronation* (Oxford, 1937), is still fundamental, though it has been considerably revised by later research. See in particular J. L. Nelson, 'Ritual and reality in the early medieval *Ordines*', *Studies in Church History*, xi (1975), 41-51; eadem, 'The earliest royal *Ordo*', *Authority and Power* ed. B. Tierney and P. Linehan (Cambridge, 1980), 29-48; R. Foreville, 'Le sacre des rois anglo-normands et angevins et le serment du sacre', *Anglo-Norman Studies*, i (1979 for 1978) 49-62.

less than as a ruler blessed by the church. His vassals acknowledged the mutual rights and duties of lordship; but they also built their ambitions around their families and were tenacious of their patrimonial rights. A wise king and lord was careful not to work against the grain.

Recent studies of the evolution of the mèdieval nobility have emphasized regional variations in development. In Normandy, where the ducal power remained strong and there were no early-established hereditary local castellans, with power based on their castle garrisons, the knights were above all a clientele bound to a lord by personal ties, drawn from families of varying wealth with some patrimonial holdings. Lucien Musset, in a penetrating study of the Norman aristocracy in the eleventh century, has shown that a change began to take place only very gradually in the second half of that century, with the increasing heritability of fiefs.[18] 'The experience gained in Normandy', he concludes, 'was to be put to advantage both in Italy and in England, when the immigrants from the duchy provided the material for a new ruling class.' Norman law, as it crystallized into parage, recognized the rights of all children to some support out of the family lands, in so far as it was compatible with maintaining the integrity of the patrimony sufficiently to support one branch of the family in keeping with its status and obligations.[19] Feudal demands, when they became defined, were met by the rule that fees were indivisible, and that no man could be lord and heir. But this was the approved custom as it appears in the *Très ancien coutumier* at the very end of the twelfth century.[20] In Orderic's lifetime conflicting claims were producing tensions that sometimes led to violence;

[18] L. Musset, 'L'aristocratie normande au xie siècle', *La Noblesse au Moyen Age; Essais à la mémoire de Robert Boutruche*, ed. Philippe Contamine (Paris, 1976), pp. 71–96.

[19] Fundamental work on Norman law and custom has been published by J. Yver, notably in 'Les caractères originaux de la coutume de Normandie', *Mémoires de l'Académie des Sciences, Arts et Belles Lettres de Caen*, N.S. xii (1952), 307–56; 'Les caractères originaux du groupe de coutumes de l'ouest de la France', *Revue historique de droit français et étranger*, xxx (1952), 18–79. Customs of inheritance are discussed by J. Le Patourel, *The Norman Empire*, *passim*; J. C. Holt, 'Politics and property in early medieval England', *Past and Present*, lvii (1972), 3–52; Bates, *Normandy*, pp. 118–28.

[20] *Le très ancien coutumier de Normandie*, ed. E.-J. Tardif, *Coutumiers de Normandie*, i (1881).

settlements slowly pointed the way to more precise legal definitions and limitations of customary rights. It is worth looking closely into the pages of Orderic's history to see how customs of inheritance could be adapted to changing needs.

Many of the knights who frequented the cloister at Saint-Evroult or Maule were heirs, like Ansold of Maule, waiting to inherit after their father's death, or members of a family without immediate prospects of inheritance, hoping to acquire rewards through service, like Ralph the Red of Pont-Échanfray.[21] The condition of these 'young' knights—the 'jeunes'—has been made familiar through the work of Georges Duby.[22] Even those who had inherited might serve out of duty to their lord, and in the hope of winning further rewards to provide for more of their children. It is impossible to read Orderic's history without realizing that during the reign of Henry I, when most of it was written, the English king's effective fighting force was his military household, made up of a wide spectrum of knights ranging from his leading vassals to the portionless sons of Norman knights, and young aspirants from other lordships in France and Flanders.[23] They were held together by strong bonds of loyalty, varying in degree for landed vassals and stipendiaries. They were rewarded with stipends, booty, the hands of heiresses, money fiefs, or fiefs in land, as the fortunes of war and confiscations permitted, and their service deserved. Those who were disappointed in their hopes, or felt they had been unjustly treated by their lord, might take their swords elsewhere—to Alfonso the Battler of Aragón, as he led his forces against the Moors to reconquer and settle the Ebro valley, or to the rulers of southern Italy, Constantinople, Jerusalem, or Antioch; to the king of Scotland and even to the king of France. Norman and Frankish society was still expanding and conquering. Fiefs could be granted without the resources of King Henry, or even of his greater vassals who maintained their own military households, being seriously depleted.

---

[21] Ralph's career is traced by M. Chibnall, *History* (1977), 16–17.

[22] Duby, *The Chivalrous Society*, pp. 112-22.

[23] See J. O. Prestwich, 'The military household of the Norman kings', *EHR* (1981), 1-37.

Sometimes, if the land granted came into the king's hand
through rebellion and confiscation, the recipient's position
was made more secure by marriage to a member of the dispossessed family, as Nigel of Aubigny was granted part of the
Mowbray inheritance and given the hand of Roger Mowbray's
former wife, Matilda of L'Aigle, in marriage.[24] The 'heir'
was not invariably the eldest son, although in time the first-
born was acknowledged to have the strongest claim on the
patrimony. But he might prefer to receive 'aquisitions' if
these were very large, as they were after the conquest of
England; again, he might wish to enter the church, or he
might be mentally retarded. There was room for manœuvre
within the family; it was desirable that the heir should be
acceptable to both family and lord, and often there was no
conflict between them. Disagreement could lead to violence
and rebellion; a good lord needed to understand men as well
as having a fine sense of how much latitude custom and right
would allow him. William the Conqueror and his two younger
sons (William Rufus only slightly less than Henry) possessed
it; Robert Curthose, his eldest son, did not.

Orderic was keenly aware of the patrimonial rights and
claims that underlay all Norman tenures. When Ascelin, son
of Arthur, insisted that he must be paid for the land taken
from his father by William the Conqueror to build the church
of Saint-Étienne de Caen, before he would allow the king's
body to be buried in his patrimony, his claim was witnessed
and approved by bishops and abbots gathered from all over
Normandy for the king's funeral. They included Abbot Mainer
of Saint-Evroult.[25] That event was merely the most dramatic
expression of the tenacity with which a family held on to
its inheritance. Aquisitions were held less securely, though
within a generation they too, if lawful, would be regarded
as patrimony. The patrimony itself was expected to descend
to the 'heir' The early part of Orderic's history covered the
period in the eleventh century when there had been consider-

[24] D. E. Greenway, *Charters of the Honour of Mowbray* (British Academy;
Records of Social and Economic History, N.S. i, 1972), pp. xvii-xviii. Cf. also
C. Warren Hollister, 'The misfortunes of the Mandevilles', *History*, lviii (1973),
18-28.
[25] Orderic, iv. 104-7; Malmesbury, *GR*, ii. 337-8; Wace, *Roman de Rou*,
ii. vv. 9279-340.

able freedom in the choice of an heir. He might be a younger son: Serlo, who inherited the patrimony of Tancred de Hauteville in the Cotentin, was not the eldest of Tancred's twelve sons, most of whom made their fortunes in southern Italy.[26] A daughter might be chosen as heir if, like Mabel of Bellême or Aubrey of Moulins-la-Marche, she made a marriage particularly desirable to the lord.[27] But, by the time Orderic actually began to write, the claims of the eldest son were becoming paramount. He often referred loosely to 'natural heirs', but he also stressed the right of the first-born, and sometimes even assumed that a son must have been the oldest because he had inherited a patrimony from his father.[28] In so doing he was interpreting the past in terms of what seemed proper to the secular lords he knew.

Claims of inheritance might be crossed by claims of lordship. Orderic wrote of 'natural lords'[29] no less than 'natural heirs'.[30] Again, he was not entirely consistent. Birth counted for a great deal in contemporary assumptions about society; men could even be thought of as 'natural servants' trying to rise above their station.[31] Most often, in Orderic's usage, the natural lord of a man was the heir of the lord to whom he had done homage. But a man could do homage to more than one lord; and conflicting obligations resulted if the lords were at war with each other. In time a conception of liege lordship, which allowed limited obligations to one lord and overriding loyalty to the liege lord, developed. Occasionally, in the later books, Orderic's reference to a natural lord implied liege lordship.[32] But he could scarcely have meant more than a superior to whom respect was naturally due when he described Abbot Robert of Grandmesnil as the

[26] Orderic, ii. 98-101, where he is incorrectly called Geoffrey.

[27] Above, pp. 22-3, 25; Orderic, iii. 132 n. 1.

[28] See Southern, 'King Henry I', *Medieval Humanism*, p. 223; Orderic, ii. 138-9, 280-1, Appendix I. On inheritance in general see J. C. Holt, 'Feudal society and the family in early medieval England', *TRHS* 5th ser. xxxii (1982), 193-212; xxxiii (1983), 193-220.

[29] Orderic, iv. 74; v. 306; vi. 22, 94, 278, 370, 372, 520.

[30] Orderic, ii. 96, 130, 314.

[31] Orderic, iii. 96. 'Naturales servi' means strictly speaking 'slaves'; here it is put into the mouth of Robert Curthose's sycophants, and may go beyond Orderic's own view. He thought of peasants as born to their lot, but did not accept slavery as morally justified (cf. above, p. 12).

[32] Orderic, vi. 178, 454.

natural lord of Robert Guiscard, duke of Apulia;[33] the lords
of Hauteville had never been vassals either of the Grandmesnil
or of the abbots of Saint-Evroult.

Once fealty had been sworn to a lord, this became the
most binding tie in secular society, as strong in England as
in Normandy, and disloyalty was the worst form of treachery.
'No good song is sung of a traitor'; and his heirs might justly
be disinherited, even if in fact such drastic action was only
rarely taken.[34] The brutal punishments of blinding and
mutilation, or life imprisonment in fetters, were accepted as
just, however regretfully, when the code of loyalty was
broken. A man might, however, fight for his lord even when
the lord's cause was unjust, provided he had not incurred an
incompatible obligation towards his lord's adversary. Orderic
sadly acquiesced in the sentence on Luke of La Barre,
because Luke had no right to fight even for his lord against
a king who had once before spared his life and allowed
him to keep his arms after surrender. Moreover, he had made
up scurrilous songs about King Henry and sung them in
public, so committing an act of *lèse majesté* that would have
been deemed treacherous by traditional English law.[35]

So Orderic accepted feudal conventions, family claims,
and even—perhaps unconsciously—royal prerogative up to
a point. But he never forgot the ethical teaching of the
church, which had shaped his conscious thoughts from boyhood. Lands might be acquired justly; but sometimes they
were taken as plunder from their rightful heirs. Plunder could
be made lawful only by reparation and penitence. Orderic
was not alone in stating William the Conqueror's case for
taking the English crown, and making the most of Harold's
perjury, while at the same time repeatedly describing the
acquisitions of the Norman lords as plunder.[36] Even if the
victory at Hastings might be read as God's judgement in
William's favour, victory alone was not sufficient: penance
and reparation and just dealing with the conquered had to

[33] Orderic, ii. 98.
[34] Orderic, ii. 314-15; M. Chibnall, 'Feudal Society in Orderic Vitalis', *Anglo-Norman Studies*, i (1979 for 1978), pp. 38-42.
[35] Orderic, vi. 352-5; *Leges Henrici Primi*, 10.1 (p. 108), 13.1 (p. 116), and see below, p. 190.
[36] e.g. Orderic, ii. 202-3; iv. 94-5; cf. Malmesbury, *GR*, i. 277-8.

follow. Like the Norman bishops who, under the guidance of the papal legate, Ermenfrid of Sion, issued penitential ordinances for all who had taken part in the battle of Hastings,[37] Orderic believed that shedding Christian blood, particularly if the motive was not obedience to a lord's command but lust for gain, could be atoned for only by personal penance and almsgiving to the church. To him Roger of Montgomery's foundation of Shrewsbury Abbey was in part reparation for having accepted an earldom he had not inherited, even though he had not fought in the battle.[38] When pondering holy writ, he interpreted Abraham's command to his companions (after the battle of the four kings) to take their portion of the spoils of the men of Sodom as a general exhortation to pious laymen. If they would not renounce worldly goods altogether, they should at least found and endow monasteries out of the possessions they had both inherited and acquired.[39]

He was particularly emphatic in his denunciation of plunder. His critical attitude to Bohemond's pursuit of his own ambitions under cover of crusade distinguishes him from other more acquiescent contemporary chroniclers. Possibly Ralph the Red of Pont-Échanfray, who had served with Bohemond in the disastrous attack on Durazzo in 1106, and had then gone on to fight for a time under the Emperor Alexius Comnenus, had opened his eyes to Bohemond's duplicity. Orderic expressed his own feelings in the speech attributed to Bohemond's companions, of whom Ralph was one: 'We are paying the penalty of our presumption, for we have embarked on a proud undertaking which is more than our birthright and beyond our strength. No hereditary right drew us to this bold enterprise . . . only lust to rule in the dominions of another.'[40]

On Bohemond's right to hold Antioch he was more hesitant. Although Alexius claimed the city as part of his Empire, it had been won from the infidels and defended against them by the courage of the Franks, 'with', as he wrote in Book X,

[37] *Councils and Synods*, pp. 581-4.
[38] Orderic, iii. 144-7.
[39] Orderic, iii. 260-3; Gen. 14: 21-4.
[40] Orderic, vi. 102-5.

'the help of God', No doubt Bohemond had made his claim in 1106, when he mounted into the pulpit before the altar of the Virgin in the cathedral church at Chartres, and urged the assembled throng to take the cross and follow him to fresh conquests; and Orderic was at first willing to see his conquest as a victory given by God, and therefore just. But when he wrote the concluding chapters of Book XIII, after the treaty concluded in 1137 between Prince Raymond of Antioch and the Emperor John Comnenus had established that Antioch was to be held as a fief of the Empire, he was able to offer an interpretation more in keeping with his views of justice in conquest. He could describe the concession as tardy reparation for a wrong that had caused forty years of war and suffering.[41]

(iii) *Marriage and Canon Law*

The church's teaching underlay his views on marriage also.[42] He accepted the rights of families and lords to arrange marriages in so far as they did not conflict with canon law. There is surely more than a touch of irony in his account of how Bertrade of Montfort was handed over in marriage by her uncle and guardian, William, count of Évreux, to Fulk of Anjou.[43] William's alleged reply to his lord, Robert Curthose, who had undertaken to negotiate the marriage in order to secure an alliance with Count Fulk, sums up Orderic's interpretation of events:

My lord duke, you ask something that is repugnant to me, for you wish me to give my niece, who was entrusted to my guardianship by my brother-in-law and is a young virgin, in marriage to a man who has already been twice married. The truth is you are solely concerned with your own interests, and think nothing of mine. You wish to use my niece as a pawn to take away my inheritance from me. Is this a just

---

[41] Orderic, vi. 506–9.

[42] A general account of the medieval marriage laws is given in A. Esmein, *Le Mariage en droit canonique* (Paris, 1981). Georges Duby's *Medieval Marriage* (Baltimore/London, 1978), is a stimulating analysis of some developments. On consent in marriage see C. Donahue, 'The policy of Alexander the Third's consent theory of marriage', *Proceedings of the Fourth International Congress of Medieval Canon Law*, ed. S. Kuttner (Vatican City, 1976), pp. 251–91.

[43] Orderic, iv. 182–7.

prosposal? I will not grant your request unless you restore to me Bavent and Noyon-sur-Andelle, Gacé and Gravençon, Écouché and the other estates of my uncle Ralph Tête d'Ane . . . and restore to my nephew William of Breteuil . . . properties which we can reasonably and lawfully prove to be ours by hereditary right.

It was clear to Orderic that Bertrade was being used as a pawn by her uncle and the duke of Normandy when she was handed over in marriage to Count Fulk, 'a man with many reprehensible, even scandalous habits, who gave way to many pestilential vices'. But when she escaped from her unwelcome husband by eloping with the married king of France and going through a form of marriage with him in defiance of papal prohibitons and excommunications, Orderic had not a word of sympathy for her. 'So the absconding concubine', he wrote, 'left the adulterous count and lived with the adulterous king until death parted them.'

Orderic was writing many years after the scandal, when canon law had gained considerably in clarity, and the union was generally condemned. William of Malmesbury shared his strictures.[44] But even at an earlier date, when most of the French bishops chose to regard Philip's repudiation of his first wife, Bertha, as legal, Orderic's attitude would probably have been much the same. The French bishop whose views were most familiar to him was Ivo of Chartres, the diocesan of the monks of Maule; and Ivo from the first refused to give approval to Philip's intended marriage unless the pope allowed it.[45] Another Norman historian, Geoffrey of Malaterra, writing in southern Italy before 1100, had made it plain that he considered Philip to be bound to Bertha. Geoffrey was not concerned with the 1092 scandal involving Bertrade; some years earlier, according to him, Philip had sent envoys to propose marriage with Emma, the daughter of Roger of Sicily. Geoffrey was explicit on the legal position, and had no regrets when the proposed marriage with Emma fell through. Philip, he said, had a lawful and highly-born wife, who had borne him a son, Louis, already designated heir to the kingdom; he had initiated legal proceedings to repudiate her, but could bring

---

[44] Malmesbury, *GR*, ii. 293, 480.
[45] Ivo of Chartres, *Correspondence*, ed. Leclercq, i. no. 28, pp. 118-19.

no charge against her except a false allegation of consanguinity, and the attempt had failed.[46]

Canon law on marriage was then in a formative stage; different views on the proper form for a legal marriage and on grounds for annulment, as well as on the secular consequences of annulment, were held by leading canonists. These were not in complete harmony with the secular laws; but compromise was often possible. The attempt to prohibit marriage within seven degrees of consanguinity would have imposed intolerable restrictions on a high proportion of aristocratic marriages at the time. Canons announcing the limitation had been promulgated in Normandy by the 1072 Council of Rouen; Orderic had copied both these and the canons of the 1095 Council of Clermont, which repeated the prohibition.[47] The Council of Rouen also legislated against secret marriages, and required priests to perform marriages only in church, after enquiring into the ancestry of both parties. But even when strictly applied, this covered only church marriages; and marriage was perfectly legal without the blessing of a priest. Many marriages took place between kinsfolk and remained unchallenged; only if one party wished to prevent or terminate the union was consanguinity likely to be alleged. The appeal had to be made to the pope, who might annul or uphold the marriage.

Orderic knew the value of suitable marriages to settle disputed claims to inheritance,[48] or even to terminate a blood feud. Geoffrey of Mortagne successfully stifled a feud between his vassals and the family of L'Aigle after the murder of Gilbert of L'Aigle with 'the sweetness of a marriage alliance'.[49] On one occasion Orderic spelled out the details of an allegation of consanguinity that prevented a proposed alliance; this was Henry I's successful plea against the betrothal of his nephew, William Clito, to Sibyl of

---

[46] Malaterra, iv. 8 (p. 90). The reference to a *libellum repudii* indicates formal proceedings for annulment. The Bertrade episode is treated at length by Duby, *Medieval Marriage*, pp. 29-45; but he does not discuss the earlier negotiations for a Sicilian marriage, which add important evidence on the earlier ecclesiastical attitude.

[47] Orderic, ii. 288; v. 12.

[48] Orderic, ii. 262, 352.

[49] Orderic, iv. 202-3.

Anjou, which would have been politically disastrous for him:[50]

> King Henry with great pertinacity . . . broke off the intended marriage, making use of threats and pleas and an enormous quantity of gold and silver and other valuables. He sent cunning advocates to allege consanguinity between the parties, as a result of which it was ruled that they ought not to be married by Christian law. For Richard, duke of Normandy, who was Gunnor's son, begat Robert, and Robert begat William the Bastard, who begat Robert the father of William Clito. On the other side Robert, archbishop and count, the brother of Duke Richard, begat Richard, count of Évreux, and Richard begat Agnes, Simon's wife, who bore Bertrade the mother of Fulk, and Fulk begat Sibyl. In this way the kinship of William and Sibyl was traced out, and the alliance which the distinguished youth had long hoped for was pronounced invalid.

The case had been settled by papal judgement, even if it owed its success to Henry's intrigues and bribes; and the ruling could be justified by citing a genealogy. Orderic stated the facts and made no comment. He must have been aware that exactly the same objection might have been raised to the marriage of Henry's own son William to Fulk's daughter Matilda, and of Henry's daughter Matilda to Fulk's son Geoffrey; he never mentioned the fact. These marriages were never challenged in the courts, and the succession to the English crown depended on them.

Orderic did not venture into the morals of marriage law. He was aware of the delicate interplay of politics and morals, and he confined himself to judicial rulings, giving support to the papal judgements against Philip in his union with Bertrade, and for Henry in his opposition to the betrothal of William Clito. Possibly, when he suggested that a proposed marriage arose from affection, he was aware of the church's insistence that free consent was necessary for a valid marriage. He explained that Henry, the son of King David of Scotland, favoured a treaty with King Stephen that gave him the hand of Adelina of Warenne, whom he loved passionately; but he also mentioned the diplomatic advantages of the treaty.[51] Canon law was making slow and partial advances

---

[50] Orderic, vi. 164-7. Henry's devious diplomacy is described by J. Chartrou, *L'Anjou de 1109 à 1151* (Paris, 1928), pp. 174-5.

[51] Orderic, vi. 524-5.

into secular territory; and in Orderic's writing the two
strands of secular custom and ecclesiastical law and ethics
were intertwined, as they were in the society around him.

(iv) *Knighthood and the Peace Movement*

As the church imposed its coronation ceremonies on
Christian kings and its church ceremony on Christian
marriages, it endeavoured also to extend its ritual to knighthood, and to control the violence in secular society by intro-
ducing peace regulations. Knighthood was, in origin, the
culmination of a purely secular professional training. The
knights were drawn principally from landed families of at
least moderate substance, and included younger no less than
older sons. Young knights from noble families might begin
their military training in a royal court; those less fortunate
had to learn the arts of war in the households of lesser lords
and castellans. Their education in secular warfare was comparable to that of the oblate monks in spiritual warfare, and
might begin at about the same age. Henry, son of Bernier,
in the *chanson* of *Raoul de Cambrai*, typically began his
military apprenticeship at the age of seven and a half.[52]
Placed as boys in the court of some lord, they were brought
up under firm discipline, practising warlike arts and games
under the instruction of a tutor (*nutricius*). These games
were dangerous; in mid-eleventh-century Normandy two of
the seven sons of Giroie suffered fatal accidents in early
youth. Arnold, the eldest, died after being thrown against
a sharp rock in a wrestling match; Hugh, the sixth son, was
struck by an ill-aimed missile, while practising throwing
javelins with his friends.[53] Even kings' sons might die young,
like William I's son Richard, who lost his life in a hunting
accident before he had received the belt of knighthood.[54]
As squires these young men attended fully trained knights
on military expeditions. Those who survived the rigorous

---

[52] J. Flori, 'La notion de chevalerie dans les Chansons de Geste du xiie siècle',
Le Moyen Âge, 4e série xxx (1975), 230. For the education of noble children
see also Barlow, *William Rufus*, pp. 14–25.

[53] Orderic, ii. 24–31.

[54] Orderic, iii. 114–15.

training and mastered the art of mounted combat went on
to test their own skill in mock battles, which gradually took
shape as tournaments, and in more serious warfare. If they
could prove their prowess and acquire the necessary equipment of a horse and armour, they would be given the belt
of knighthood.

The hazardous life of the young household knights has
been described at length by Georges Duby, in his study of
youth in aristocratic society.[55] Often turbulent and dis-
orderly, they nevertheless shared a sense of fellowship in
arms, and were a highly-trained, thoroughly professional,
body of men. They provided a large part of the audience
for the *jongleurs*, who voiced their accepted ethic of valour
and prowess in battle, of loyalty and honour and lavish
hospitality. But they mingled in court and castle with
another group of young men: the clerks and chaplains
attached to the lord's household, who were for the most
part drawn from the same landed families as the young
knights, but had a different view of morality in war. The
knights whom the clerks held up as ideals were men like
St Gerold of Aurillac,[56] who had avoided bloodshed as far
as possible, or St Maurice and the Theban legion who, though
Roman soldiers, had refused to carry out an edict command-
ing the persecution of Christians.[57] A small minority of the
knights who heard them embraced the church's teaching with
such enthusiasm that they renounced the career of arms and
took the monastic habit. The majority recognized some at
least of the restraints of the secular code, especially where,
by demanding loyalty to a lord, these agreed with feudal
custom. In time, too, the moral code of the church became
embodied in the developing canon law. When the two codes
were brought sufficiently into agreement they became
enforceable, not only by ecclesiastical censures such as excommunication and interdict, but also by the secular
penalties of distraint and dispossession.

The peace movement stemmed originally from church
councils, notably the 994 council of Limoges, described by

[55] Duby, *The Chivalrous Society*, pp. 112-22.
[56] See the *Vita* by Odo, abbot of Cluny (Migne, *PL*, cxxxiii. 646-7).
[57] Erdmann, *The Origin of the Idea of Crusade*, pp. 12-14.

Adhémar of Chabannes.[58] The declared intention of the
Peace of God, to renew the peace that Christ had left with his
apostles, had a strong emotive appeal, and from time to time
stirred up outbursts of popular enthusiasm and repentance
that might be harnessed to particular causes; but it was too
broad and general to lead directly to lasting change. The
Truce of God was aimed more particularly at the aristocracy
and their dependants; it recognized that warfare could be
legitimate, but tried to limit the days on which fighting
was permissible, and to give protection to certain categories
of non-combatants. In Normandy, where the Truce was promulgated in 1047 in a council at Caen presided over by the
duke, the legislation was given a special twist to reinforce
ducal authority and justice. Originally at least the the duke
was not bound by it; it became therefore a moral instrument
for restraining private war. Men were required to take an oath
to observe it: a solemn oath, which from the first was sworn
on relics.[59] The duty of enforcement was first placed on the
bishops; but when the Council of Lillebonne renewed the
Truce in 1080 there was a further provision, that if anyone
refused to respect the bishop's sentence the bishop should
make this known to the lord on whose land the offender
lived, and if the lord failed to take action the bishop might
lawfully have recourse to the duke's vicomte.[60] Full details
of the Truce were included in the canons of the 1096 Council
of Rouen.[61] It was to extend from Septuagesima Sunday
until dawn on the Monday after the octave of Pentecost,
and from sunset on the Wednesday before Advent until
the octave of Epiphany; and at every other time of year from
sunset on Wednesday until dawn on Monday, and on all the
feasts of St Mary and the apostles with their vigils, during
which time no man was to attack or wound or kill another,
or take distraint or plunder. Besides this, full protection
at all times was to be extended to all churches and their
churchyards, all monks, clerks, nuns, women, pilgrims,
merchants and their households, and all men ploughing or

[58] Adémar de Chabannes, *Chronique*, ed. J. Chavanon (Paris, 1897), iii. 35,
p. 158.
[59] M. de Bouard, *Annales de Normandie* (1959), p. 181.
[60] Orderic, iii. 26–7.
[61] Orderic, v. 20–1.

harrowing with their oxen and horses, and all the lands of religious houses and money of the clergy. Every man who was aged twelve or more was to swear to observe the Truce, and to assist any bishop or archdeacon, with arms if necessary, to enforce it.

So extensive a truce was frequently violated; but efforts were made to enforce it, and it gave an added sanction to the duke's attempts to abolish private war and stamp out the last traces of the blood feud.[62] There was a widespread belief among defenceless peasants that in time of war they and their possessions would be safer in a church; and this may not have been due solely to the greater strength of stone buildings. The picture drawn by Orderic of Henry I's Easter communion in the church of Carenton in 1105, when he and his household knights were crowded into corners of a building filled with the household goods and baskets of peasant refugees, is unforgettable.[63] Sometimes respect for sanctuary restrained a marauding band. Once during a raid Richer of L'Aigle and his men held their hand and spared a terrified group of country people, who had thrown themselves on the ground by a wayside crucifix.[64] But the discipline of large armies could easily break down, leaving soldiers free to loot and pillage and burn churches. Even a disciplined band of troops might resort to a deliberate scorched earth policy, or make calculated raids into disputed territory, to demonstrate to the inhabitants that their accepted lord was incapable of defending them. 'First lay waste the land, then defeat your enemies', was a strategy that often commended itself to an invader, even if a clerical writer would not put such a recommendation into the mouth of any belligerent who was considered just.[65] But William the Conqueror deliberately devastated land round Hastings to force Harold into battle;[66] and William Rufus's knights systematically laid

[62] See Haskins, *Norman Institutions*, pp. 38, 278, for the limitation of the blood feud.

[63] Orderic, vi. 60-3.

[64] Orderic, vi. 248-51.

[65] *Jordan Fantosme's Chronicle*, ed. and trans. R. C. Johnston (Oxford, 1981), pp. 32-5.

[66] Ann Williams, 'Land and power in the eleventh century; the estates of Harold Godwineson', *Anglo-Norman Studies*, iii (1881 for 1980), 171-87, shows

waste the region around Lucé-le-Grand by uprooting vines and cutting down fruit trees, when the invasion of Maine was brought to a halt.[67] It seems that the dukes of Normandy respected the Truce most readily within their own domains.

In France, until the reign of Louis VI, the church had even less support from the secular ruler. Ivo, bishop of Chartres, took the lead in his own diocese by trying to apply the principles he had learned from his study of canon law. On the question of war he took his personal stand on the principle stated in a series of church councils from 1054 onwards, that no Christian should shed Christian blood; even when he was enduring harsh imprisonment in the castle of Hugh of Le Puiset, he wrote to the people of Chartres categorically forbidding them to make war to obtain his release. He would rather, he said, endure prison and even death than allow the massacre of human beings to secure his freedom; they must pray, and not fight, for him.[68] He dutifully excommunicated these knights who broke the Truce of God; but a letter to Philip I, in which he explained that he could not bring an armed force to escort the king because almost all the knights who were available had been excommunicated for breaking the Truce, suggests that excommunication alone was not a very effective weapon.[69] Among the lands given to Saint-Evroult were some that had become depopulated by devastation in war; they were offered to the abbey in the hope that church protection might bring enough security to attract new settlers.[70] Some were in the diocese of Chartres, others in the French Vexin; both territories lay outside the frontiers of Normandy, and King Philip was not able to offer the effective protection that might have come from a strong duke of Normandy.

If the Truce of God on its own was somewhat fragile, it nevertheless helped to mitigate some of the worst brutalities of war. Secular justice and feudal custom introduced other restraints. The mobility of young, and even older, knights,

the great extent of Harold's Sussex estates; for the devastation by William cf. *The Bayeux Tapestry*, ed. Stenton, pl. 52.

[67] Orderic, v. 258-61.
[68] Ivo of Chartres, *Correspondance* ed. Leclercq, i. no. 20, pp. 86-9.
[69] Ibid., no. 28, pp. 118-19.
[70] Orderic, ii. 152-3; iii. 202-5.

who might take service with any lord from Normandy or
Flanders to Constantinople, Italy or Spain, tended to produce
a kind of freemasonry of knighthood. Added to the well
established and profitable custom of holding prisoners to
ransom rather than enslaving or permanently imprisoning
them, it reduced mortality in all but the most bitter wars.[71]
Orderic, a sincere Christian who knew the realities of
knightly life, was aware of both influences. He wrote in
explanation of the very few casualties in the battle of
Brémule, 'I have been told that in the battle of the two kings,
in which about nine hundred knights were engaged, only
three were killed. They were all clad in mail and spared each
other on both sides, out of fear of God and fellowship in
arms; they wished rather to capture than to kill those they
had routed.'[72] Similarly, when he described how the French
defenders of Chaumont had repulsed the Norman attackers
by shooting down their horses, he wrote, 'The garrison
defended their walls vigorously, but never forgot their duty
to God or their common humanity. They took care out of
mercy to spare the bodies of the attackers, and turned their
anger against the costly chargers of their enemies.'[73] Fellowship in arms and common humanity represented the secular
ethic; fear of God and duty to God, the teaching of the
church. And even narrow self-interest encouraged many
victors to look for ransoms rather than revenge, and to show
magnanimity towards brave knights who might at a later date
be enlisted in their own household troops.

Where possible, they also avoided killing the horses, which
represented a valuable capital investment, well worth capturing alive. The desire to achieve victory and capture spoils
with a minimum of bloodshed may in part account for the
practice of jousting during sieges and before battles, whenever both sides consisted of knights who were similarly armed
and trained. Single combat between champions was often
invited; it provided mutually beneficial training for the
knights involved, gave the victors an opportunity of capturing

[71] See Contamine, *La guerre au Moyen Age*, ch. x.

[72] Orderic, vi. 240-1.

[73] Orderic, v. 218-19. Orderic's attitude to war is explored by C. J. Holdsworth, 'Ideas and reality: some attempts to control and defuse war in the twelfth
century', *The Church and War* (*Studies in Church History*, vol. xx), pp. 59-78.

booty, and enabled both sides to test the strength of their opponents before deciding whether to risk a pitched battle or to continue with a siege. Such single combats were a major theme in epic songs, as in the first stage of the engagement at Roncevaux in the *Chanson de Roland*;[74] but chronicles show that they had an important function in sober reality. William of Malmesbury even thought it worth noting when they had not taken place; before the battle of Lincoln, King Stephen's knights attempted 'that prelude to the fight which is called jousting, in which they were accomplished'; but they had to abandon the attempt when they saw that their opponents were fighting 'not with lances at a distance, but with swords at close quarters'.[75] Jousting might turn sour, and the conventions were by no means always observed; but the comments of the chroniclers show what was both morally acceptable and tactically desirable.

Other restraints were applied partly by feudal custom, partly by the developing concept of chivalry. It was normally acceptable for a man to fight for his lord, even though, if he were the vassal of two different lords who were fighting against each other, he had to supply contingents to both sides. This was a necessary restraint on the ill-treatment of prisoners of war, in an age when treachery might be punished by blinding and mutilation. The lord for his part had duties to his men, whether vassals or stipendiary troops. If the commander of a beleaguered garrison sent out a desperate call for help and received none, he was entitled to make the best bargain he could with the besieging forces. In favourable conditions the defenders might count on being allowed to go free, keeping their arms and horses, on the understanding that they would not fight against their conquerors in the future.[76] Here, as so often in this tough and realistic society, military skill and courage earned their reward. Knights of outstanding ability might hope to be spared, if they kept the rules. The position of the garrison which defended the citadel of Le Mans for William Rufus against

[74] *La chanson de Roland*, ed. J. Bedier (Paris, 1927), vv. 1188-260.
[75] Malmesbury, *Hist. Nov.*, p. 49.
[76] See for example Orderic, vi. 28-9, 178-9; *Letters of Lanfranc*, ed. Clover and Gibson, pp. 124-7.

Helias of Maine in 1100 was a perilous one; hated by the townspeople, whose houses they had burnt during the earlier stages of the fighting, and uncertain whom they could reckon as their lord after the death of Rufus, they were not safe even in an impregnable fortress with an abundant store of food. But they had fought with courage, and they negotiated with skill. Messengers sent to Robert Curthose and King Henry I brought back the information that each had his hands too full to wish to burden himself with a war in Maine. The garrison therefore made peace with Helias and recognized him as their lord; he in turn gave them a safe passage through the crowds of angry citizens and took them into his service.[77] The French knights who were allowed to leave Pont-Audemer with their arms after holding it against King Henry were less fortunate, for they continued to fight against the king and were recaptured. This time they were brought to trial and sentenced to be blinded, so that they could never fight again.[78]

This was feudal justice, combined with fellowship in arms. It would be wrong to look too early for the chivalrous concepts of later courtly epics and the liturgy of the church. The ritual blessing of arms began in coronation ceremonies, where there was a special case for dedicating a king's sword and banner for the defence of the church and of justice, and the protection of the weak. Gradually the practice of blessing arms was extended to other swords. But bloodshed, even in a just cause, was for long regarded as a sin to be expiated. Even though William I carried a banner blessed by Alexander II when he embarked on the conquest of England,[79] a council of Norman bishops presided over by a papal legate imposed heavy penances on all who had shed blood during the English war.[80] There was no inconsistency in this; it resulted from normal penitential teaching. Although in time it became possible to regard certain wars as holy wars, in which the shedding of enemy blood was justifiable and even justifying, such theories came very slowly, and were

[77] Orderic, v. 302-7; cf. Orderic, iv. 132-5 for the departure of Odo of Bayeux and other rebels through an angry crowd after the siege of Rochester.

[78] See above, p. 126.

[79] Erdmann, *The Origin of the Idea of Crusade*, pp. 188-9.

[80] *Councils and Synods*, pp. 581-4.

only loosely connected with a more chivalrous concept of knighthood.[81]

Knighthood, as it appears in the earliest *chansons*, has been described as a kind of corporation.[82] It was not egalitarian: it had its grand masters and masters who commanded the troops, its companions (the knights), and its apprentices (the squires); it had its professional code, its rites and its patron saints. It was not a caste; entry was by merit, not by birth. To a great extent this is a true picture of early knighthood in historical reality. Whatever social or religious implications were later read into it, in origin it was professional and secular. These were its dominant characteristics in Normandy and northern France in the late eleventh and early twelfth centuries.

The knights serving a Norman lord were bound together by fellowship in arms and shared a common professional training; on the battlefield skill and courage counted more than birth. Knights took pride in their horses, but they were prepared to fight on foot if they gained an advantage thereby. The use of mixed forces of mounted and dismounted knights was a common practice in Norman and French battles of the early twelfth century. Dismounted knights could be relied upon to fight more resolutely, since escape was difficult, if not impossible;[83] but in addition they were exposing their attackers' horses to a danger from which they had saved their own. A mounted enemy charge could be thrown into confusion by archers shooting down the horses; and the mounted reserve would then sweep in to capture the unhorsed knights of the opposing force. The first shock of the fighting fell upon those who had dismounted, and often the best knights under royal or noble commanders were the ones to dismount.[84] There was no question of any distinction

---

[81] On the just war see J. A. Brundage, 'Holy war and the medieval lawyers', in Murphy, *The Holy War*, pp. 99–140.

[82] Flori, *Le Moyen Âge* (1975), pp. 436–8.

[83] King Louis VI just managed to escape alive on a borrowed horse after dismounting his knights during the second siege of Le Puiset and being surprised by a sortie of the garrison (Suger, *Vita Ludovici*, xxi. pp. 160–1). William the Lion was captured at Alnwick because his wounded horse fell and pinned him down (*Jordan Fantosme's Chronicle*, vv. 1776–805).

[84] Examples of such tactics occurred at Tinchebray (Orderic, vi. 88–91; *EHR*, xxv (1910), 296; *Chron. de Hida*, p. 307); Brémule (Orderic, vi. 234–43; *Chron.*

of class in this division of knightly function. Certainly infantry existed; when large armies had to be raised they contained some non-knightly elements, such as Welsh or Scottish auxiliaries,[85] or men in charge of the baggage. But it was only later in the twelfth century that more lightly armed, mounted, men who were not knights, sometimes known as *servientes loricati*, played a significant part in battles.[86] At the same time, knighthood began to have much more social significance. This, however, was after Orderic's day.

In Orderic's Normandy the importance of Henry I's household troops in all his military engagements emphasized the professional in contrast to the social aspect of knighthood. This does not mean that all knights were of equal social status. A certain minimum standard was normal, since most of them came from free families with enough landed property to provide a horse and armour, if necessary by obtaining a loan. But above the minimum, grades existed; both the knights and the chroniclers who recorded their family histories were very conscious of birth and standing. Qualifying adjectives crept in; distinctions were made between *nobiles* and *nobiliores* or even *nobilissimi*, and individuals were sometimes described as *gregarii milites, pagenses milites,* or *legitimi milites*.[87] These different grades within the profession depended partly on birth, partly on marriage. Marriage could raise the status of a humble knight. Geoffrey of Malaterra, describing Norman conquests in southern Italy, related how a certain *gregarius miles* named Ingelmar showed

---

de Hida, pp. 316-18; Suger, *Vita Ludovici*, xxvi. pp. 196-9; H. Huntingdon, pp. 241-2); and Bourgthéroulde (Orderic, vi. 348-51; Torigny, Interpolations (Marx, pp. 294-5)). Battle tactics are discussed by J. Bradbury, *Anglo-Norman Studies*, vi (1984 for 1983).

[85] These appear at the battle of Lincoln (John Beeler, *Warfare in England, 1066-1189* (Ithaca, New York, 1966), p. 109), and the battle of the Standard (H. Huntingdon, pp. 263-4).

[86] A valuable study of medieval warfare is given by Philippe Contamine, *La Guerre au Moyen Âge* (Paris, 1980); it contains an extensive bibliography.

[87] Cf. Contamine, *La Guerre au Moyen Âge*, p. 161. Outside Germany, where serf knights were common, the evidence for knights of unfree origin is scarce. Glanvill's *Tractatus de legibus* (ed. G. D. G. Hall (Edinburgh and London, 1965), v. 5, pp. 57-8) refers to the possibility of men of villein origin being freed and made knights. Some *chansons* (e.g. Aspremont) also regarded this as possible; but how far it represented contemporary reality is doubtful (Flori, *Le Moyen Âge* (1975), pp. 407-36).

such military prowess in the service of Count Roger of Sicily that, although he was of low birth, the count rewarded him with the hand of a daughter of the count of Boiano. The marriage was arranged so that the high birth of Ingelmar's wife might give him greater distinction among his companions in arms, and the bride's complaints that it was disparaging to her went unheard.[88]

Orderic was keenly aware of social grades among the knights. He used the term *gregarii* on several occasions. It was flung as a taunt by the haughty young noble, Waleran of Meulan, at the highly trained royal household troops, just before his defeat at their hands at Bourgthéroulde.[89] It was thought appropriate for the fugitives and casual mercenaries—men not members of permanent household troops—whom the exiled Robert Curthose collected to help garrison the French castle of Gerberoy.[90] By contrast, Orderic called the father of his fellow monk, Robert of Prunelai, *legitimus eques*; plainly he had a claim to dignified lineage.[91] High birth or a brilliant marriage could be a source of pride. But they did not have any immediate effect on a knight's role in battle; and initially there was no restriction of birth on those who were invested with the belt of knighthood.[92]

When chroniclers writing in the early twelfth century referred to a man as being given the belt of knighthood, the ceremony was usually performed by the lord in whose court he had trained or served, frequently a king. If the ruler were a woman, she might act. Cecilia, the widow of Tancred, prince of Antioch, knighted a number of squires after the disastrous battle of Darb Samada, when knights were urgently needed.[93] But less distinguished lords could act if necessary; in essence what was done was to give arms, horses, and means of subsistence. Anselm of Bec, in one of his analogies, mentioned the essential equipment of a knight.[94] First of all came the horse, 'which is so necessary for him that it

---

[88] Malaterra, iii. 31, p. 76.   [89] Orderic, vi. 350.
[90] Orderic, iii. 108.   [91] Orderic, vi. 150.
[92] See J. Flori, 'Les origines de l'adoubement chevaleresque', *Traditio*, xxxv (1979), 228–39.
[93] Orderic, vi. 108–9.
[94] *Memorials of St. Anselm*, pp. 97–102.

could rightly be described as his faithful companion. For
with his horse he both charges and puts to flight the enemy,
or, if need arise, escapes from his own pursuers.' The trapp-
ings of the horse were bridle and saddle; the horse at this
date was unarmoured. The knight himself would have
hauberk, helmet and shield for protection, lance and sword
for attack. 'He cannot', Anselm concluded, 'properly be
called a true knight if he lacks any one of these.' In the
chansons the sword had a special significance, and was often
given a name—Durendal, Haute Claire, Joyeuse; it would
be worn at court as well as on the battlefield. It had a special
significance in the ceremonial of knighting, though until
the ranks of knighthood closed in a later period the use of
the sword was not confined to dubbed knights.[95] Similarly,
although the bow was not included in the traditional equipment of a knight, the use of bow and arrow had not been
relegated to archers of a lower status. Skilled archers made up
part of the mounted royal household troops at Bourgthéroulde. Knights of the highest birth practised archery,
though they may have used their skills chiefly in the hunt.
Robert Curthose was reputed to be a deadly archer, and so
was Walter Tirel, a noble French knight who accompanied
William Rufus on his fatal hunting expedition in 1100.[96]

Very gradually during the eleventh century an ecclesiastical
element was introduced into the ceremonial. It began with
the blessing of arms, with formulas taken from coronation
rites. The use of a complete written church ritual for blessing
a new knight remained very rare; only one example has been
discovered earlier than the thirteenth century.[97] At Cambrai,
a little before 1093, a ritual was devised, which is of considerable interest although at the time it made very little impact.
It contained prayers for blessing lance, banner, sword, shield,
and the knight himself; the formulas were adapted from
earlier coronation rituals. After the benedictions, the bishop
himself girded the knight with his sword, to be used against
the enemies of Christ's church. Basically, the ceremony was

[95] Flori, *Le Moyen Âge* (1975), p. 225.

[96] Orderic, ii. 356–7; v. 288–9.

[97] J. Flori, 'Chevalerie et liturgie', *Le Moyen Âge* 4e série, xxxiii (1978),
274–8, 436–8.

the simple admission of a knight to his profession, much as
a lay lord would have performed it, with a superimposed
Christian meaning. But since the handing over of arms by
a priest had symbolic significance, in time church writers
succeeded in adding a spiritual meaning to a ceremony that
was secular in origin.

In Orderic's day there is no reason to suppose that the
ceremony would normally have taken place in a church, even
when the new knight was a king's son; the court was a more
appropriate setting. Orderic wrote, without specifying any
place, that King William's son, Henry, was invested by
Lanfranc; William of Malmesbury and the Anglo-Saxon
chronicler, more precisely and probably more accurately,
wrote that Henry was knighted by his father in the royal
court at Westminster.[98] But Lanfranc may have played some
part in the ceremony. As a king's son, born in the purple,
who might one day have to use the sword blessed on this
occasion for the defence of justice, Henry was no ordinary
knight; Orderic, writing with hindsight, must have been
anxious to suggest the prefiguration of a coronation rite.
Nowhere else did he imply any ecclesiastical participation
in the granting of arms to a knight. By the middle of the
twelfth century churchmen had succeeded in imposing
a more spiritual ritual on the normal ceremony of initiation
to knighthood, just as they had done with marriage.[99]
John of Salisbury assumed in the *Policraticus* that the ceremony would take place in a church. On the day a knight was
to be invested, he would lay his sword upon the altar,
showing by his action that he offered the service of his sword
to God. The act itself was sufficient, and was not accompanied
by any spoken declaration. 'It is not necessary', John
explained, 'that he should make any profession in words.
Who would require such a profession of a man who is
illiterate, and who ought to be trained for arms rather than

[98] Orderic, iv. 120-1; Malmesbury, *GR*, ii. 468; *A.-S. Chron.* s.a. 1086. William
of Malmesbury (*GR*, ii. 360) says that Lanfranc had brought up William Rufus and
made him a knight. Orderic may have transferred the more ecclesiastical ceremony, which seemed to foreshadow a coronation, to Henry I to stress the legitimacy of his rule; but it is possible that Lanfranc was made responsible for the
upbringing of both boys.
[99] See above, pp. 130-2.

for letters?'[1] This view may explain why written rituals for the admission of knights did not become generally used until much later.

Chivalry, whether the secular ideal of the *chansons* or the religious ethic of the initiation ceremonies, was one expression of the attempt to limit hostilities to 'just' wars. Moralists had categorized certain wars as just since Roman times, even if the concepts of Cicero were a good deal narrower than those of Augustine or Gratian, or the writers of *chansons*. But in the course of the eleventh century another concept made its appearance; the holy war.[2] This, when first launched, was in part an attempt to turn the aggressiveness of society against the enemies of the faith; it was directed against the groups and races who existed outside the Christian world.

---

[1] John of Salisbury, *Policraticus*, ed. C. C. J. Webb (2 vols. Oxford, 1909), vi. 10 (ii. p. 25).

[2] For a brief account of the development see Contamine, *La Guerre au Moyen Âge*, pp. 423–68, and references there cited.

7

The World Outside

(i) *Saracens*

Writers of homilies and treatises depicted monks as the *milites Christi*, engaged in unremitting daily battles with demons. A typical story was set down by a Cluniac monk, Jotsaldus, in the eleventh century: he described a vision in which demons were seen to be lamenting because the souls of the condemned were being freed from their torments by the prayers of religious men.[1] Anselm of Bec, with his characteristic clarity and brevity, described the whole world as a battleground between God and the devil. Within God's kingdom Christianity was a strong city that the devil might break into occasionally to carry off weaker souls. Within the city was a castle, manned by monks who were safer still, unless they ventured outside; but only in the keep, defended by angels, was safety absolute. Outside the city dwelt Jews and pagans, whom the devil had wholly in his power.[2]

To Anselm's contemporaries in most of Western Europe, all non-Christians were outside their familiar world. Anselm himself did not advocate the use of force against them, and others were divided in their views. Jews, indeed, were settled and protected in many cities; they traded freely with Christians, and doctrinal debate was possible between the learned of both faiths. Up to the end of the eleventh century attacks on Jews were isolated and limited; a typical example was their expulsion from Mainz by King Henry in 1012.[3] The Saracens, more numerous and more dangerous, were in

[1] Jotsaldus, *De vita et virtutibus sancti Odilonis abbatis*, Migne, *PL*, cxlii. 926-7.
[2] *Memorials of St. Anselm*, pp. 66-7.
[3] *Annales quedlinburgenses, MGH SS*, iii. 81; Anna Sapir Abulafia, 'An eleventh-century exchange of letters between a Christian and a Jew', *Journal of Medieval History*, vii (1981), 154-5. Normally Jews in the Empire enjoyed imperial protection.

a different position. They were resisted as invaders; when attempts at reconquest began in Spain the participants were the forces recruited as vassals and mercenaries by the Spanish kings. Some Normans, including Baudry de Guitry and possibly Ralph of Tosny fought in these wars during the reign of William the Conqueror; many went as pilgrims to Compostela. The motives of these men was a mixture of aggression and professional training, land-hunger, penitence, and pilgrimage. By 1063 some foreshadowing of crusading ideas can be detected in the expedition that led to the capture of Barbastro; Pope Alexander II granted a form of indulgence to participants, and may have sent a papal banner.[4] But the event that acted as a catalyst to these confused ideas was Urban II's appeal at Clermont in 1096 for a united attempt to recover Jerusalem from the infidel, twenty-five years after the Selchükid Turks had inflicted a crushing defeat on the forces of the Emperor of Constantinople, and had become the dominant power in Asia Minor and Palestine. Even then, though far more western knights became involved in battles against the infidel, the Saracen world was remote from the great majority of Christians, including most of those who recorded the history of these stirring enterprises.

The concept of a holy war as something not merely just, but justifying, only slowly gained ground, and even then remained at first a moral rather than a legal concept.[5] Christian attitudes to war, always ambivalent, continued to have a strong element of pacifism, shading through passive resistance to the acceptance of war as just, provided it was waged to resist aggression or recover lost rights. But the way had been prepared for a holy war; the need to find an outlet

---

[4] The growth of the crusading ideal in the eleventh century was traced by Karl (Carl) Erdmann in 1935 in *Die Entstehung des Kreuzzugsgedankens* (Stuttgart), a seminal book of lasting value. Over forty years of research have led to the modification of some of his views; the translation by Marshall W. Baldwin and Walter Goffart, *The Origin of the Idea of Crusade* (Princeton, 1977) contains useful bibliographical notes. For the expedition against Barbastro see pp. 136-40, 288-90.

[5] The subject of the just war and the holy war has given rise to much recent study. See in particular Frederick H. Russell, *The Just War in the Middle Ages* (Cambridge, 1975); *The Holy War*, ed. T. P. Murphy (Columbus, Ohio, 1976). For some legal and theological views of war see J. A. Brundage, 'Holy war and the medieval lawyers', in Murphy, *Holy War*, pp. 99-140.

for the violence in society led ultimately to religious leaders from Urban II to St Bernard seeing the *milites Christi* not merely as men engaged in spiritual battles against sin and the devil, but as knights fighting a war of aggression against the enemies of Christendom.

Three or four hundred leading churchmen heard Pope Urban's sermon at Clermont, and carried reports of its contents home to their several provinces.[6] Different individuals seized on whatever points in his long and eloquent plea seemed to them most important. Some wrote their own account of the proceedings; the reports of others were filtered through the minds of the chroniclers who recorded them. Orderic's account owed much, but not all, to Baudry of Bourgueil; it was certainly derived from more than one source and interpreted in his own way.[7] Jerusalem, sanctified by Christ's sepulchre, had been overrun by Turks, Arabs, and other infidel peoples, who had destroyed churches and slaughtered and enslaved Christians. Property given to support holy men and the poor had been unlawfully seized by pagan tyrants. The call was for Christians to be the instruments of divine vengeance. They set out on pilgrimage, after confessing their sins, to make expiation to God and restore Jerusalem to the followers of Christ. They took the cross, but even when Orderic wrote, over twenty years later, there was no word for a crusade. He occasionally called the men 'cruciferi', but referred to them most frequently as pilgrims, or the army of Christ. When, in his preface to Book IX, he tried to sum up the importance of the great events he felt compelled to describe, he saw the journey to Jerusalem as a pilgrimage to visit the tomb of the Messiah, and recover the holy city from the vile Saracens; it was a single great enterprise in which western peoples were marvellously united in a common cause.[8] Their triumph was God's triumph; but so was the conquest of sin in each individual soul.

Pilgrimage as an act of penitence and devotion was something with which Orderic had been familiar all his life. The

---

[6] See P. Rousset, *Les origines et les caractères de la première croisade* (Neufchatel, 1945), p. 58; D. C. Munro, 'The speech of Urban II at Clermont', *American Historical Review*, xi (1906), 231-42.

[7] Orderic, v. 14-19.   [8] Orderic, v. 4-7.

monks of his abbey remembered with affectionate admiration the departure of their first abbot, Thierry, for the pilgrimage to Jerusalem on which he died.[9] Yet, in common with many bishops and abbots, including Anselm of Bec and Hildebert of Le Mans, he recognized that many duties were imposed upon a man by his place in society. Hildebert was later to dissuade Geoffrey of Anjou from going on a pilgrimage to Compostela, writing, 'You have laid yourself under a vow, but God has laid on you an office. Your vow demands a journey, but God requires obedience . . . Consider well whether the fruit of this journey can compensate a breach of that obedience.'[10] His office as count came from God, and he had a duty to his people. Similarly Orderic thought it right that Helias, count of Maine, should defer fulfilling his vow to go to Jerusalem, when William Rufus refused to guarantee the integrity of the county of Maine during his absence, and even threatened to invade it. He put an eloquent speech stating the case into the mouth of Count Helias:

God has seen fit to entrust to me the stewardship of Maine, which I should not weakly relinquish for any light cause, for fear of leaving God's people at the mercy of predators . . . I will not abandon the cross of our Saviour, which I have taken up as a pilgrim, but will have it engraved on my shield and helmet and all my arms . . . Fortified by this symbol I will advance against the enemies of peace and right.[11]

Although in time crusades were to be turned against Christian aggressors, this is less a foretaste of a much later development than a powerful restatement of the case for a just war, in a society where men were held to be destined by their birth to serve God according to the requirements of their 'order' or office. In this society even pilgrimage, a potent ideal, might become an evasion of a harder duty.[12]

Geoffrey, bishop of Vendôme, wrote of a monk who had returned from Jerusalem that he would have done better to

[9] Orderic, ii. 68-73; iii. 334-7.
[10] Migne, *PL*, clxxi. 181-3 (i. 15); P. von Moos, *Hildebert von Lavardin* (Pariser historische Studien, 3, Stuttgart, 1965), pp. 144-6; cited R. W. Southern, *The Making of the Middle Ages* (London, 1953), p. 95.
[11] Orderic, v. 228-31.
[12] G. Constable, 'Monachisme et pèlerinage au Moyen Âge', *Revue historique*, cclviii (1977), 18-19; reprinted, *Religious Life and Thought*, ch. III.

have stayed in his monastery and led a good life there: that was a surer way to the heavenly Jerusalem than visiting the terrestrial one.[13] He told Odo, abbot of Marmoutier, that with his own ears he had heard Pope Urban call on the laity to go on pilgrimage to deliver Jerusalem, and at the same time discourage monks from undertaking a pilgrimage so full of danger to their vows.[14] According to Robert the Monk, who had also been present at Clermont, the pope had said that any clergy joining the expedition should have the permission of their superiors, and even the laity should not go without the blessing of a priest.[15] This was a restatement of accepted practice, in some danger of being overturned by the enthusiasm and hysteria of the moment. Forty years earlier, Abbot Thierry of Saint-Evroult had not felt free to undertake a pilgrimage until he had secured the consent of his bishop.

In popular thinking, the idea of pilgrimage remained dominant, alongside a steadily growing, very confused, belief that pilgrims who were also knights of Christ were assured of paradise if they died in battle against the infidel. These views were expressed in the crusading songs.[16] The earliest of these to survive, *Jerusalem mirabilis*, a Latin song from the cloister of Saint-Martial de Limoges, probably composed for the first crusade, sings of the duty of pilgrims to sell their lands and go to the most blessed city to rescue the temple of God and destroy the Saracens. But a vernacular troubadour song, *Chevalier, mult estes guariz*, which called on French knights to follow Louis VII in 1148, already made its different appeal confidently in the refrain, 'He who goes with Louis, what has he to fear from hell? For surely his soul will dwell in paradise with the angels of the Lord.' This view may have owed something to the encouragement of monks who were kinsfolk and friends of the crusading knights. To the monks who saw themselves as *milites Christi*, striving to earn a martyr's crown by their warfare against Satan and his legions, it was only a short step to see the

[13] Migne, *PL*, clvii. 127–8 (iii. 24).

[14] Migne, *PL*, clvii. 162–3 (iv. 21).

[15] *Historia Iherosolimitana*, *RHC Occ*. iii. 729–30.

[16] R. L. Crocker, 'Early Crusade songs', in Murphy, *Holy War*, pp. 78–98, especially pp. 82–5.

secular knights of Christ as martyrs when they fell in war against the Saracens. In time Orderic came to write of them in these terms. Reports of the crusading indulgences helped to feed these views in untrained minds, unable to grasp the subtleties of penitential teaching; even the theologians and canon lawyers only slowly worked out the implications of the indulgences.[17]

The Saracens in the Holy Land were distant peoples, who to most men and women in western Europe inhabited a world of fantasy. There was almost total ignorance about their religion; many even believed that they worshipped Mohammed as a god.[18] Even though some Norman outlaws like Hugh Bunel and his brothers had taken service in their armies in the late eleventh century, and after the launching of the first crusade contingents of knights from almost every province of France and the Low Countries had gained experience of fighting against them,[19] only the permanent settlers in Jerusalem, Antioch, or Edessa learnt much about their way of life. Most knights accurately observed and reported the way the Saracens fought; adapting their own tactics was necessary for survival. Otherwise the stories that filtered back to the men and women at home, even when they contained some accurate facts about individuals involved in negotiating the release of prisoners, had far more in common with the Arabian Nights. To many writers, as to the men who composed the pilgrim songs for the crusaders, the Saracens were not so much real people as a projection into the material world of the demons against whom they waged their spiritual battles.[20] When they described such atrocities as the sack of Jerusalem they did not visualize the slaughtered enemy as human beings.

In Spain and even southern Italy, where Moslems and Christians lived in closer contact for long periods and there were some cultural exchanges (particularly through the Mosarabs and Jews),[21] the situation was different. Orderic

[17] J. A. Brundage, *Canon Law and the Crusader* (Madison, 1969).
[18] See for example Orderic, v. 166-7.
[19] Orderic, v. 156-7.
[20] Crocker, 'Early Crusade songs' (Murphy, *Holy War*, pp. 96-7).
[21] Marie-Thérèse d'Alverny, 'Translations and translators', *Renaissance and Renewal*, pp. 438-44, revised some traditional views on cultural contacts with Spain.

wrote of the early conflicts in Spain, until crusading fervour took over after the council of Toledo in 1118, in realistic terms.[22] To the Normans, Spain was a land of settlement like southern Italy, England, or Scotland. Norman knights took service with rulers who were anxious to recruit stipendiary knights; many who went to fight there were young men waiting to inherit an ancient patrimony, or hoping to acquire lands to settle. Often they returned disappointed, but their complaints were more of Spanish ingratitude than of Saracen barbarity. Among the friends and patrons of Saint-Evroult, Rainald of Bailleul went, but returned to his Norman patrimony. Robert Bordet of Cullei and his brave wife, Sibyl, went and stayed longer, trying to hold a lordship in Tarragona. Rotrou, count of Mortagne, was a first cousin of King Alfonso the Battler of Aragón; early in the twelfth century he responded to his cousin's appeal for auxiliaries, and in spite of initial disappointments, returned later with a contingent of knights from Mortagne and Perche to help in the reconquest and settlement of the Ebro valley. At first, in Orderic's narrative, the Sarcens figure simply as oppressors. They are shown demanding tribute, even acting unjustly and brutally, but allowing Mosarabs to baptize their children and practice their own religion. They are barbarous enemies, not demons. Only in the last decade, particularly after the siege of Fraga, did Orderic see the war in Spain as a holy war of Christian knights to drive back the infidel; and by that time the stories of returning warriors had been partly taken over by *chansons*.[23]

(ii) *Jews*

The groups of non-Christians most familiar in the West at the time of the first crusade were the Jews. Up to the eleventh century, in spite of a few mainly local outbreaks of hostility and violence, Christian and Jewish communities

[22] Orderic, vi. 394-419, describes some events in Spain. Although later historians sometimes traced crusading ideas back to the 1063 expedition against Barbastro, which became the subject of a twelfth-century *chanson*, Orderic's realistic view is more typical of contemporary attitudes (cf. Erdmann, *The Origin of the Idea of Crusade*, pp. 136-40).

[23] See below, pp. 202-8.

had achieved a fair measure of peaceful co-existence. Groups were settled in many of the largest cities of northern France, including Rouen, Blois, Le Mans, Orleans, Paris, Rheims, Sens, and Troyes. Their principal occupation was trade, and the activities associated with it. Tightly organized local communities that provided for their own social and religious needs, they relied on the protection of local counts whenever they settled outside the territory effectively controlled by the king of France.[24] For the Jews of Rouen and Le Mans this meant the duke of Normandy and the count of Maine.

Their protectors expected in return certain benefits, of which the most important were a general stimulus to trade and urban life, and the payment of taxes. While ecclesiastical writers greeted the occasional conversion of a Jew as a cause for rejoicing, churchmen no less than secular lords were opposed to forcible conversions, and at times helped to safeguard their way of life. Between 1007 and 1012 there were outbreaks of hostility against the Jews, arising possibly from fears about the spread of heresy. A few edicts in various parts of northern Europe gave them the alternative of conversion or expulsion or, very occasionally, even of death.[25] It was probably about this time that Duke Richard II of Normandy was charged with attempting the forcible conversion of Jews; Hebrew chroniclers record an appeal against him made by Jacob b. Yekutiel, a Jew of Rouen. Jacob is alleged to have said that the duke had not the jurisdiction necessary to force the Jews from their faith, which could be done only by the pope at Rome; and, according to the Hebrew account, he took his case to Rome and obtained a papal decree putting an end to forced conversions.[26] This toleration of another people's customs even in matters of religion was to come under increasing strain in the next hundred years, but it left its mark on the behaviour of many secular rulers and churchmen for a very long time. William Rufus came under attack for ordering children who had been converted (most probably by force) to Christianity to return

[24] Robert Chazan, *Medieval Jewry in Northern France* (Baltimore and London, 1973), pp. 10–29.

[25] R. Chazan, 'Initial crisis for Northern-European Jewry', *Proceedings of the American Academy for Jewish Research*, xxxviii–xxxix (1970-1), 101-18.

[26] Chazan, *Medieval Jewry*, pp. 13-14.

to the faith of their fathers. The Emperor Henry IV authorized forced converts to return to Judaism in 1097. Count Roger of Sicily was so strongly opposed to the conversion of his Saracen troops that, according to Eadmer who had met them when they accompanied the count to Bari in 1097, they dared not listen to the persuasive teaching of Anselm, much as they wished to do so.[27]

For the Jews in many parts of Europe, the first crusade marked a serious setback in their fortunes. Widespread hostility broke out, and there were appalling massacres of Jews in the Rhineland.[28] Only one incident is recorded in northern France; and, apart from a brief notice in one continuation of the *Annales Rothomagenses*, that incident is reported only in the autobiography of Guibert of Nogent.[29] According to Guibert, those who had taken the cross began to complain to each other, 'We are setting out to attack the enemies of God in the East, and here before our eyes are Jews, of all races the worst foes of God; this is doing our work the wrong way round.' So, 'seizing their weapons, they rounded up the Jews in a certain church either by force or guile, and put to the sword, regardless of age or sex, all except those who agreed to accept Christianity'. Guibert was able to give details because on that occasion William, the young count of Eu, rescued a Jewish boy and took him to his widowed mother, Helisende. The boy was baptized with the name of William, and placed in Guibert's own abbey of Saint-Germer de Fly, to protect him from his kinsfolk, who wished to recover him for their faith. Here he became an exemplary monk.

This is the only attack on Jews in northern France at

[27] See below, p. 155; and for imperial policy *The Jews and the Crusaders*, ed. Shlomo Eidelberg (Wisconsin, 1977), pp. 98-103, 167 n. 15.

[28] Albert of Aix condemned the massacres, which the archbishop of Mainz had tried in vain to prevent, commenting that the pilgrims slaughtered the Jews rather through greed for their money than for the sake of God's justice, and that consequently they were themselves cut to pieces, because God is a just judge and does not wish for forced conversions (*RHC Occ.* iv. 292-3, 295). Pope Alexander II had anticipated the danger to Jews in expeditions against the infidel when, in 1063, he forbade the knights going to fight in Spain to oppress the Jews (JL 4528, 4532, 4533; Erdmann, pp. 137-8).

[29] F. Liebermann, *Ungedruckte Anglo-normannische Geschichtsquellen* (Strasbourg, 1879), p. 47; Guibert, *De vita sua* ii. 5 (Benson, pp. 134-7; Labande, pp. 246-9).

the time of the first crusade for which satisfactory evidence exists, and it is likely to have been an isolated one. Hostility built up as the bands of crusaders straggled across Europe, often tempted to loot by their own privations. Normandy was one of the points of departure, where the forces were still well disciplined and adequately supplied. Moreover, Guibert's account does not give a clear statement of the numbers actually killed; many may have bought time by professing willingness to be converted and then appealing to the duke. If they did, it would account for some strange stories in the histories of William of Malmesbury and Eadmer. Malmesbury accused William Rufus, who exercised ducal authority in Normandy during his brother Robert's absence on crusade, of impiety for taking money to induce certain Jews who had apostasized to relinquish their new religion.[30] Eadmer made similar accusations, adding a story about a young Jewish convert named Stephen, who, claiming to have been converted by St Stephen the protomartyr in a vision, refused to return to Judaism in spite of the king's threats.[31] Stephen's conversion may have been genuine; if the others were forced, William Rufus appears to have acted in accordance with established practice, by protecting the customs and religion of a minority group settled in his domains and exercising the right of levying money from them. His predecessor, Duke Richard II, had been compelled to abandon forced conversions at the beginning of the century. But Rufus had an unfortunate taste for impious jests, which encouraged monastic chroniclers to put the worst possible interpretation on his motives. Eadmer was more reticent about Roger I's refusal to allow the conversion of his Saracen troops, saying only that it was a matter between Roger himself and God.[32]

French Jews never regarded 1095-6 as a watershed in their history, as their German counterparts did; for them the first major catastrophe was the massacre at Blois in 1171. The economic and intellectual development of Jewish communities

[30] Malmesbury, *GR*. ii. 371. He alleges that Rufus encouraged a disputation between Jews and Christian bishops and clerks, and said in jest that he would embrace Judaism if the Jews got the better of the argument.

[31] Eadmer, *Hist. Nov.*, pp. 99-101.

[32] Eadmer, *Vita Anselmi*, pp. 111-12.

in Normandy and the neighbouring provinces continued into
the twelfth century. Negative evidence that the outbreak at
Rouen was on a relatively small scale, and was successfully
damped down by William Rufus, comes from the silence of
Orderic Vitalis. He tells us nothing whatever about the attack
on the thriving Jewish community at Rouen;[33] he was chiefly
aware of Jews at a different, purely intellectual level.

This was a period when Christian exegetes and theologians
were actively engaged in discussions with Jewish scholars
for two main reasons. Like Jerome, they needed to understand the technical terms in the Old Testament with the
help of the Jews; and their search for 'Hebrew truth' led
them to interpret the books of law by relating the precepts
they contained to Jewish practices.[34] Besides this, the Jewish
interpretations of Scripture challenged some of the central
tenets of the Christian faith, and these provided a powerful
stimulus to Christian thinkers to define their own beliefs
more explicitly in contemporary terms. The *Disputations*
with Jews written at this time were largely expositions in
a particular literary form of dialogue for the edification of
Christian hearers; but often they originated in real discussions
with Jews, and the writers may have hoped both to make
converts and to prevent apostasies.

The *Disputatio Iudei et Christiani* of Gilbert Crispin,
monk of Bec and abbot of Westminster, arose from friendly
discussions with a learned Jew from Mainz who had settled
in London.[35] The unbelievers in Anselm's *Cur Deus homo*
may have been generalized adversaries rather than individuals;
there is no doubt from the substance of their attack on the
central doctrine of the Incarnation that they were Jews.
'The unbelievers', says Boso, at the beginning of Anselm's
dialogue, 'deride our simplicity, objecting that we do God an
injury and disgrace him when we assert that he descended

[33] The silence of the great Jewish commentator, Rashi, and other Jewish
sources is also significant. See *The Jews and the Crusaders*, ed. Eidelberg, pp. 137
n. 2, 166 n. 3.
[34] See, for example, B. Smalley, 'Ralph of Flaix on Leviticus', *RTAM*, xxxv
(1969), 66-9; reprinted *Studies in Medieval Thought and Learning*, ch. V.
[35] J. A. Robinson, *Gilbert Crispin*, pp. 81-2; and *The Works of Gilbert
Crispin, Abbot of Westminster*, ed. G. R. Evans and Anna Sapir Abulafia (British
Academy, *Auctores Britannici Medii Aevi*, forthcoming).

to a woman's womb and was born of a woman.'[36] Odo, bishop of Cambrai, in his *Disputation* against the Jew, Leo, represented the Jew as saying that the Jews considered Christians crazy for thinking that God endured being imprisoned for nine months in a womb.[37] Guibert of Nogent also wrote a treatise on the Incarnation against the Jews; this, he said, pleased his fellow monk William, the converted Jew, so much that he made a devout compilation of arguments for the faith.[38] William's work has not survived; but the homilies attributed to him show a very strong and pious devotion to the Virgin Mary; and the cult of the Virgin was undoubtedly stimulated by opposition to Jewish attacks.

Orderic was familiar with some of this literature, particularly with the works of the monks of Bec. A copy of Gilbert Crispin's *Disputatio*, made under Orderic's supervision, was in the library of Saint-Evroult.[39] He spoke with admiration of Anselm's works, including his *Cur Deus homo*.[40] Saint-Germer de Fly seems, surprisingly, to have lain outside his intellectual orbit, though it was within two miles of the priory of Neufmarché. Unlike his contemporary, William of Malmesbury, he never made a compilation of miracles of the Virgin, and he may not have known the popular stories that developed on the theme of Jewish hostility to her, and her triumphs over her enemies. But in the regular round of scriptural meditation and exposition that made up a large part of the life of every monk he constantly heard and read of the practices of Jews. William of Merlerault, whose homilies were composed for the monks of Saint-Evroult, refered to Jewish customs in his discussions of the meaning of scriptural texts.[41] The jars of water mentioned in the miracle of Cana were set out, William explained, because it

[36] Anselm, *Opera*, ii. 50; Southern, *St. Anselm*, pp. 90-1.

[37] Migne, *PL*, clx. 1105-12. On the whole question see Robert Worth Frank Jr., 'Miracles of the Virgin, Medieval anti-Semitism, and the Prioress's Tale', *Essays in Early English Literature in honor of Morton W. Blomfield*, ed. L. D. Benson and S. Wenzel (Kalamazoo, 1982), pp. 179-84.

[38] Guibert, *De vita sua*, ii. 5; and see Leclercq, 'Prédicateurs bénédictins aux xie et xiie siècles', *Revue Mabillon*, xxxiii (1943), 59-65.

[39] Rouen, MS 1174, fos. 106-115v. Orderic's handwriting occurs in this manuscript.

[40] Orderic, ii. 294-7.

[41] On William's homilies see Leclercq, *Revue Mabillon* xxxiii (1943), 48-59.

was customary for Jews, particularly Pharisees, to have at
their feasts jars of water for washing their hands or their
mouths.[42] He spoke of their marriage customs in discussing
the marriage of Joseph and Mary.[43] It is true that in his
allegorical expositions he sometimes suggested that the Jews
attacking Christ signified the demons who tried to kill Christ
in the hearts of men;[44] but only the most simple-minded
of his hearers were likely to confuse the literal and allegorical
meanings of holy writ.

Certainly Orderic wrote of the Jews almost exclusively
in a historical context: being led from Egypt by Moses,
enduring the Babylonian captivity, obeying the law of Moses
in their dietary practices.[45] Where, in his account of the first
crusade, he spoke of the Jews as the persecutors of Christ
or of St Stephen, he was simply copying Baudry of Bourgueil,
who had added these comments to the more detached
account of the anonymous *Gesta Francorum*.[46] Only in one
place in his work is there a possible suggestion of animosity
against contemporary Jews. This is in his account of the
reception accorded to the son of Peter Leonis at the council
of Rheims in 1119. The young man had been held as a
hostage by the archbishop of Cologne, and was restored to
freedom in the council. He was brought in by the archbishop's
envoy, 'a dark-haired, pale youth, more like a Jew or a
Saracen (*Agarenus*) than a Christian, dressed in splendid
garments, but physically deformed. At the sight of him seated
beside the Pope, the French and many others laughed scorn-
fully, and called down imprecations on his head, out of
hatred of his father, whom they knew to be an infamous
usurer.'[47]

This is a difficult passage to interpret. Orderic described
what he himself had seen and heard at Rheims in 1119: an
outburst of hostility shown by the French and many others
at the appearance of the son of Peter Leonis, and angry
murmurs about the financial dealings of the boy's father.

[42] Alençon, MS 149, fo. 16v.
[43] Alençon, MS 149, fos. 7v–8.
[44] Alençon, MS 149, fo. 7.
[45] Orderic, ii. 274; iv. 24; v. 6, 372.
[46] Orderic, v. 156, 168; *RHC Occ.* iv. 97, 102.
[47] Orderic, vi. 266–9.

He wrote the passage at least sixteen years later, when the boy's brother had become the rival pope Anacletus II; and he may have read back into the earlier episode some of the hostility to the whole family of the Pierleoni that then prevailed among Innocent II's supporters. Modern commentators have tended to examine the episode for signs of anti-Jewish feeling, or even a foretaste of anti-Semitism. But Orderic's reference to Jews was a passing one: he linked them explicitly with the infidel Saracens (the reputed sons of Hagar) as enemies of the Christian faith; and he may have linked them implicitly with those other enemies of the faith who were guilty of the heresy of schism. He did not refer to the fact that the boy's great-grandfather had been a converted Jew; and indeed in 1119, as F.-J. Schmale has rightly stressed, not even the enemies of the Pierleoni held their Jewish descent against them. The criticisms Orderic heard were directed against the financial dealings of the boy's father. Here again, Schmale's interpretation of the undercurrents of politics is revealing; he suggested that a treaty of Calixtus II with the Genoese in 1121, which was underwritten by representatives of both the Pierleoni and their great rivals, the Frangipani, heralded a change in papal policy, previously heavily reliant on the Pierleoni.[48] Might not the truth be that opposition to the Pierleoni was already making itself felt in curial circles in 1119, and seeking justification in charges of usury against Peter Leonis? If so it might explain why Calixtus II, a prudent and practical pope, cautiously began shifting ground two years later. Perhaps modern preoccupation with the problem of anti-Jewish feeling had caused historians to overlook an interesting clue to the growth of factional opposition in the papal curia at this time.[49] Even if Orderic's interpretation can be explained partly in the light of the later schism, the evidence of his

[48] F.-J. Schmale, *Studien zum Schisma des Jahres 1130* (Forschungen zur Kirchlichen Rechtsgeschichte und zum Kirchenrecht, 3), Cologne and Graz, 1961, pp. 22-3.

[49] Schmale, *Studien zum Schisma*, p. 71 n. 190, argues cogently that Orderic's remarks should not be read as an expression of anti-Jewish feeling. The interpretation of A. Graboïs ('Le schisme de 1130 et la France', *Revue d'histoire ecclésiastique*, lxxvi (1981), pp. 610-11), who finds an expression of anti-Semitism in this passage, seems to me unacceptable in the light of Orderic's normal attitude to Jews.

eyes and ears still indicates that there were stirrings of rival political factions at Rheims.

Normally Orderic showed nothing of the violence against Jews that appears in the writings of some of his contemporaries. This may have been partly determined by his own experience; he had little to say about the affairs even of Christian townsmen and merchants, with whom he had little contact. Again, there were no sensational apostasies in his own region during his lifetime. By contrast Guibert of Nogent brought into his autobiography the family history of the count of Soissons who, though nominally a Christian, was reputed to be a notorious blasphemer and supporter of Jews, and whose mother was said to have poisoned her brother with the help of a certain Jew.[50] The Jew had been brought to trial and burned. Guibert also readily retailed gossip about black magic and unnatural vice, and made uncritical accusations against both Jews and heretics.[51] Orderic either never heard, or did not choose to repeat, such stories. William of Malmesbury, another historian who attacked the Jews, did so for a different reason. His denunciations of them as an 'infidel people', and an 'accursed people', occur notably in his collection of the *Miracles of the Virgin*. They reflect the popular reaction to the explicit denial by Jewish writers of the whole doctrine of the Incarnation, which many Christians saw as a cruel and obscene personal challenge to the Mother of God.[52] Orderic made no collection of these miracles, and no copy is known to have been in his library. Instead, the Jews he encountered in his reading were the theological opponents of Anselm and Gilbert Crispin, who were introduced into intellectual disputes so that their arguments might be civilly, but firmly, refuted. His attitude is a reminder that the more militant approach to non-Christians often associated with

[50] *De vita sua*, iii. 16 (Benson, pp. 209-10; Labande, pp. 422-5).

[51] *De vita sua*, iii. 17 (Labande, p. 428 n. 4).

[52] *El libro 'De laudibus et miraculis Sanctae Mariae' de Guillermo de Malmesbury*, ed. José M. Canal (Rome, 1968), pp. 73-6; Peter Carter, 'The historical content of William of Malmesbury's "Miracles of the Virgin Mary" ', *The Writing of History in the Middle Ages*, ed. Davis and Wallace-Hadrill, pp. 145-53, discusses the reasons for William of Malmesbury's anti-Jewish writings; he sees them partly as a bookish fervour, resulting from study of the Prophets and the classics.

the crusading movement only very slowly became general, and only partially replaced older customs of thought and action. Co-existence of Christian and Jewish communities within the great cities of northern France, though at times precarious, and made possible only by the toleration and protection of the various secular powers, had continued far too long to disappear overnight. The Norman kings valued the services of the Jews of Rouen and London, and were strong enough to protect them if need arose. Orderic's attitude, shown in his writing, is added evidence that the Jews of northern France and particularly Normandy continued to be left in peace to pursue both their economic and their intellectual interests for half a century after the first crusade.

(iii) *Heretics*

As the crusaders followed Bohemond from Durazzo towards Constantinople, they turned aside north of Castoria to attack a 'fortress of heretics', pillaged it, and burnt it with all its inhabitants, who appear to have been Paulicians. 'Indeed these pilgrims', wrote Orderic, 'held all Jews, heretics, and Saracens, whom they called enemies of God, to be equally detestable.'[53] The motives for attacking them and plundering their fortress may not have been purely religious, for the knights were experiencing difficulty in purchasing provisions; but the episode shows how easily the swords of the *milites Christi* could be turned against any of the opponents of the Christian faith. The three groups named were the same as those against whom scholars drew the sword of the intellect: Peter the Venerable was writing in a well established tradition when, a generation later, he produced treatises attacking the beliefs of the Jews, the Saracens, and the followers of Peter of Bruys. The titles by which his treatises are known are significant: *Contra Iudeos, Contra Sarracenos, Contra Petrobrusianos*. The first two were long established, identifiable groups, but heresy was a hydra-headed monster.[54] Individual leaders and their followers

[53] Orderic, v.44; cf. *RHC Occ*. iv. 23.

[54] The distinction was not absolutely clear cut; Peter the Venerable wrote of the 'heresy of the Saracens', and made a reasoned attack on their doctrinal errors, especially their denial of the Trinity (*Letters of Peter the Venerable*, ii. 275-8).

might be cut off from the church; others, with different tenets and different types of following, sprang up to take their place. Heresy might take many forms; it was not immediately recognizable, and it was sometimes associated with social movements. Not surprisingly, contemporaries used the term loosely to cover such different manifestations as doctrinal error, moral turpitude, and revolt against authority.

When describing doctrines condemned in the early councils of the church and denounced by the Fathers, chroniclers were on sure ground. Arians, Eutychians, or Pelagians were heretics. Orderic, who used the word heretic very sparingly, had no hesitation in applying it to such men; indeed he found it in the works of Bede and other earlier historians who were his sources.[55] In his own day the position was more confusing; but he discovered in the work of Berengar of Tours one clear example of heresy of a traditional type.[56] The implications of Berengar's teaching on the eucharist were certainly misunderstood and misrepresented by his critics; but the teaching had been clearly condemned in church synods at Rome, Vercelli, and Tours. Among the opponents who attacked him with great learning were Lanfranc, whose treatise *On the Body and Blood of the Lord* passed through Orderic's hands, and Durand of Troarn, a respected Norman abbot. 'Some considered him a heresiarch', Orderic wrote, and he added that Berengar had been forced to burn the books containing his errors for fear of being burned himself.[57] Berengar's views, and the aggressiveness with which he first asserted them, provoked debate in centres of learning from Rome to Normandy; they were in fact more subtle than most of his adversaries allowed, and though decisively rejected for the time being, they had the great merit of forcing the defenders of orthodoxy to clarify their own ideas. No Norman historian could have failed to be aware of the smoke of that controversy. But from Orderic's point

---

[55] Orderic, iii. 58, 64, 72; vi. 382.

[56] Important recent works on the controversy with Berengar include Gibson, *Lanfranc*, pp. 63–97; J. de Montclos, *Lanfranc et Bérenger. La controverse eucharistique du xie siècle* (Louvain, 1971); Stock, *Implications of Literacy*, pp. 273–315; these give further references to the voluminous literature on the subject.

[57] Orderic, ii. 250–3.

of view the dispute was settled before he began to write; and the eucharistic debate was his only direct contact with intellectual aspects of heresy.

In common with many churchmen, he saw the rejection of the church's law, and defiance of papal authority, as a form of heresy. Simony to him was 'simoniacal heresy', and he wrote of the pope's enemies in Rome and the antipope Wibert of Ravenna as heretics.[58] He did not apply the term to anyone when he was writing during the course of the schism that began in 1130 and ended only with the death of Anacletus II in 1138. This may have been a necessary caution, since in spite of the general acceptance of Innocent II in France and the Anglo-Norman realm, the Sicilian Normans and some other individual friends of Saint-Evroult resolutely supported Anacletus to the end.[59] After 1138 he invariably called Anacletus a schismatic, but not a heretic.

Orderic showed little or no interest in the heresies that sometimes became associated with civic disturbances. It may seem surprising that he had nothing to say about the preaching of Henry of Lausanne in Le Mans, which led to attacks on the canons of the cathedral in 1116, open controversy with the bishop, Hildebert of Lavardin, and ultimately to Henry's condemnation by the council of Pisa in 1135.[60] Orderic was deeply interested in the events in Le Mans during the Norman occupation, and described in some detail the election of Hildebert, who was to him a peerless poet and a subtle and learned hagiographer and theologian.[61] But after the Norman garrisons were withdrawn from the city in 1100, and Count Helias resumed full authority as a descendant of a native line of counts, Le Mans drops out of Orderic's narrative, to be mentioned only when a new bishop was elected, or the cathedral was burnt. The preaching of the monk

---

[58] Orderic, ii. 238; iv. 10, 26. For simony as heresy, see H. E. J. Cowdrey, *The Age of Abbot Desiderius* (Oxford, 1983), pp. 84-6.

[59] For further details see Orderic, i. 94-5.

[60] For the trouble in Le Mans see *Actus pontificum cenomannis in urbe degentium*, ed. G. Busson and A. Ledru (Archives historiques du Maine, ii, 1902), pp. 407-37; R. Manselli, 'Il monaco Enrico e la sua eresia', *Bullettino dell'Istituto Storico Italiano per il Medio Evo e Archivio Muratoriano*, lxv (1953), 1-63; R. Manselli, *La religion populaire au Moyen Âge* (Montreal and Paris, 1975), pp. 142-6; P. von Moos, *Hilbert von Lavardin*, pp. 12-14.

[61] Orderic, v. 236-9.

Henry made a great stir locally, and led to events fully
recorded in the chronicle of the cathedral. Henry was a
Cluniac monk in deacon's orders, who came to Le Mans
and obtained permission from Bishop Hildebert to preach in
Lent in 1116. A strict ascetic himself, he entered the city
barefoot and bearded as a penitent, carrying a cross, and
preached poverty and penitence. Like Vitalis of Savigny
and Robert of Arbrissel he attracted a crowd of men and
women, some of whom were very wealthy. What appealed
to the masses was his call to the poverty he visibly practised
himself. But when he attacked the wealth of the higher
clergy, riots broke out and the canons of the cathedral feared
for their lives. By this time critics were beginning to question
some of his views on the sacraments of baptism and marriage.
Hildebert was called back from a journey to Rome and found
the city in a tumult. Henry withdrew; and, after Hildebert
had met him and found him unable even to recite his
breviary, he was ordered to leave the diocese. He moved
away to Poitou and Aquitaine. It was there, in a more fertile
breeding-ground for heresies, that he came under the
influence of Peter of Bruys and developed heterodox views
that were condemned by Innocent II in the council of Pisa
in 1135, and firmly refuted by Peter the Venerable in his
Contra Petrobrusianos.[62] Orderic recorded nothing at all of
his preaching or condemnation, although he mentioned the
reforming decrees of the council of Pisa, and had close
links with Cluny.

A historian's assumptions can sometimes be deduced from
his omissions. It is difficult to believe that Orderic, with
points of contact in Le Mans, Pisa, and Cluny, had never
heard of Henry; but he did not think him important. Unlike
Vitalis of Savigny, who 'raised his voice like the trumpet of
Isaiah's prophesies, showing the Christian people their trans-
gressions', and 'often confounded haughty warriors and
undisciplined rabbles, and caused wealthy ladies delicately
clad in silk garments and fine lambskins to tremble when he
attacked their sins with the sword of God's word',[63] Henry
never founded a religious order. Unlike Berengar, a learned

[62] See *Letters of Peter the Venerable*, ii. 287-8.
[63] Orderic, iv. 332-3. Some of Orderic's omissions are more surprising than

and influential teacher, he did not expound doctrine for the learned, and so challenge debate immediately at the highest level; his ideas on sacraments were confused and naïve, and were only clarified sufficiently to be refuted long after he had left Maine and come under the influence of Peter of Bruys. At that time the greatest threat to the church came from the schism which divided Europe from 1130 to 1138, and caused confusion in every diocese or abbey where adherents of the two papal claimants brought about divided elections. Heresy was not a serious danger in northern France at that date; it was strongest in the urban centres of southern France and Italy, where it fed on popular unrest and anti-clericalism.

Orderic showed little interest in urban history. His ideological world consisted of orders of knights, peasants, and secular and monastic clergy; the real world he knew was the world of these people, particularly the monks and the knights. If, copying from Baudry of Bourgueil, he mentioned that Bohemond's followers regarded Saracens, Jews, and heretics alike as enemies of God, this was no more than a passing reference. He came to accept the legitimacy of a holy war against the infidel in his later accounts of events in Spain and the crusading states, in which the knights he knew were involved. Apart from this, the real holy wars were, in his view, fought with the sword of the spirit against sin and the devil; in these the principal protagonists were monks, and among their weapons was the liturgy.[64] If he had made a collection of miracles of the Virgin, he might have come into contact with a widespread mode of thought that saw contemporary Jews as personal enemies and persecutors of the Virgin Mary and her son Jesus; he did not do so. And heresy hardly touched the world he knew, though schism and disobedience leading to excommunication did. He had no grounds for wishing to turn the violence in society against Jews or heretics, and in this he reflected the outlook of the

his omission of Henry of Lausanne; he recorded nothing about Robert of Arbrissel, a compelling preacher, who founded Fontevrault.

[64] Cluniac liturgy as 'ritual aggression' is discussed by Barbara Rosenwein, *Viator*, ii (1971), 129-57. Her view, though interesting, over-emphasizes the aggressive elements in the liturgy, and would not be applicable to Saint-Evroult, an abbey subject to Cluniac influences but not actually a member of the order.

men, both clerical and lay, amongst whom his life was spent. Christian swords were needed to help rulers preserve peace and protect the poor and helpless; the just war against rebels and oppressors was to him far more of a daily reality than the holy war.

PART IV

THE HISTORIAN AND HIS WORLD

8

The Record of the Past

A historian writing in the eleventh or early twelfth century was never at a loss for a definition of history. Isidore had provided his classical description: the Greek ἱστορεῖν meant to see or investigate,[1] and the earliest historians had recorded only the evidence of those who had been present and had seen the events; the word of an eyewitness was to be preferred to hearsay. Again, according to Isidore, annals were a branch of history, recording the memorable events of single years. But between history and annals there was a distinction; the concern of history was with the present age, of annals with past ages. Sallust wrote history; Livy, Eusebius, and Jerome wrote both annals and history.[2] He did not quite say that to-day's history becomes tomorrow's annals, though the deduction follows naturally. A further complication, that of chronicle, was introduced at another point in Isidore's *Etymologies*: chronicle meant, in Latin, *temporum series*, the succession of ages, such as Eusebius wrote in Greek and Jerome translated.[3]

As so often happens, an apparently clear and simple definition, when examined critically from a number of different points of view, becomes confused and complicated, particularly when the subject of the definition is immensely varied. Isidore had to cover works as diverse as those of Thucydides and Herodotus, Livy and Sallust, the Old Testament Books of Kings, Josephus and Trogus Pompeius, Eusebius, Cassiodorus, Jerome, and many more.

Even the Greeks who provided Isidore's definition had not been in agreement about the legitimate content of history. Herodotus, using 'his eyes, his judgment and his talent for

[1] *Isidori Hispalensis Episcopi Etymologiarum sive Originum libri xx*, ed. W. M. Lindsay (Oxford, 1911; Scriptorum classicorum bibliotheca oxoniensis), I.41.

[2] Isidore, *Etymol.* I.44.

[3] Isidore, *Etymol.* V.28.

enquiry', had collected oral traditions of the recent past from many countries. To him, in the words of A. D. Momigliano, 'the first duty of the historian was to collect and preserve traditions; respect for tradition was placed higher than criticism'.[4] To Thucydides, whilst respect for oral tradition was retained, contemporary history was paramount, because the historian should either be present at the scene or use the reports of those who had been present. He did not entirely reject erudite research using written sources, but he excluded it from true history; and this view dominated later classical historiography. It was left to the hellenizing Christians, above all Eusebius, to bring back the critical examination of written records into the scope of ecclesiastical history. And from Eusebius sprang a long tradition of universal church history, continued first of all directly by Jerome and Prosper of Aquitaine. Even without the further complications of Augustine's philosophical speculations on time and history, the definition of Thucydides preserved by Isidore did not square with the tradition of Eusebius. Nevertheless it had to be accommodated with it. Not surprisingly, a historian at work in the eleventh or twelfth century usually plucked the appropriate definition from whichever page of Isidore suited his immediate convenience, and then turned to the serious task of selecting and shaping the materials he had assembled from written records, oral testimony, and his own personal experience. The materials changed their character with each generation; the problem of what to select and how to present it was, for each writer, a new problem. He might, almost in the same paragraph, call the same work *historia, chronographica, annalis historia*; many of the books finally produced defied compression into any one of the definitions of Isidore.

For those whose scope was wide enough, however, one fundamental distinction remained; it was implicit in Isidore and was clearly enunciated by William of Malmesbury in his preface to the *De gestis regum*: 'The earlier part of my

---

[4] The development of Greek ideas on historiography is discussed by A. D. Momigliano, 'The place of Herodotus in the history of historiography', *History*, xliii (1958), 1-13, and 'Historiography on written tradition and historiography on oral tradition', *Atti della Accademia delle Scienze di Torino*, xcvi (1961-2), 1-12, reprinted in *Studies in Historiography* (London, 1969), pp. 127-42, 211-20.

history', wrote William, 'rests of the authority of the writers I have copied, the later on what I have seen myself or heard from reliable informants.'[5] One called for skill in selection and knowledge of chronology; the other for wide ranging and reliable contacts. It also demanded the ability to reduce oral or visual information accurately to writing for the first time. And, as Isidore said, the discipline of history was a part of grammar;[6] and it had certainly been treated by Sallust, an admired model in the Middle Ages, as a part of rhetoric.[7] History never became a subject of formal study in the medieval schools in its own right, but it could not escape being influenced by the elementary arts of the Trivium.

The eleventh and early twelfth centuries were a time of intense historical activity. Historical study did not die out completely in western Europe after the Carolingian renaissance; but it lay dormant in many regions and came to life again at different times in monasteries and cathedral schools. Usually it was a spontaneous growth, stimulated in monasteries at least by the daily activities of monks in church, scriptorium, and chapter house. A medieval scribe rarely copied any work other than the Bible exactly as he found it in his exemplar; he corrected or added details from his own knowledge. Sometimes these took the form of marginal notes, which the next copyist might incorporate in a fresh version; sometimes they consisted of new paragraphs inserted in the text, or whole chapters added at the end. Even liturgical works might be adapted to local needs. Historical works were particularly liable to be altered by the addition of facts or traditions discovered in another source that seemed to be relevant. So a monk engaged in the work of copying might graft on to the Chronicle of Bede the dates of Lombard rulers taken from Paul the Deacon, or insert decretals from the collections of Pseudo-Isidore into the lives of the appropriate popes in the *Liber pontificalis*. A continuous record of the past events was being built up, and in

---

[5] 'a viris fide dignis audivi', Malmesbury, *GR*, i. 3.

[6] Isidore, *Etymol.* I. 41.

[7] See B. Smalley, 'Sallust in the Middle Ages', *Classical Influences on European Culture A.D. 500–1500*, ed. R. R. Bolgar (Cambridge, 1971), p. 175.

time it led to the conscious compilation of a more universal chronicle.

The best known chronicles, those of Marianus Scotus and Sigebert of Gembloux, came from the Empire, where con-tinuity from the earlier Roman Empire was an attractive theme for any historian. But they were by no means alone. The genesis of the earliest universal history produced in northern France by Hugh of Fleury can be traced to the impressive revival of historical study at Fleury-sur-Loire, the abbey that claimed to have the body of St Benedict.[8] The record of the miracles of St Benedict, begun in the ninth century by Adrevald, supplied an incentive to historical writing. Though initially a work of hagiography, it at least placed the translation of the saint's body and the miracles associated with it in a framework conceived on the lines of a universal chronicle, and provided synchronisms of the dates of eastern Emperors, popes and Frankish kings. A real historical revival began in the time of Abbo, abbot of Fleury, in the late tenth century, and was continued by a succession of historians from Aimoin through his pupils Helgaud and Andrew to Hugh of Fleury himself a hundred years later. Abbo had kindled an interest in history when he made or procured an abbreviation of the *Liber pontificalis*; but it was his pupil Aimoin who played the greatest part in making Fleury a live centre of historical writing. Born in Aquitaine of a family of local lords, he was placed as a boy in Fleury, where he spent most of his life in building up the library. Collecting, copying, and enlarging earlier histories gave him the stimulus and training to compile and compose histories of his own. His development as a historian seems, in the words of Robert-Henri Bautier, to have been due to his own natural ability.[9] Fleury owed to him a chronicle of the Franks up to 653, a *Gesta abbatum* (now lost), a new book of the miracles of St Benedict, written with a far greater regard for the historical background, and a biography of Abbo, which

[8] For the historical revival at Fleury see R.-H. Bautier, 'La place de l'abbaye de Fleury-sur-Loire dans l'historiographie française du ixe au xiie siècle', *Études ligériennes d'histoire et d'archéologie médiévales*, ed. René Louis (Auxerre, 1975), pp. 25–33.

[9] 'Sa formation nous semble due à son génie propre' (Bautier, *Études ligériennes*, p. 29).

adopted the outline plan of the papal biographies in the *Liber pontificalis*. Part of his work at least was to be adapted for use in the *Grandes Chroniques de France*, when they began to be compiled later at St Denis. When Hugh of Fleury composed his two great chronicles, known as the *Historia ecclesiastica* and *Historia modernorum regum Francorum*,[10] which between them outlined the chronology of events from the foundation of Nineveh up to 1108, he had a strong historical tradition on which to build, and a library containing many historical works and early Frankish annals.

If Fleury was the earliest French abbey to foster a true historical revival, others came hard on its heels as centres of historical study. Amongst them was the abbey of Saint-Pierre-le-Vif at Sens, which had very close relations with Fleury. Here the tradition of historical writing went back to the early eleventh century, when a short History of the Franks was put together about 1015, and the monk Odorannus, who showed his versatility by writing on law, liturgy, exegesis, and music, also compiled a chronicle for the period 678 to 1015 and wrote a life of Queen Theodechilde.[11] Within a hundred years a universal chronicle from the birth of Christ to 660, and a Frankish chronicle from 675 to 1096, had been put together by the abbot, Arnold, working in 1108-9.[12] Like Aimoin, he devoted much time to building up the library of the abbey and supervising the work of the scribes. Even as abbot he handed out the numbered quires to individual monks after the pages had been trimmed, and had the finished sections brought back to him for inspection.[13] Both he and Hugh of Fleury belonged to the second generation of compilers of world chronicles, which included Hugh of Flavigny, Ekkehard of Aura, and Sigebert of Gembloux. Neither attained the eminence and wide circulation of Sigebert, though they equalled the most outstanding of the first generation, Marianus Scotus. They

[10] Migne, *PL* clxiii, 805–937. A new edition is being prepared by R.-H. Bautier.

[11] Odorannus de Sens, *Opera Omnia*, ed. R.-H. Bautier and Monique Gilles (Paris, 1972, CNRS).

[12] *Chronique de Saint-Pierre-le-Vif de Sens, dite de Clarius*, ed. R.-H. Bautier and Monique Gilles (Paris, 1979, CNRS). The editors identify the author of this chronicle as the abbot, Arnold, not Clarius (pp. x–xii).

[13] Ibid., pp. 188–95.

showed the strength of the spontaneous movement towards producing such histories, which arose from the practical work of copying and reducing to order various series of annals and collective biographies, stimulated by the desire to continue the work of Eusebius, Jerome, or Bede. Any attempt to see a pattern or impose a philosophical form on the narrative came only later, with Hugh of St Victor and Otto of Freising.[14]

In England the most influential universal chronicle was at first that of Marianus; a copy was carried there by the Lotharingian scholar, Robert, when he was appointed bishop of Hereford in 1079. It became the basis of the great Worcester chronicle.[15] In Normandy the work of tracing a continuous history at least from the birth of Christ was attempted first by Orderic Vitalis, on a framework derived partly from Bede's Chronicle and the *Liber pontificalis*, and later by Robert of Torigny, who built on the work of Sigebert. But all these writers grafted on to the central chronology the histories of various peoples—Franks, Lombards, Normans, and English—and of particular communities to which they themselves were attached. They were struggling to find a new form in which to describe the development of the many peoples and societies that made up the Christian church. If the products of their labours sometimes seem shapeless and confused, it must be remembered that they were largely self-taught as historians, and worked empirically with materials that had been put together at different dates on varying principles, and were very uneven in scale and value.

Most of the early writers of a universal chronicle came to it by way of more local studies. At Fleury the accumulation of miracles round the reputed tomb of St Benedict was a stimulus to historical writing, and the *Liber pontificalis*, containing a continuous series of papal biographies, provided

---

[14] For a discussion of some universal chronicles see R. W. Southern, 'Aspects of the European tradition of historical writing: Hugh of St. Victor and the idea of historical development', *TRHS*, 5th ser. xxi (1971), 159–79; Peter Classen, '*Res gestae*, Universal History, Apocalypse: Visions of Past and Future', *Renaissance and Renewal*, pp. 398–403.

[15] For a detailed analysis of the Worcester chronicle see M. Brett, 'John of Worcester and his contemporaries' *The Writing of History in the Middle Ages*, ed. Davis and Wallace-Hadrill, pp. 101–26.

a central framework of dates for papal history up to the ninth century. Odorannus of Sens began his historical work with a brief life of Queen Theodechilde, the foundress of his abbey; and notes on the endowment, privileges, and relics of the house were an important element in his short chronicle. His chronicle was in turn one of the sources that Abbot Arnold wove into his universal history, along with the more detailed history of his own administration. In England, where the chronicle of Marianus provided a ready-made framework for other historians from the early days of the post-conquest historical revival, John of Worcester inserted into it, stage by stage, a series of different documents, beginning with events in the history of England and a number of saints' lives, and he progressively incorporated other records from Canterbury, Malmesbury, and Durham as they came to his hand.

Writers in each region were influenced partly by their intellectual training and the books of the historians they had read, partly by the historical interests of the society in which they lived. In England the Norman conquest gave a special colour to the historical revival that began some twenty-five years later; the sense of loss of lands and traditional rituals 'drew English monks together in defence of their past'.[16] In Normandy, a country with a resurgent aristocracy advancing from conquest to conquest, one of the strongest influences was the sense of lineage; the intense interest in family history was fostered both by *chansons* in court or castle, and by narrative charters, recording the ancestry of founders in religious houses. At the highest level, the history of the Norman dukes merged into the history of the Norman people.

Norman historical writing began at the turn of the tenth century with Dudo of Saint-Quentin. His history of the Norman 'dukes' from Rollo to Richard I, though written in the ornate, post-Carolingian Latin of the French schools where he had studied, recorded in epic style the oral history of the early Normans, extolling even their pagan virtues.[17]

[16] R. W. Southern, 'The sense of the past', *TRHS*, 5th ser. xxiii (1973), 247.

[17] See Eleanor Searle, 'Fact and pattern in heroic history: Dudo of St Quentin', forthcoming in *Viator*.

Half a century later this overt paganism was not to the taste of monk historians in the reformed monasteries. Dudo was used; but William of Jumièges, who wrote the most widely read history of the Norman dukes, omitted the more distasteful passages of Dudo, abbreviated and reinterpreted others, and added his own independent account of the later dukes up to William I.[18] His work provided the most popular basis of Norman history for the next century; recopied, interpolated, extended, in Saint-Ouen, Saint-Evroult, Bec-Hellouin, and many other Norman abbeys, it was soon circulating in England and France as well, and survives in over forty manuscripts. It required adaptation with changes in political circumstances; the uncertainties of the Norman succession meant that references to Robert Curthose as the son destined to succeed his father had to be adapted to Robert's fortunes at the time any new copy was made. Some chroniclers interpolated a few popular stories in praise of the dukes, or added information relevant to their own abbeys; others, notably Robert of Torigny, who added a new chapter on Henry I, extended it in time. Orderic, who began work on it before 1109, but made some revisions as late as 1113, added miscellaneous material. Much related to his own abbey, the families whose history was involved with its foundation, and the deeds of their kinsfolk in Italy. But he included facts of general interest, taken from other chronicles, and some oral traditions. Some material may have been put together by John of Rheims; some seems personal to him. When he wrote of the marriage of Edward the Confessor and Edith, 'It is said that they both preserved their virginity all their lives', he was repeating a story current in the English court shortly after Edward's death,[19] which he might have picked up from his teacher in England, the noble Siward; it was less likely to have circulated in Normandy until somewhat later. Such interpolations had satisfied many chroniclers before him; but the *Gesta Normannorum ducum* of William of Jumièges was never suitable as a base for

[18] His work is discussed by E. M. C. van Houts, *Gesta Normannorum ducum* (Groningen, 1982).
[19] Marx, p. 161; and see Barlow, *Edward the Confessor*, pp. 256-9; the sources of the story of his chastity are, however, uncertain.

a universal chronicle, and as Orderic's own historical knowledge and aspirations grew, he put aside his interpolations, and wrote his slowly evolving history of the church as a completely separate work.

Why did Orderic call his great work 'The Ecclesiastical History'? He himself gave it this title, and did so in the first book he wrote, when its final shape had not been determined. Possibly the influence of Bede was paramount; he might also have had Eusebius in mind, but the example of Eusebius became more appropriate after he had widened the scope of his history. His theme, expounded in the opening sentences, was the vine of the Lord of Hosts, which represented the church with true Christians as its branches. Orderic's concern at first was with the church in Normandy, and he could then have claimed to be writing an ecclesiastical history of the Norman people, as Bede had written one of the English people. But starting from the monastic movement in Normandy he enlarged his work, as Peter Classen wrote, 'in concentric circles',[20] taking in more and more regions and a wider sweep of time. To include the deeds of laymen was entirely consistent with the title: laymen, if good Christians, were branches of the vine; indeed it was the metaphor of the vine that held together a vast, very loosely organized work.

Originally Orderic collected materials for a separate chronicle, as Bede had done, and he used Bede's chronicle from the Incarnation as the basis of his own *chronographia*, as he called it. The *chronographia* was a highly original compilation; in it he ultimately included a life of Christ, carefully built up from the gospels, together with canonical and apocryphal lives of the apostles, annals of the Lombard, Frankish, Norman, and English peoples, and a series of papal biographies, mostly from the *Liber pontificalis*.[21] At the same time he was composing a history of his own times (including a history of his monastery) which ran to eleven books. When towards the end of his life he put the two works together, and turned the expanded chronicle into Books I and II of a single *Ecclesiastical History* in thirteen books, the two

---

[20] P. Classen, *Renaissance and Renewal*, p. 389.
[21] See Orderic, i. 45–63 for the structure and sources of the *Ecclesiastical History*.

components were loosely but persuasively joined by the metaphor of the vine. Invoking the parable of the vineyard, he wrote that God represented the husbandman and holy Church the vineyard, which God cultivated all over the world, and in which Christians toiled up to the last hour. So the opening sentences of Book I were linked with the epilogue that closed Book XIII, which gave the widest possible interpretation to the metaphor. For in the epilogue Orderic saw his own life as a monk from boyhood in terms of one of the labourers employed from the morning hour. He had born the burden and heat of the day, hoping for the reward of eternal salvation. His work ended with a prayer that he might live in such a way as to deserve it.[22] The church whose history Orderic wrote consisted of the church triumphant as well as the church militant; its history was traceable in the succession of ages in time, but it belonged also to eternity. Orderic's vision was a total one. He offered an explanation of his choice of title in his preface to the completed work:

I have set out to investigate and record the fortunes of the Christian people in this present time, and therefore I have ventured to call this work the *Ecclesiastical History*. For although I cannot explore Macedonian or Greek or Roman affairs and many other matters worthy of the telling, because as a cloister monk of my own free choice I am compelled to unremitting observance of my monastic duty, nevertheless I can strive with the help of God and for the consideration of posterity to explain truthfully and simply the things which I have seen in our own times, or know to have occured in nearby provinces.[23]

This clings to conventional language and seems a little confused, since it combines a chronicle of a thousand years (which could hardly be called the record of his own times) with a work of history as the Greeks understood the word, which we would call contemporary history. But Thucydides could be more successfully reconciled with Eusebius in fact than in theory by a sufficiently eclectic writer. And given Orderic's interpretation of the vineyard of the Lord of Hosts, which comprised both the total life of the church and the individual life of every Christian, he could not appropriately have called his work by any other name.

[22] Orderic, vi. 554–6.   [23] Orderic, i. 130–3.

The thirteen books represented Orderic's picture of what Bede had called the sixth age of the world. The first two books, he might have claimed with William of Malmesbury, rested on the authority of the writers he had copied.[24] He had selected, arranged, and corrected materials, torn between the wish to give a true chronology and the temptation to include almost any source that came to his knowledge and appealed to his imagination. He was able to resist the lure of the apocryphal gospels: the materials for his *Life of Christ* came from the canonical scriptures, without a trace of the stories in the so-called Gospel of Nicodemus, which had been copied at Saint-Evroult under his supervision.[25] But he eagerly seized on the legends in the long series of apocryphal lives of the apostles, written from the second century onwards. From Pseudo-Clement through Pseudo-Abdias in the sixth century to Pseudo-Aurelian in the eleventh, all were delightful to him. He wrote of the collection of lives now known as Pseudo-Abdias (because the preface to the lives of Simon and Thaddeus attributes the work to Abdias, bishop of Babylon), 'I do not know the author of this book, but I believe that telling the marvellous deeds it records would be a worthy undertaking'.[26] The miracles and marvels attributed to the apostles, accepted uncritically, were much to the taste of his age. The Bollandists of a later generation dealt with them as they deserved.[27] Orderic would have regretted, but could not have rejected this. The whole picture was part of his attempt to set out fairly the history of the church, in the hope of helping later writers to interpret the will of God as manifested in history. Although occasionally drawing a moral, he did not presume to offer a general interpretation from his partial knowledge. He did his best with his written sources, and then left them to stand the test of time. His personal addition to the unfolding chronicle of the Christian church, which had been summarized in Books I and II, lay in the eleven succeeding books of mainly contemporary

[24] Malmesbury, *GR*, i. 3.
[25] Rouen MS 1343, pp. 23–33. See Orderic, i. 50, 202–3.
[26] Orderic, i. 54–5, 178, 190.
[27] For the work of the Bollandists see M. D. Knowles, 'Great Historical Enterprises: The Bollandists', *TRHS*, 5th ser., viii (1958), 147–66.

history. Their veracity rested on his ability to record faithfully any notable events that he had seen himself, and on the reliability of his informants.

9
Contemporary History

(i) *The Interpretation of Evidence*

A historian who saw all human history as part of God's plan
for creation might easily have been tempted into writing
apocalyptic history, and distorting his evidence to fit into
a grandiose scheme. Orderic never gave way to that temptation. Occasionally he suggested that particular events, such as
the misfortunes of unjust men, were manifestations of God's
providence; normally his attitude was the one succinctly
expressed by Gerald of Wales, that God's ways are always
just, but often hard to understand.[1] One result of his training
in biblical study was that he naturally handled events at two
levels: the moral and the historical. He deliberately avoided
the third, the allegorical, and contented himself with writing,
'I find many things in the pages of Scripture which, if they
are subtly interpreted, seem to resemble the happenings of
our own times. But I leave the allegorical meanings appropriate to human customs to be interpreted by scholars.'[2] Moral
interpretations, on the other hand, are everywhere. In his
account of the early days of his own abbey he wrote, 'The
old enemy never ceases to disturb the peace of the church
with every kind of trial, and uses those who are moved by
worldly ambition to torment the men who fight single-
mindedly for the faith and make a brave stand for the cause
of virtue.'[3] When the prior, Robert of Grandmesnil, a proud
and passionate man from a wealthy aristocratic family, built
up a faction against the gentle and unworldly abbot, Thierry,
he acted, in Orderic's eyes, at the instigation of Satan. As
Orderic saw the world, all human acts had significance in

[1] See *Itinerarium Kambriae*, in *Giraldi Cambrensis Opera* ed. J. S. Brewer,
J. F. Dimock and G. F. Warner (RS 1861-91), vi. 111, 147 ('occulto Dei judicio,
sed nunquam injusto').
[2] Orderic, iv. 228-9.
[3] Orderic, ii. 64-5.

the perpetual battle of demons for the souls of men. But they also had their place in the visible changes of everyday life. The greater part of his work was concerned with events at their literal, historical level.

So rebellion might be the result of sin; but it was also the work of the disinherited or overambitious. Wars might be just or unjust in terms of human no less than divine law; the historian could at least investigate the claims that lay behind them, or the apparently trivial incidents that sparked off an ancient feud. His assessment of right and wrong is evidence of the ethical values and social customs of his age. Orderic wrote in the midst of the most momentous changes in Anglo-Norman government and society, when the rights of succession in kingdom and duchy were still imperfectly defined, when customs of succession were merely in the process of hardening into law, and when church reform was only very slowly making headway in all areas of ecclesiastical influence, from the election and investiture of prelates to the solemnization of matrimony and the blessing of warriors and their arms. His work is a touchstone for the values of his world.

When William, duke of Normandy, was crowned king of England on Christmas day, 1066, two offices were for the first time united in a single person. Neither in England nor in Normandy were the rules of succession finally settled. They remained uncertain for the whole of Orderic's life, and he was writing over a period of more than thirty years, against a background of changing power and authority. Normandy, considered in isolation, had the simpler problem of the two: succession had normally gone to the eldest son or brother of the duke. But Robert the Magnificent had taken precedence over the young son of his brother Richard III; and the fact that his own son and successor, William, was a bastard had complicated the issue by keeping alive the potential rights of illegitimate sons. England presented a far more difficult problem, quite apart from the complications of first Danish and then Norman conquests. The traditional components in a lawful succession have been described as 'eligibility by birth, designation by the late king, election or recognition by the secular and ecclesiastical magnates, and consecration by the church'.[4] In the changing political climate it is interesting to see what weight was attached to each by contemporary historians, and how they interpreted, or twisted, the evidence to justify or condemn a particular succession. The most suitable candidate for the English crown might not necessarily be the right duke for Normandy; yet what was to happen if political expediency required the two offices to be permanently linked?

When Orderic began writing history, the events of 1066, 1087, and even 1100 were far behind him. He was not yet certain of the ultimate fate of Robert Curthose, defeated at Tinchbray, but not deprived of the title of duke; and the claims of Robert's son, William Clito, kept the uncertainty alive until long after Henry I's only legitimate son had gone down in the *White Ship*.[5] The succession remained as much an open question for historians as it did for King Henry himself. Some stated their principles consistently, others changed their minds.

Orderic had most to say on the first Norman succession in 1066, the legitimacy of which had already been attacked and upheld with every shade of argument when he was still only a boy. In his account of the first months of conquest and William's coronation he made use of the narrative of William of Poitiers, but added his own characteristic interpretations. Whereas William of Poitiers wrote as a wholehearted apologist of the conquering Normans, Orderic repeatedly stressed the will of God. He made much of the prayers of the Normans whilst they waited to embark at Saint-Valéry;[6] he alone recounted the episode of the *malfosse*, when the Norman victors, pursuing the defeated English too hastily across treacherous country, suffered losses in a deep, concealed ditch.[7] Like William of Poitiers, he stressed Harold's loss of right through his perjury, but added an illuminating sidelight in his story of Gyrth's attempt to

[4] Barlow, *Edward the Confessor*, p. 54.

[5] For a recent assessment of the threat from William Clito see S. B. Hicks, 'The impact of William Clito upon the continental policies of Henry I of England', *Viator*, x (1979), 1–21.

[6] Orderic, ii. 168–71.

[7] Orderic, ii. 176–7; and see R. A. Brown, 'The Battle of Hastings', *Anglo-Norman Studies*, iii (1981 for 1980), 18–19.

dissuade Harold from going into battle: in an imaginary speech Gyrth is represented as saying, 'I have taken no oath and owe nothing to Count William; therefore I can boldly join combat with him for my native soil. But you, my brother, should wait peacefully wherever you like for the outcome of this war, lest the fair freedom of the English should perish with you.'[8] William of Poitiers wrote of the final submission of the English after London capitulated: 'The bishops and other magnates joined together to beg him to accept the crown, for they were accustomed to obey a king, and wished to have a king as their lord.'[9] The emphasis is different in Orderic's expanded version:

So by the grace of God England was subdued within the space of three months, and all the bishops and nobles of the realm made their peace with William, begging him to accept the crown according to English custom. No less insistent were the Normans . . . And this too by God's will was the wish of the general populace for they had never obeyed anyone except a duly crowned king.[10]

A little later he set down a more general expression of right in a speech attributed to Guitmund, abbot of La Croix-Saint-Leufroi, who had declined ecclesiastical preferment in England:

Not one of your forebears before you has enjoyed royal authority, and such honour has come to you not by hereditary right but by the free gift of almighty God and the friendship of your kinsman Edward. Edgar Atheling and several others of the royal line are, according to the laws of the Hebrews and other peoples, nearer heirs to the English crown. When they were set aside the chance of advancement fell to you, but the judgment of God . . . waits till the day when you must render account of your stewardship.[11]

All this was tending towards the dramatic death-bed speech, in which Orderic summed up the achievements of the king's reign, and added the arrangements he made at the last moment for the succession of his sons:

I invested my son Robert with the duchy of Normandy before I fought against Harold at Senlac; because he is my first-born son and has received the homage of almost all the barons of the country the honour

[8] Orderic, ii. 170–3.
[9] William of Poitiers, ed. Foreville, pp. 216–17.
[10] Orderic, ii. 182–3.   [11] Orderic, ii. 276–9.

then granted cannot be taken from him . . . I name no man my heir to the kingdom of England; instead I entrust it to the eternal Creator to whom I belong and in whose hand are all things. For I did not come to possess such dignity by hereditary right, but wrested the kingdom from the perjured Harold with bitter strife and terrible bloodshed, and subjected it to my rule after killing and driving into exile all his supporters. I treated the native inhabitants of the kingdom with unreasonable severity, cruelly oppressed high and low, unjustly dis-inherited many, and caused the death of thousands by starvation and war, especially in Yorkshire. I dare not hand on the royal authority that I secured with so many sins to anyone save God alone. I hope that my son William, who has always been loyal and obedient to me from his earliest years, may prevail in the way of God and flourish in the kingdom, if such is the divine will.[12]

He then sent William to England with a letter for Archbishop Lanfranc, asking the archbishop to crown him king.

All Orderic's comments on the reign of the first Norman king were written with hindsight. On the level of human law he gave particular weight to hereditary right, to consecration by the church, and to acceptance by the governed. When he widened the basis of consent from the prelates and magnates specified by William of Poitiers to include all the native English he may have echoed boyhood memories of the attitude of humbler Englishmen towards their ruler: they would obey only a properly crowned king, not a military conqueror. Turning to Normandy, he stressed feudal homage. Robert Curthose had been invested with the duchy and had received the oaths of the Norman barons before his quarrel with his father;[13] William, however much he regretted this, could not undo it, particularly as Robert was his eldest son and had been designated his heir. England was a different matter; Orderic made much less than some other writers of the question whether Edward the Confessor had named Harold or William as his heir,[14] and he allowed William only a con-ditional designation of Rufus. Here, indeed, he moved to

---

[12] Orderic, iv. 92–5.

[13] The position of Robert Curthose has been investigated by R. H. C. Davis, 'William of Jumièges, Robert Curthose and the Norman succession', *EHR*, xcv (1980), 597–606.

[14] William of Poitiers repeatedly stated that Edward had designated William his heir; he also refuted Harold's claim to have been designated by Edward on his death bed (ed. Foreville, pp. 30–1, 100–1, 172–9). The Bayeux Tapestry gives some support to Harold's claim (*The Bayeux Tapestry*, ed. Stenton, pl. 33).

the level of divine law, and his account of the scene is a suggestive one.

How did Orderic know what might have happened as William lay dying? Are there any elements of literal truth in his account, or is it an extension of what, in the light of subsequent events, William ought to have said—a moral interpretation that has parted company with any literal and historical sense? Certainly some ideas very characteristic of Orderic's outlook are developed at length: in particular an English born boy's recollections of the bitterness of dispossessed Englishmen, and his horror at the accounts of William's relentless harrying of the north, which had made an indelible impression on his earliest memories. Since he believed that William's rule had the approval of God, it was natural for him to believe also that William felt penitence and tried to make reparation for his cruelty. But he might also have known something of what really happened, for amongst those present at the deathbed was Gilbert Maminot, bishop of Lisieux, Orderic's own diocesan.[15] Even though it can scarcely be supposed that an individual young monk ever had the opportunity of talking with his diocesan bishop, and Orderic's only direct personal contacts with Gilbert may have been his ordination as sub-deacon at the bishop's hands, and Gilbert's visit to the abbey to help in dedicating the new church in 1099, stories may have spread through the monastery from the abbot, who had sufficient opportunities of contact. And we know that Orderic had talked to members of the bishop's household; he had been told by one knight who acted as watchman there about Gilbert's comments on the falling stars seen at the time of the council of Clermont.[16] Moreover, there is one particular statement that suggests Orderic may have had some accurate information about the scene. It relates to the insignia.

When Orderic described William's surrender of the kingdom to God rather than any individual he used the expression *fasces huius regni*. The phrase may have had a purely abstract meaning. But *fasces* were symbols of office. And we know that William gave the crown that he wore at all important ceremonies and his sceptre and *virga* to his

---

[15] Orderic, iv. 80–1.   [16] Orderic, v. 8–11.

own abbey of Saint-Étienne de Caen.[17] Later, William Rufus bought them back, and a short treatise, *De obitu Willelmi*, probably written towards the end of the reign of Rufus, tried to maintain that the dying king had given them to his son.[18] But the evidence of a charter, drawn up shortly after William gave lands in England to the abbey in exchange for the insignia, proves that the abbey had indeed received them. The handing over of treasures was a concrete and visible act, into which various symbolic meanings could be read. Carolingian and early Capetian rulers had sometimes bestowed insignia on a favoured royal foundation;[19] but William was the first Norman duke to wear a crown, and others might have read a deeper meaning into a straightforward bequest. By sending his son Rufus to England with a letter for Lanfranc he made quite clear what his intentions were. Yet Rufus undoubtedly attached great importance to the insignia, and was prepared to part with lands at a time when his need for money was pressing in order to recover them. Orderic's account does no violence to the facts; he may have believed that the king's gift of the insignia to an abbey implied a surrender of his royal rights to God. Whether or not he correctly interpreted the intentions of individuals, he revealed something of the views of clergy, barons, and humbler Englishmen.

The assumptions of knights and barons led him to attach great importance to rules of inheritance, in which the eldest son had a special, but not an overriding, right to be designated heir; and to the obligations of homage, which held firm unless they were renounced by mutual consent, or violated by one side. But kingship both included and transcended lordship. It may have been Orderic's biblical studies that made him suggest that Old Testament precedents might be sought for the right to claim the crown; such precedents,

[17] This is clear from a charter of William Rufus to Saint-Étienne de Caen (Musset, *Abbayes caennaises*, no. 24, pp. 132-4).

[18] A strong case for this date was made by Annebert Sapir and Ben Speet, *De obitu Willelmi* (Historisch seminarium van de universiteit van Amsterdam, Werkschrift 10, Amsterdam, 1976), pp. 30-4, 56-7. They drew attention to the importance of the Caen charter. For the treatise *De obitu* see also L. J. Engels, 'De obitu Willelmi' in *Mélanges Christine Mohramann* (Utrecht/Antwerp, 1973), pp. 209-25; E. M. C. van Houts, *Gesta Normannorum ducum*, pp. 98-106.

[19] See above, p. 53.

though sometimes used as supporting arguments, rarely carried much weight in England at the time.[20] But coronation mattered, and to Orderic it was of supreme importance. He was indeed extremely reluctant to approve any arguments for deposing an annointed king. Harold's death in battle was represented as God's judgement on his perjury; in any case it was not a deposition. William's victory was shown as a sign of God's will; he remained morally subject to God's judgement on the last day for the acts of his government, but once crowned he was king until he died. Robert Curthose might have presented a problem had he ever become king of England; as duke of Normandy he could be set aside. Orderic repeatedly insisted on his incompetence, and described with graphic detail his inability to keep the peace and protect the church and the poor. Similarly, however much sympathy he may have felt for the fate of Robert's son, William Clito, who was denied his paternal inheritance, Clito was responsible for rebellion and war. 'In vain are human efforts to achieve anything, when God's ordinance has disposed otherwise.'[21] There was one Norman king, duly crowned, whom Orderic was prepared to defend in all his acts; that was Henry I, and Clito, like his father, struggled against him to no purpose. Nevertheless, though Orderic frequently invoked God's will in justifying Henry's acts when they seemed contrary to accepted custom, he attributed his success directly to such factors as his profound wisdom, military prowess, and abundance of wealth and friends.[22] His belief in Henry as a just king approved by God remained unshaken in everything he wrote, both during his reign and after his death. But his belief in the importance of coronation in making a king comes out strongly in Stephen's reign.

Orderic had not expected Stephen to become king. When Matilda's son, the future Henry II, was born, Orderic wrote of him as one destined for royal rule.[23] When Henry I died

[20] Robert, earl of Gloucester, was said to have been fond of citing the hereditary right of the daughters of Zelophehad (Numbers: xxxvi) in support of the right of his half-sister, Matilda, to the English crown (*The Letters and Charters of Gilbert Foliot*, ed. A. Morey and C. N. L. Brooke (Cambridge, 1967), pp. 61-2).

[21] Orderic, vi. 368-9.

[22] Orderic, vi. 368-9.

[23] Orderic, v. pp. xii, 201 n. 5, 228 n. 2.

Orderic felt that Stephen's elder brother, Theobald, had a greater right than Stephen by birth;[24] at the very end of his work he described how, after Stephen's defeat and capture at Lincoln, the magnates offered Theobald the duchy and kingdom, but he 'as a wise and pious man' renounced his right in favour of Geoffrey of Anjou on certain conditions.[25] In spite of this, from the moment that Stephen was crowned at Winchester, Orderic referred to him as king; the very last mention of him in the epilogue, when he was still imprisoned in fetters, called him king of England.[26] In saying that Theobald had surrendered his royal right to Geoffrey on certain conditions (which in fact were never fulfilled) he may have envisaged no more than a residual right to transmit the crown.

One problem for which there was no easy solution was the linking of Normandy to England. From the death of William the Conqueror in 1087 until the death of Robert Curthose in 1134, a defender of Robert's legitimacy might have argued that the two offices of king and duke were in different hands. From 1095 till 1100, whilst Robert was absent on crusade, William Rufus held Normandy in return for the substantial loan he had made to his brother; but though he exercised the duke's authority in the province there was no question of his assuming the title of duke or count. For many years after the victory at Tinchebray in 1106 Henry I ruled Normandy without using the ducal title in his charters;[27] and though he had begun to do so by 1120 Orderic never gave it to him until Robert Curthose was dead.[28] He entirely approved Henry's rule in Normandy, which gave some measure of peace to the war-torn province; but he saw it either as a special dispensation of God or as an extension of the royal power, which did not exclude Robert's empty title.[29] It was by royal right that Henry promulgated measures to

[24] Orderic, vi. 454–5.
[25] Orderic, vi. 548–9.
[26] Orderic, vi. 550–1.
[27] Orderic, vi. 99 and n. 3; C. N. L. Brooke, G. Keir and S. Reynolds, 'Henry I's charter for the City of London', *Journal of the Society of Archivists*, iv (1970–3), 561–4.
[28] Orderic, i. 161.
[29] Orderic, vi. 92–5, 138–9, 176, 178.

secure the peace in Normandy immediately after the battle
of Tinchebray. When he held his court in Normandy, it was
the royal court for all business. If there was no irony in
Orderic's statement that Luke of La Barre, the vassal of
another lord, was punished for crimes that included composing and singing scurrilous songs about the king, Henry
was undoubtedly exercising royal power in Normandy; by
ancient English custom any contempt or slander of the king
placed a man in the king's mercy and was punishable by
him.[30] Once Robert had died, Henry's title was secure until
his own death opened the whole question of succession to
both kingdom and duchy once more.

Orderic emphasized the union between the two whenever
possible. He knew how much the Normans who held estates
on both sides of the Channel wished to owe allegiance to
only one lord. He advanced this as the reason many had
rebelled against William Rufus at the beginning of his reign.
The motives attributed to them were shrewdly observed:
Robert was the first born, he was more pliable in character,
and they had already sworn fealty to him. Customary right
and self-interest combined to persuade them that William
must be the one to be deposed.[31] Similarly, when the magnates heard that Stephen had already been crowned king,
they decided to accept him as duke of Normandy, even
though they would have preferred his older brother Theobald,
and Henry I's daughter Matilda was asserting her claim by
force of arms in the Hiémois.[32] Orderic never mentioned
the complicating factor that most of the magnates had
already sworn fealty to Matilda, though he certainly knew
that David of Scotland had taken such an oath at King Henry's
command.[33] He was, however, grappling with the difficulty
any historian must experience when trying to write in the thick
of events, with very imperfect techniques of investigation.

Law and justice were subjects with which, as a historian
convinced that God had some divine plan for mankind,

[30] *Leges Henrici Primi*, ed. L. Downer (Oxford, 1972), 10.1 (p. 108), 13.1
(p. 116).
[31] Orderic, iv. 122-5.
[32] Orderic, vi. 454-5.
[33] Orderic, vi. 518-19. Other contemporary historians discussed the oaths at
length; see Malmesbury, *Hist. Nov.*, pp. 4-5; John of Worcester, pp. 26-8.

Orderic was deeply concerned. Yet even the canonists were only beginning to introduce concord into a mass of discordant canons; and more than half a century was to pass before secular judges and administrators put together the earliest 'coutumiers'.[34] A few tags from Roman law books were beginning to pass into currency, and the pamphlets generated by the investiture contest in Germany gave a stimulus to abstract political thought. But such things lay outside Orderic's intellectual experience. He had to feel his way towards abstract concepts by applying his knowledge of Scripture and the writings of the Fathers and earlier historians to his own experience of political reality and feudal and ecclesiastical custom. It was clear to him that the king, although in one sense a feudal lord, was very far from being merely *primus inter pares*. He had royal power, and exercised it in Normandy no less than in England. But it was his duty to use that power to rule justly according to God's will. If he failed to protect the weak and honour the clergy, if he waged wars of aggression to conquer where he had no hereditary right, he was guilty of sin, and would be answerable for it. The final reckoning might come only on the Day of Judgement; on the other hand individual men might act as the instrument of God's justice. But whereas Orderic was ready to see the king as such an instrument when he punished Robert of Bellême and removed Robert Curthose from the exercise of the office in which he had failed so lamentably, he hesitated to approve any attack on even the most inadequate anointed king.

His dilemma appears in his references to tyranny. Isidore's definition provided a literary model that showed how subtly the word tyrant had changed its meaning. Originally, as Isidore pointed out, simply the Greek word for a king, it had come to imply cruelty, wickedness, and lust by the time he compiled his *Etymologies*.[35] All these shades existed in

---

[34] In Normandy the *Très ancien coutumier* was compiled about 1200 (*Les coutumiers de Normandie*, ed. J. Tardif, i (Rouen, 1881)); in England the treatise known as Glanvill, which has been called a 'coutumier' (J. Yver, 'Le bref anglo-normand', *Tijdschrift voor Rechtsgeschiedenis*, xxix (1961), 324; P. Hyams, 'The Common Law and the French connection', *Anglo-Norman Studies*, iv (1982 for 1981)), was written at the end of the reign of Henry II.

[35] Isidore, *Etymol*, I. xxxi, II. xxix. 7, IX. iii. 19-20.

Orderic's use of the term, with the added implication of
unjust usurpation.[36] He used it freely of powerful lords who
oppressed their vassals or subjects and were brought to book
by the kings they had defied: men such as Thomas of Marle,
against whom Louis VI campaigned in France, Odo of
Bayeux in his secular capacity as earl, or particularly that
arch-villain in Orderic's eyes, Robert of Bellême. Robert
was described as tyrannical no less than twenty times, whereas
Orderic never applied the word to Robert Curthose, whose
principal failing was inadequacy. Pagan kings were automatically classified as tyrants, and Harold Godwinson, once
adjudged a perjured usurper who had been crowned by an
excommunicate, was readily consigned to the same category.
The rebellious earls of Hereford and Norfolk were said to
have aimed at tyranny, not at just rule. But Orderic never
used the term in a general sense of any of the Norman kings.

William the Conqueror and his son Rufus might act
tyrannically by expelling properly elected abbots or bishops,
or intruding prelates who were tyrants rather than pastors,
such as Thurstan of Caen at Glastonbury. Here the element
of injustice, of transgressing a higher law, seems to be important in his conception. Canon law was a reality to him,
whether he copied the canons of councils into his history,
listened to the preliminaries to an abbatial election in his own
monastery, or witnessed the consequences of excommunication or interdict in a neighbouring diocese. A German king
might be excommunicated and even deposed. But within the
Anglo-Norman realm where his main interest lay no such
crisis was ever quite reached, and Orderic was able to deal
with any disagreement of secular and ecclesiastical authorities
pragmatically as it occurred. This reflected the realities of
everyday life in that realm. Freedom of election, as
originally interpreted, did not exclude nomination by the
ruler, provided that neither family interest nor bribery had
any part in it, and the office had been canonically vacant
in the first place. And the king expected to enforce the law
if the local ecclesiastical authorities failed to do so; this
was set down as a custom in the 1080 canons of Lillebonne.[37]

[36] See Orderic, i. Index Verborum, *tirannicus, tirannis, tirannus.*
[37] Orderic, iii. 26–7.

Even when reformers demanded more complete independence in principle, both Paschal II and Innocent II were prepared to accept Henry I's overriding of the letter of the law in some matters, as long as he appointed and supported suitable prelates.[38]

It was not surprising that the monk-historian Orderic did not attempt to shape a general theory of political right, or suggest a hierarchy of laws. In the last resort he turned to a penitential interpretation of a king's actions. Whilst loudly condemning the morals of William Rufus, and declaring that his squalid life and dreadful death showed him to be past redemption,[39] he did not suggest that the fatal arrow was the instrument of God's will. Indeed, he avoided any general condemnation of his rule; though Rufus oppressed the poor and 'bestowed ecclesiastical honours like hirelings's wages', at least he had 'brought rebels to heel with the rod of justice' and been a brave and famous knight.[40] Writing in the thick of the civil war in England he was critical of Stephen's failure to take effective action to protect Normandy, but he would say nothing to undermine his claim to the crown. He simply accepted the fact that he was king. He must surely have known of the oaths to Matilda taken by the Anglo-Norman magnates, since he knew of King David's oath, but he chose to keep silent. Any general judgements of legal right appear only faintly, almost unconsciously, in his language. He never called any of Stephen's acts tyrannical. It is worth noting incidentally that he made no mention of the fact that Stephen had sought papal approval for his assumption of the crown; but perhaps he did not know about it.

Writers of contemporary history, whether they were describing events or assessing causation, were limited by their techniques of using the sources available to them, and conditioned then as now by the literary conventions of their day. Historians might delve into the archives of their own abbeys in defence of their property and privileges; and many, including Orderic, copied some letters and decrees of councils

---

[38] See Migne, *PL*, clxiii. 376-7, ep. 423 (but when Paschal II wrote this letter his patience was running out); Orderic, i. 74, and sources cited n.1).

[39] Orderic, v. 292-5.

[40] Orderic, v. 200-3.

into their histories for the sake of the record. In writing
accounts of past events they were content most of the time
to summarize and rearrange the work of earlier historians,
or preserve oral traditions. This was an ancient and accepted
method.[41] Occasionally they attempted a general interpretation of a recent development. Orderic sometimes did so,
particularly in the parts of his work that originated in
separate treatises, such as his account of the new monastic
orders.[42] Here he was in his element; he could write with
penetration and understanding of the historical changes
behind the new movements. He knew that the influence of
St Columbanus had been strongly felt in Normandy alongside that of St Benedict, and that the rule of St Benedict
had been adapted to meet changing needs in different climates. When he pointed to the late Merovingian and early
Carolingian period as the time when manual work in the
fields began to give way to more liturgical devotion and study
for choir monks, he was correctly dating the changes he
described. There was some research behind his treatise, for
he cited several early saints' lives and the letters of Gregory
the Great; but he used oral traditions also, and seems not to
have known the earliest life of St Évroul, with its references
to the mixed rule used in his own monastery.[43] In this
treatise, although in common with most men north of the
Alps at this time, he was deceived by a forged *Life of St Maur*
produced in the abbey of Glanfeuil,[44] the historian appears
at his best: as an interpreter of a profound change in contemporary monasticism, which he viewed in its historical
setting, without partisan rancour. He had sufficient authentic
sources, and the traditions he knew were soundly based.

His accounts of the causes of wars and feuds, if written
from less intimate knowledge, sometimes showed the ability
to go behind the immediate pretext for hostilities to the

[41] This method of writing past history had been the normal practice of Greek
and Roman historians; and in spite of an increased interest in documents shown
by the more antiquarian monastic writers the tradition remained dominant. Cf.
Momigliano, *Studies in Historiography*, pp. 130-1.

[42] Orderic, iv. 312-37.

[43] Orderic, i. 208-9; iii. 363-4; see above, pp. 101-5.

[44] L. Halphen, 'La "Vie de Saint Maur" ', *Revue historique*, lxxxviii (1905),
287-95.

more remote origins of discord. In explaining why William I attacked the French Vexin in 1087, he went back half a century to an alleged grant of the whole Vexin to Robert the Magnificent by King Henry I of France, before describing the frontier raids that sparked off the war.[45] This went deeper than the accounts of some other historians, notably William of Malmesbury, who attributed the outbreak of war (as a climax of unexplained hostilities) to a coarse joke made by Philip I at King William's expense.[46] But at times Orderic was content to take the superficial, even frivolous, explanation. He attributed a private war between the lords of Tosny and the counts of Évreux to the intrigues of their wives: Countess Helwise of Évreux was, he alleged, offended by slighting remarks made by Isabel of Conches, and persuaded her husband to take up arms. Yet his account of the war and settlement shows plainly, if only implicitly, that rights of inheritance were at stake, and that William Rufus, always anxious to increase his influence in Normandy, was ready to fish in troubled waters.[47]

Sometimes when a historian offered a frivolous motive although he knew of a better one his intention was to shift the blame for a rash undertaking from the shoulders of an admired figure. To blame a wife was an ancient device. Evil counsellors, too, were often convenient scapegoats. Orderic carefully shielded from blame the kings he held in high esteem. Although he openly condemned William the Conqueror's brutal harrying of the north, he defended his actions whenever possible. Firmly convinced that Waltheof was innocent of treachery, he contrived to suggest that he was accused by his wife and condemned through the machinations of powerful enemies in the king's court.[48] He attributed the capture of Earl Morcar and the killing of Earl Edwin to evil counsellors who deceived the king and were angrily

---

[45] For a full discussion see Orderic, iv. pp. xxx–xxxiv.

[46] Malmesbury, *GR*, ii. 336, 'contractis inimicitiis cum rege Francorum, aliquantisper se continuit; cujus abutens patientia, Philippus fertur dixisse, "Rex Angliae jacet Rotomagi, more absolutarum partu fœminarum cubile fovens", jocatus in ejus ventrem quem potione alleviarat'.

[47] Orderic, iv. 212–17; in the final settlement William of Breteuil made Ralph of Tosny's son, Roger, his heir; unfortunately Roger died shortly afterwards.

[48] Orderic, ii. 320–3.

condemned by him.[49] For Henry I his admiration was greater. If Henry's methods were sometimes harsh, he acted to enforce justice, and was dealing with men who could be even harsher to those who fell into their clutches. Orderic liked to represent him as a just king, only occasionally misled or prevented from taking some necessary action by self-seeking counsellors. During Henry's lifetime he wrote, 'He governed the realm committed to him by God well and prudently through prosperity and adversity; among all the distinguished rulers of Christendom he is considered outstanding for his preservation of peace and justice. In his days the Church of God has enjoyed riches and honour, and every religious order has flourished greatly.'[50] He had even greater cause to respect and praise King Henry after his death, when order broke down, Angevin troops overran the countryside near to Saint-Evroult, and even the abbey's own patron looted the nearby villages and very nearly burned the abbey over his head as he wrote his history.[51]

One part of a historian's skill consisted in blending tradition and experience in his narrative. It was equally important for him to use all available literary devices to present it elegantly and persuasively. Style was an essential element in historical writing, and the classical tradition of rhetoric, however much watered down in the course of centuries, was still a powerful influence. Even when Cicero praised history as the light of truth and the guide of life, he insisted that it needed the creator's art. The ideal of the nineteenth-century 'scientific' school of writing, to present history 'exactly as it happened', even if attainable at any time would have been as unthinkable in medieval Europe as in ancient Rome. Roman education, as T. P. Wiseman has shown in an illuminating study, was conditioned by rhetoric.[52] Historians wrote for a sophisticated audience, trained in debate from their schooldays, who appreciated all the subtleties of oratory and

[49] Orderic, ii. 256-9.

[50] Orderic, v. 294-5.

[51] Orderic, vi. 452-3, 458-63. His high opinion of the king was shared by other historians, including Suger of Saint-Denis and William of Malmesbury. See Suger, *Vita Ludovici*, cap. i, p. 14; Malmesbury, *GR*, ii. 485, 488-9.

[52] T. P. Wiseman, *Clio's Cosmetics* (Leicester, 1979). pp. 27-40 (citing Cicero, *De orat*. II. 36 on p. 38).

assumed that an orator's business might at times be to make a case rather than to present the truth. Historians had a duty to present the truth, but they were expected to do so in language that was persuasive and lively; in other words to write rhetorically. The use of imagined speeches was a popular device; in such speeches a historian was allowed to invent as an orator would invent, and his readers were assumed to be sufficiently sophisticated to know what he was doing. The invented speech survived as one of the most enduring legacies of ancient rhetoric until at least the eighteenth century.[53] It changed its content and character to conform to the education of the historian and the expectations of his readers. Always perilously balanced on a knife-edge between truth and falsehood, it could, if used with honest intent and understanding of the reader's expectations, enhance without falsifying.

Orderic used speeches in many ways, with considerable skill.[54] In his hands they reveal the art of the historian, epic poet, homilist, and advocate alike. They explain motive and show two sides of a question; at times their function is that of the modern historian's footnote, applied to the needs of a mainly aural audience. They help to tell a story and to celebrate the heroism of the knightly hero facing hopeless odds against the infidel, like Roland and Oliver. They justify the harsh punishments meted out by a peace-loving king, invite the pity of the reader for acts of unjust cruelty, and take on the voice of the preacher to condemn oppression. They are so prominent a feature of his historical writing that it is worth pausing to consider why, very occasionally when they might have been used to effect, he did *not* use them.

Why, for instance, did he write, after describing the reconciliation of Henry I and Robert Curthose when they met between their encamped armies at Alton, 'I cannot record the words of their conference, for I was not present, but I have learnt by hearsay what was the outcome of the counsels of these noble brothers'?[55] Normally he had no hesitation in describing debates that had taken place before he was born,

---

[53] See Orderic, i. 80 n. 1.
[54] See Orderic, i. 79-84.
[55] Orderic, v. 318-21.

or in distant lands that no one could imagine he had ever visited. Again why, in describing the denunciation of Henry I and his representatives made by King Louis VI and the French at the Council of Rheims in 1119, did he record no reply by the Normans and simply admit that they were shouted down?[56] When he described the private meeting of Henry I with Pope Calixtus shortly afterwards at Gisors he was ready enough to provide the king with an eloquent defence of all his actions, from disinheriting and imprisoning his brother to engaging in a war in which Évreux and its cathedral were reduced to ashes.[57] There is no simple answer; but he seems to have been careful to use speeches only when they were plausible (within the accepted conventions) to himself no less than to his readers. He had to believe that these words, or others to the same effect, might have been spoken, and to be particularly sure in recording significant historical events that men still living would not give him the lie.

Morally convinced of the justice of Henry I's rule, he was restrained from outright falsification by his respect for attested actions that might reveal (however obscurely) the will of God. But it is by no means certain that he did not occasionally turn a blind eye. His justification of Henry's cause depended upon what was agreed at Alton, when Robert Curthose, who had come to claim the kingdom of England with a powerful army behind him, withdrew without striking a blow.[58] It was the first step that led to Robert's gradual expulsion from Normandy, which was his by inheritance. Other chroniclers gave some account of the agreement, but Orderic alone asserted that Robert and Henry agreed to help each other to recover all the 'domains' of their father (whatever that might mean) that had been lost since his death, and to 'punish the wicked men who had fomented discord between them'. Robert's alleged failure to carry out this agreement was to be cited by Orderic each time Henry campaigned against him. He made much, in addition to this,

[56] Orderic, vi. 256-61.

[57] Orderic, vi. 282-91.

[58] This was noted by David, *Robert Curthose*, p. 133 n. 66, p. 135 n. 74, where he draws the conclusion that caution is necessary in accepting some of Orderic's statements.

of Robert's failure to protect the church and the defenceless poor; but he could hardly have presented Henry as the instrument of God's will if he had broken a solemn oath to his brother. Given Henry's skill in propaganda, the ultimate source of Orderic's information, whatever the channels by which it reached him, was probably Henry himself. There is no need to doubt the truth of his statement that he had learnt the outcome of the meeting by hearsay, and had recorded what he had heard. But his deliberate turning away from a potentially magnificent dramatic scene suggests a reluctance to probe too deeply into what might have been, at best, ambiguous or misleading promises.

The events at Rheims were of a different kind, for Orderic's account was written from the angle of an eye-witness; and there can be no doubt that he himself was the eye-witness.[59] His narrative is full of visual and aural details. The clergy attendant on the pope wore dalmatics; the pope preached in Latin; Cardinal Cuno quoted Genesis from memory. The speeches he recorded were summaries of what he had actually heard, not rhetorical devices to express different viewpoints or to convey his own interpretation. He reported in full the speech made by King Louis, 'tall in stature, pale, and corpulent', when he advanced to the papal throne and laid charges against the king of England, beginning, 'He has violently invaded Normandy, which is a part of my realm, and has treated Robert, duke of Normandy, atrociously, without justice or right. He has done all kinds of wrongs to this man, who is my vassal and his brother and lord, and has finally captured him and kept him in prison for many years.' A long string of other vehement charges followed; but when Geoffrey, archbishop of Rouen, rose to reply, Orderic did not attempt to expound the arguments he might have wished to offer, but reported that he was shouted down as soon as he began to speak, 'because the defence of the victorious prince was unacceptable to his many enemies there'. A little later in the proceedings he related how, when Audoin, the bearded bishop of Évreux, complained that Amaury of Montfort had driven him out of his episcopal seat and burned his cathedral, Amaury's chaplain

[59] Orderic, vi. 254–77.

made a spirited defence, condemning the bishop and the king of England as the men responsible for the war and the destruction of the city. Orderic recorded no reply to the charges, saying that the French took Amaury's part against the Normans and an uproar arose with everyone speaking at the same time; it was quelled only when Pope Calixtus intervened with an eloquent plea for peace. In any of Orderic's imagined, rhetorical debates the Normans were never shouted down. But he was not prepared to fly in the face of truth by inventing a speech when he knew from the evidence of his own senses that no speech had been made. Instead he provided a full defence of Henry's actions later, in a rhetorical speech attributed to the king during his meeting with the pope at Gisors after the council broke up. He could do this with a clear conscience. The speech was not merely plausible, but probably accurate in substance, since Henry was always ready with arguments and the pope showed himself satisfied by refraining from taking any action against him.

It is interesting to compare Orderic's handling of events at Rheims and Gisors with the work of another historian writing a generation later: John of Salisbury's reconstruction of the Angevin claim to the English crown, made before Pope Innocent II at the 1139 Lateran council.[60] John had not been present; writing round about 1167, almost thirty years after the council, he was mainly concerned to explain why, although Innocent had originally confirmed Stephen's right to the crown, neither he nor any pope after him would ever give approval to the coronation of Stephen's son. According to his account, Arnulf, bishop of Lisieux, had stated the case against Matilda, arguing amongst other things that she was illegitimate because her mother had been a nun. To this Matilda's advocate, Ulger, bishop of Angers, angrily replied that her mother's marriage had been publicly celebrated in church and solemnly confirmed as valid. But we know from a letter of Gilbert Foliot, written to Brian fitz Count shortly after the council, that John's facts were not quite right.[61]

[60] John of Salisbury, *Historia Pontificalis*, ed. M. Chibnall (Edinburgh, 1956), pp. 83–5.
[61] *The Letters of Gilbert Foliot*, ed. Morey and Brooke, pp. 65–6.

Gilbert had been present at the council; in his letter he stated ruefully that Ulger had made no reply to the attack. He went on to say that he had heard it argued since then by Matilda's supporters that the marriage was unquestionably lawful, because it had been celebrated by Anselm himself, the holiest of men. Gilbert was simply reporting what he himself had seen and heard in Rome, and commenting on it, much as Orderic had reported events at Rheims. John, writing history later, may genuinely have believed that Ulger had indeed put forward the arguments that only occurred to others afterwards. But he had been educated in the schools of Paris and was far more deeply read in classical literature than the cloister-bred Orderic; and even Peter, abbot of Saint-Rémi at Rheims, the 'dearest friend and master' for whom John wrote his papal history, was capable of appreciating many of the subtleties of classical rhetoric. The arguments John attributed to Ulger were plausible; they were elaborated later and, since they helped to influence the decisions of Innocent II's successors, they were relevant to his purpose. He was a historian 'writing rhetorically' for learned men who would not misunderstand him. Orderic wrote a generation earlier for a less literate audience, and in a rhetorical tradition tempered by monastic study. Both of them worked within historical conventions more acceptable at that time than they would be at the present day.

Most twelfth-century historians felt free to reshape their material in approved literary form. But the material itself was very uneven in value. Even though the accepted convention was that they should record only what they had seen themselves or learned from a reliable witness, the reliability of some testimony approved by them was open to suspicion. It was strangely compounded of accurately observed detail and moral or heroic fantasy, and they rarely attempted to separate the two. William of Malmesbury, for example, told the story of the witch of Berkeley complete with visible demons who came to carry the witch away from her locked coffin in the midst of chanting monks, exactly as he claimed to have had it from a reliable witness.[62] Orderic occasionally

[62] Malmesbury, *GR*, i. 253–5. William defended a story which he thought his readers might well disbelieve by saying, 'Ego illud a tali viro audivi, qui se

named an informant when recounting marvels and miracles; the vision of Hellequin's hunt, with the sombre company of souls undergoing the torments of purgatorial fire, came to him on the authority of Walchelin, the learned priest of Saint-Aubin, Bonneville.[63] In this remarkable passage the details of the sins of Landry, the corrupt advocate of Orbec, and William of Glos, steward of the great William of Breteuil, who had lent money to a poor miller on usurious terms, are so precisely described that one cannot doubt the good faith of the priest. Whatever medical, psychological, or other explanation may be offered for the vision as a whole, the men who appeared in it were the men he knew, and their sins were as stark and positive as if they had come to him straight from the confessional.

There is a similar mixture of accurately observed fact and fantasy of a different kind when Orderic's informants were the knights who were guests and benefactors of Saint-Evroult, and described their adventures in battle. Battle scenes, in Orderic, were of two kinds: combats near home, particularly in Normandy, and distant battles waged against the infidel in Spain or the Holy Land. In Norman battles romantic epic did not intrude, though grammar and rhetoric did. Any narrator was handicapped by the shortcomings of his classical vocabularly; developed to describe battles of Roman armies, which were largely infantry, it had no word for the cavalry unit of feudal warfare, the vernacular *conroi* of a small group of mounted knights. So writers were obliged to describe fighting units in a mixture of terms, fluctuating between *acies, agmen, cuneus,* and so forth, not one of which on its own quite accurately described what the formation really was.

In spite of this handicap, Orderic's descriptions of battles fought near home enable us to reconstruct the actions.[64] He received reports directly from eye-witnesses, probably very soon after the engagements. At Brémule, indeed, when

---

vidisse juraret, cui erubescerem non credere', adding, 'Ista incredibilia non judicabit qui legerit beati Gregorii Dialogum'. There may, however, be a touch of irony in such protestations.

[63] Orderic, iv, 236-51.
[64] Orderic, vi. 234-43, 348-51.

the Normans defeated the French, friends of his abbey were fighting on both sides; the knights of Maule were among the French knights who escaped capture by throwing away their cognizances and shouting the Norman battle cry, as they rode off in mock pursuit of their own men. When Orderic used speeches in these accounts they were short and to the point, and helped to explain the disposition of the forces, as in his description of the battle of Bourgthéroulde. The tactics adopted by the king's household troops were outlined by their leader, Odo Borleng: 'The best plan is for one section of our men to dismount and fight on foot, while the rest remain mounted ready to join combat. Let us also place a rank of archers in the first line and compel the hostile troops to slow down by wounding their horses.' Other speeches showed how Amaury of Montfort, recognizing the danger of charging against an enemy on his chosen field, urged caution; and how Waleran, the reckless young count of Meulan, would have none of it, with disastrous consequences for the rebels. Here rhetorical conventions bring the action to life and clarify the battle tactics.

(ii) *Poetry and History*

Rhetorical conventions belonged to a well-established tradition of historical writing. So too did the belief that there was common ground between epic and history. Greek and Latin poets and historians dealt with similar themes: 'the famous deeds of men, whether at Thebes or Troy or Salamis'. Many early writers of history indulged in what has been aptly called 'creative historiography'.[65] Vergil's Aeneid was quarried by later historians in search of historical fact and examples of noble conduct. Franks and English alike sought for Trojan ancestors to enhance the reputation of their ruling houses. By the twelfth century every writer of early history had a wealth of literary allusion at his finger tips, and poets were at work providing fresh semi-authentic material for the writers of contemporary history.

Royal and baronial courts were a seeding ground for both vernacular song and vernacular history, for knights delighted

[65] Wiseman, *Clio's Cosmetics*, pp. 145, 149.

in the deeds of their ancestors as monks treasured the legends of their saints. Heroic poems to be sung in camp and at court had their origins in long campaigns, almost on the battle-field. According to William of Malmesbury a *jongleur* accompanied the Norman forces at the battle of Hastings and sang a *cantilena* about Roland to encourage them to deeds of valour.[66] The oldest version of the *Chanson d'Antioche* was composed in the course of the first crusade.[67] A knightly poet like William, duke of Aquitaine, could compose his own songs to entertain his friends with tales of his adventures and trials; most knights had to rely on *jongleurs* to commemorate them. So *jongleurs* had a place in every court with any pretension to culture or distinction. The earliest *chansons* had taken shape by the beginning of the twelfth century;[68] it was only a short step from them to the more historical vernacular verse histories, such as Gaimar's *Estoire des Engleis*, composed shortly before 1140 for his patron, Ralph fitz Gilbert, and a little later to the *Roman de Rou* of Wace, designed to be sung at the court of Henry II.

The morality of epic differed from that of history; it accepted brutality and was full of the sheer joy of combat. But the writers of Latin history, even the monk historians, could not avoid being influenced by the *chansons*. How quickly elements taken from them might creep into the accounts of eye-witnesses and so into the pages of serious history appears repeatedly in Orderic's work. Nowhere is the speed with which the blending took place more remarkable than in his description of the battle of Fraga, fought in July 1134, when the forces of King Alfonso the Battler of Aragón were almost annihilated by the Moors.[69] It was written not later than the spring of 1137, within two or three years of the battle; and the truth of parts of it can be confirmed by comparison with independent Spanish and Arab sources.

The battle took place when the Aragonese had mounted

---

[66] Malmesbury, *GR*, ii. 302.
[67] Orderic, v. pp. xvi–xvii.
[68] For courtly literature and the origins of the *chansons* see R. Bezzola, *Les Origines et la formation de la littérature courtoise en occident* (Paris, 1960); E. Faral, *Les Jongleurs en France au moyen âge* (Paris, 1910); Italo Siciliano, *Les Origines des chansons de geste* (Paris, 1951).
[69] Orderic, vi. 410–19.

an offensive against Moorish settlements in the Ebro valley, and their victorious forces were held up for a year by the siege of Fraga. Orderic relates that at first all went well for the king; forces of Almoravides sent from Africa to raise the siege were defeated in a three day battle, thanks partly to Robert Bordet, count of Tarragona, and other vassals, who arrived fresh on the field of battle and routed the weary pagans, capturing many prisoners and securing rich booty. The citizens then sued for peace; but the king, who had already sworn on the holy relics in his field chapel that he would take the city by storm, haughtily refused to accept surrender on any terms, and insisted that he would massacre the inhabitants of Fraga to the last man. The besieged then sent a desperate plea for help to 'Ali ben Yousuf in Africa, and 'Ali's son brought together contingents from Africa, Cordova, and other parts of Spain. He advanced towards Fraga with five columns of men, sending one ahead with supplies for the city, to lure the Christians into an ambush. Alfonso's forces were led by Bertrand of Laon, count of Carrión, Centule of Béarn and Aymer of Narbonne amongst others; in spite of the efforts of the count of Carrión to persuade the king to wait until the full power of the enemy had been revealed, Alfonso recklessly and arrogantly sent them to attack the supply train. The other four columns of Saracens closed in; the whole Christian army was cut to pieces; only the king—yielding to the persuasion of one of his bishops to save his life for the defence of his kingdom— escaped alive with ten knights.

On his way from the fatal field, he met fresh contingents of French and other vassals hurrying to reinforce his army. Here Orderic, with a sublime indifference to geography, transported them across rivers and mountain ranges to take vengeance. They caught up with the Saracens at the coast, found them loading up their ships with about 700 Christian captives, as well as with captured booty and the heads of the slain, fell upon them with great slaughter, released the captives, and gave Christian burial to the severed heads. 'So', Orderic concluded, 'the triumph of the pagans was turned to mourning, and the Christian army blessed God in all his works.' Alfonso himself, however, was so worn out with hardship and sorrow that he died shortly afterwards.

Many of the facts given by Orderic up to the moment that the king escaped from the battlefield can be checked in other sources. The author of the twelfth-century Aragonese *Chronica Adefonsi* described the relics kept in a chapel in the king's camp outside Fraga, and the oath taken on them, and added that Alfonso refused to accept an offer of surrender from the citizens because he wished to massacre them to the last man. He also said that the Christians won two victories before the final disaster; these may be equivalent to Orderic's three-day battle, in which at first the king gained the advantage, and then, as the pagans continued to resist, Robert Bordet and other vassals arrived in time to deliver a *coup de grâce*. The Aragonese chronicler gave the same list of leaders who died in the final battle as Orderic did, and stated that the king escaped with only ten knights.[70]

Further confirmation comes from Arab sources. Ibn-el-Athir named the provinces from which the Saracens were mustered, described the trick by which the Christians were persuaded to attack prematurely and so fall into an ambush, and attributed the reckless attack to the king's pride, although he spoke with generous admiration of his courage and fighting qualities.[71] And all sources, including charters such as the one drawn up 'after that wholesale, disastrous slaughter of Christians at Fraga, in which almost all perished by the sword, and only a handful, half dead from exhaustion, escaped with the king',[72] were agreed on the total disaster of the field of blood.

But what of the postscript, the king's vengeance on the infidel? Only one other historical source described such an episode: the Chronicle of Saint-Étienne de Caen, and the compiler may have taken some of his details from Orderic.[73]

[70] *Chronica Adefonsi imperatoris*, ed. L. S. Belda (Madrid, 1950), chs. 53–8, pp. 44–7.

[71] Ibn el-Athir, *Annales du Maghreb et de l'Espagne*, trans. E. Fagan (Algiers, 1898), pp. 553–5.

[72] J. M. Lacarra, 'Documentos para la reconquista del valle del Ebro', *Estudios de Edad Media de la Corona de Aragón*, iii (1947–8), no. 180, p. 574.

[73] *Recueil des historiens des Gaules et de la France* (nouv. edn., ed. L. Delisle, Paris, 1869–1904), xii. 779–80). The Vatican MS of the chronicle also contained (before rebinding in the twentieth century) the only surviving early copy of

There were, however, variations; the Caen chronicler put the triumphant intervention of Robert Bordet after the main battle, and linked Robert with the king in the final vengeance. He also added as a colourful detail that the lives of a few Saracens were spared to enable them to take back to King 'Ali in Africa the boats filled with heads of slaughtered Saracens. These variations may be due either to reworking brief notes taken from Orderic, or to hearing the story in a slightly different version from a similar oral source. Essentially it was Orderic's story as told in Normandy; and the only place where we can find any echo of it elsewhere is in the *chansons de geste*. The crucial question is whether the eyewitnesses who told the story told it simply and factually, or with the heroic trimmings already added.

Saint-Evroult was very well placed for eyewitness accounts of events in Spain; one powerful neighbour and benefactor, Rotrou, count of Perche, led a force of vassals to the Spanish wars. But Robert Bordet, count of Tarragona, is the most obvious source for this episode. Robert came from Cullei, a property of the abbey of Saint-Evroult from the time of its foundation; the monks had a personal interest in the knights of the region, which extended to providing their war horses. When Robert Bordet was first enfeoffed with Tarragona, a Christian outpost under constant threat from the Moors, he came back to Normandy to try to raise forces of knights.[74] What more likely than that he came, or sent representatives, to raise more men in 1134, after the disastrous slaughter at Fraga? Mention of rich booty captured in the first battle might have served to whet the appetites of potential recruits. He would have an added interest in softening the diaster by providing an epilogue of vengeance and triumph; an interest that was paralleled by the convention of the *jongleurs* that a *chanson* should end on a note of success: *finir beau*.

The resemblance between Orderic's account of the battle and some passages in the various *chansons de Guillaume* has

Books VII and VIII of Orderic's *Ecclesiastical History*, which was certainly known at Caen, even if Book XII, containing this episode, was not copied (MS Vat. Reg. lat. 703A).

[74] Orderic, vi. 402-5.

been noted by a number of scholars.[75] There is certainly
a parallel between it and *Aliscans*, and it has been suggested
that Orderic had heard a cantilena about the battle of Larchamp in a version different from the one known to us. This
probably misrepresents the way he worked; he had little use
for the stories of *jongleurs*. He consciously rejected their
version of the life of St William of Gellone in favour of an
ecclesiastical *Life*, stressing the much greater truthfulness of
monks.[76] He did, however, trust an eyewitness; and *jongleurs*
were at work during long campaigns no less than at home,
enhancing the battle exploits it was their duty to sing, and
sometimes being prepared to add or suppress stories of individual exploits on the battlefield in return for an adequate
reward. Surely the explanation is that Robert Bordet had
heard a cantilena in the making, and had incorporated details
from it in the narrative he told at Saint-Evroult, and possibly
also at Caen. Perhaps, if the Caen chronicler had heard a
later version of the story and grafted it on to a narrative
taken in the main from Orderic, the legend had been im-
proved in the telling; perhaps Robert Bordet had given a pair
of precious gloves to some *jongleur* to ensure that it should
be so.[77] However that may be, we have in Orderic's narrative
a blending of traditions: the true record of men who had
been near to the events described, together with their views
of the ideals and aspirations of knighthood, which were far
removed from the brutal reality. Their experience and outlook helped to condition his vision of the world in which
he lived.

[75] The parallel was first noted by O. Densusianu, *La prise de Cordres et de
Sebille* (Paris, 1896), pp. xlvi-xlviii. F. M. Warren, 'The battle of Fraga and Larchamp in Orderic Vital', *Modern Philology*, xi (1913-14), 339-46, carried on the
discussion; but his suggestion that Orderic worked over various sources and
followed models, after hearing a cantilena unknown to us, is utterly implausible.
[76] Orderic, iii. 218-19; he did not suspect that the monastic version was
a recent forgery.
[77] Lambert of Ardres, *Historia comitum Ghisnensium, MGH SS*, xxiv. 626-7,
mentions a *jongleur* who refused to sing in praise of a patron who had denied
him a pair of costly gloves.

10

History and Society

In principle, Orderic's world took in the whole of Christendom, but there were geographical, linguistic, and cultural boundaries to his knowledge of it. Manuscripts moved freely wherever Latin was understood; men, as vernacular languages developed and emphasized differences in culture, moved less easily across linguistic barriers.[1] By the twelfth century there was a deep gulf between lands of Germanic and Romance speech; and, though a contingent of knights from Lotharingia joined the first crusade and played their part under Count Rainald of Toul in the second battle of Antioch, the crusading movement did little to bridge it. The written Latin chronicles of Sigebert and Marianus passed easily from the Empire to become incorporated in histories written in the Frankish lands; but oral accounts were easily garbled or misunderstood. Even when Orderic by chance gleaned some accurate information about German affairs he was prepared to believe the wildest rumours. His description of the imperial election following the death of Henry V, which may have reached him through the attendants of the widowed Empress Matilda when she returned home to England, reads in places like a chapter of romance.[2] It is hard to see how a sober historian, after recording more or less correctly that the archbishop of Mainz took the initiative, and that forty chosen knights named three dukes from whom the emperor was to be chosen, could then state that the archbishop threatened with instant decapitation anyone who disagreed with the final choice; but that is what Orderic wrote. He could never have believed such a thing of an Anglo-Norman assembly; but the Empire was to him little more than a literary kingdom, and in his imagination the familiar rules of feudal custom did not apply.

[1] See in particular Southern, *Making of the Middle Ages*, ch. I.
[2] Orderic, vi. 360–5.

Within the Romance speaking regions, which extended from Scotland to Sicily and from Spain to Jerusalem, news was carried by a variety of agents, especially monks, pilgrims, and knights. Benedictine monks were vowed to stability; but the growth of great international orders such as those of Cluny and Cîteaux caused a regular movement across Europe from house to house, and even independent abbeys might have a network of widely scattered dependent priories. Prayer unions expanded the network; the journeys of monks carrying mortuary rolls were a familiar part of monastic life.[3] Religious houses gave hospitality to pilgrims and learned news from them at the same time. Jerusalem, Compostela, Monte Gargano, Rome, and Saint-Gilles were among the favourite centres of pilgrimage, and there were innumerable local and regional shrines. Pilgrims included not only humble men and women, but renowned abbots such as Pontius of Cluny, and leading magnates like Fulk, count of Anjou. Like the monks with their mortuary rolls, they carried news and helped to build common traditions as they travelled from place to place. Their importance to chroniclers has frequently been noted. Saint-Evroult, linked in prayer with some eighty houses,[4] as well as being a centre of hospitality and of a local cult, owed much information to such agents.

The share of knights in spreading tradition as well as news has been less fully explored. Yet many of them were extremely mobile, particularly as young men; and all of them might campaign through the length and breadth of the domains of the various lords they served. Orderic's history reveals how much he learned from them; in particular the knights of the royal household troops made him familiar with their professional pride, sense of honour, and social aspirations, with the life of castle garrisons, the course of sieges, the tactics of battles. Many occur with their cognomens in his history and nowhere else. Bertrand Rumex,[5] Odo Borleng,[6] and their like were men who had won fame for their skill

---

[3] For the transmission of information see *Letters of Peter the Venerable*, ii. 23-9; L. Delisle, *Rouleaux des morts* (Société de l'histoire de France, Paris, 1866).

[4] See above, Map II.

[5] Orderic, vi. 192.

[6] Orderic, vi. 348-51.

with the spear or some other weapon, or their resolution in a tight corner; they came of good families, but had not acquired or inherited any personal property from which to take a name. Their ambition was to earn the grant of some land and found a family. Some were younger sons from the castles of Pont-Échanfray, or L'Aigle, or La Ferté-Frênel, in the neighbourhood of Saint-Evroult; they might be linked in fraternities with the abbey and were frequent visitors, bringing their news. As long as royal garrisons were holding the citadel of Le Mans, Orderic learned a great deal about the course of events there, including personal anecdotes and private jests; once the Norman garrisons had been withdrawn, Le Mans practically dropped out of his history. It was probably from a source of this kind that he gleaned the story of how Ranulf, earl of Chester, and William of Roumare tricked the king's garrison and captured the castle of Lincoln in 1141.[7]

It would be interesting to know what individuals made up the large permanent force of household knights that Conan, son of Gilbert Pilatus, the wealthiest citizen of Rouen, 'arrogantly maintained against the duke', and where they found employment after Conan's rebellion and summary execution in 1090; Orderic had remarkably full details about some episodes in the fighting.[8] And it was surely from royal household knights that he learned of the assassination plot at Gisors in 1123, when Robert of Candos, castellan of the king's castle, narrowly escaped with his life.[9] This story gives one of the rare glimpses of town life in Orderic's history. Robert was summoned to a plea in the house of Pain of Gisors, who packed the town with knights wearing cloaks to hide their hauberks. It was market day, and the knights mingled with the throngs of peasant men and women hurrying in to market from all the neighbouring villages; they were welcomed in the houses of the citizens, who knew nothing of the plot and greeted them as friends. But Robert was delayed because his 'pious wife Isabella' had household matters to discuss with him, and the conspirators struck too soon.

[7] Orderic, vi. 538–9.
[8] Orderic, iv. 220–7.
[9] Orderic, vi. 342–5.

Baudry, a ringleader, arrived last at the court, and gave the signal for attack before Robert, unarmed and unsuspecting, had even reached the market-place; he escaped back to the castle in safety. This is a knight's eye view of history: the peasants and townsfolk are there in the background; the nature of the law-suit is unimportant; but the identity of the knight Baudry is assumed to be self-evident. One touch may come from another source: Robert's pious wife Isabella was well known as a benefactor of Bec-Hellouin.[10] Her fortunate intervention may have reached Orderic from a monastic line of communication.

Naturally he collected news also from the kinsfolk of the greatest magnates who had become monks at Saint-Evroult; but the household knights, many of whom were of less than noble status, brought him information at a practical, professional level, and made his *Ecclesiastical History* incidentally one of the best sources for early twelfth-century military history, particularly in Normandy. The importance of these knights, both in the social structure as the element of 'youth' and in the armies of the day as a professional élite is now well known;[11] they deserve to be recognized also as disseminators of news. Since they formed a substantial part of the audience for vernacular stories, from the early *chansons de geste* to the later popular legends,[12] they tended to dress up their news in their own social and ethical values, as expressed for the semi-literate by the *jongleurs* who travelled from camp to court. Their language was changed to Latin from the vernacular, but their values and interpretations of motive were modified only by a greater insistence on a Christian ethic as their 'news' passed through the mind of a literate monk. With such sources, the traditional defini-

[10] She and her husband together gave Bec the church of Goldcliff in Gwent, and established a dependent priory there (M. Chibnall, 'The English possessions of Bec in the time of Anselm', *Actes du IVe colloque international anselmien* (Paris, CNRS, 1985), p. 279.

[11] See Duby, *The Chivalrous Society*, pp. 112-22; J. Prestwich, 'The military household of the Norman kings', *EHR*, xcvi (1981), 1-35.

[12] J. C. Holt, *Robin Hood* (London, 1982), pp. 62-5, and ch. vi, argues for the importance of the fourteenth-century household as audience in the elaboration of the later legend of Robin Hood, and suggests that earlier legends, such as those of Hereward the Wake, Eustace the Monk, and Fulk fitz Warin, were adapted to the different kind of household existing in the twelfth century.

tions of history handed down through the centuries were reinterpreted in every generation in the writing of contemporary history. Orderic, with his remarkable receptivity, was alert to all of them.

It was Bede, not Orderic, who wrote in the preface to his *Ecclesiastical History of the English People*, 'So I humbly beg the reader, if he finds anything other than the truth set down in what I have written, not to impute it to me. For in accordance with the true law of history, I have simply sought to commit to writing what I have collected from common report, for the instruction of posterity.'[13] What Orderic collected from the common report of Norman knights and magnates was history as they knew and valued it: the exploits of the Norman race, and of their own ancestors, to which they added their own deeds in battle, often embellished as they wished them to be remembered. Another Norman historian, Geoffrey of Malaterra, defended such aspirations when he wrote, citing Sallust, that the desire for fame lifts men above the level of brute beasts, and so justifies the recording of great deeds.[14] Count Roger of Sicily liked to be entertained by listening to the deeds of the Normans, as Geoffrey recorded them. Vernacular historians such as Gaimar and Wace prudently selected particular incidents to flatter the lay hearers of their own day, knights no less than counts.[15] Small wonder if Orderic, spending his whole life in a cloister peopled to a great extent by the sons of the knightly class, unconsciously absorbed much of their outlook, even when he consciously tried to adapt it to an acceptable framework of Christian ethics. So the *gens Normannorum* was constantly remembered in his history. According to Isidore's definition of the word *gens*, 'A people is a multitude sprung from a single source.'[16] The illusion of of common descent might still be preserved when, in the reign of William the Conqueror, William of Jumièges wrote his history of the deeds of the Norman dukes; almost all the

---

[13] Bede, *Ecclesiastical History*, Preface, pp. 6–7.

[14] Malaterra, p. 4.

[15] See M. Bennett, 'Poetry as history? The "Roman de Rou" of Wace as a source for the Norman conquest', in *Anglo-Norman Studies*, v (1983 for 1982), 21–39.

[16] Isidore, *Etymol.* IX. ii. 1.

Norman counts were offshoots of the ducal family. But it was fast becoming an illusion in Orderic's active lifetime, half a century and more later; by then the *gens Normannorum* survived only as a topos behind the shifting realities of Anglo-Norman-Breton-Picard-Flemish-French intermarriage. The conquest of England, and Henry I's marriage with a princess of English descent, made the Normans widen their historical interests; Orderic's notes for his historical work included genealogies of the kings of England.[17] Gaimar in *L'Estoire des Engleis* helped the Norman nobility to annex the Old English past as a part of their own history, whilst still cherishing their Norman traditions.[18] A significant number of manuscripts of both the *Gesta Normannorum ducum* of William of Jumièges and Dudo's *Historia Normannorum* were copied in twelfth-century England.[19]

These men were Orderic's informants; their outlook, with its reverence for ancestry, coloured the secular side of his history. It affected his language when, for instance, he used the word *felicitas* to imply descent from the Frankish imperial house.[20] It coloured his rhetoric, when knights addressed each other in the style of Roland and Oliver. There was no conscious distortion on his part; if he had been at Fraga in 1134, as he was at Rheims in 1119, he would have known what was said and done, and would have confined his account to that, however much he might have wished that the unspoken right answer had been given, or that the happy ending had followed the disastrous defeat. This we may surely deduce from his careful reporting of what he had himself seen. He wrote in his preface to the fifth book that he would rather have described miracles and marvels if the bishops and rulers of his own day had been as holy as the Fathers of old, but since the altercations of prelates and

---

[17] Orderic, iv. p. xvii.

[18] Southern, *Medieval Humanism*, pp. 154–5.

[19] The list of MSS of William of Jumièges compiled by E. M. C. van Houts, *Gesta Normannorum ducum*, pp. 195–60, includes six early MSS copied in England. The manuscript tradition of Dudo's *Historia Normannorum* is described by Gerda Huisman in *Anglo-Norman Studies*, vi (1984 for 1983).

[20] See Pierre Bouet, 'Le *Felicitas* de Guillaume le Conquérant dans les *Gesta Guillelmi* de Guillaume de Poitiers', *Anglo-Norman Studies*, iv (1982 for 1981), 40.

bloody wars of princes provided most of the material for a historian of his own times he resigned himself to recording them, in the hope that God's hidden purpose might become clear to men of future ages when they read his words.[21] As a contemporary historian, he was struggling to record what actually happened, always a difficult task; he could not shake off the assumptions of his own day.

What gives his work its remarkable richness and diversity is the blending in it of secular and ecclesiastical culture. It cannot be compressed into a single genre. The attempt to divide medieval historical writings into different categories, and to classify them as history, chronicle, universal history, ecclesiastical history, *res gestae*, legitimization history, and so forth is something of more concern to modern critics that it ever was to twelfth-century writers.[22] They were prepared to pay lip service to the ancient categories in their prefaces; sometimes, like Orderic or Otto of Freising, they themselves proposed a title.[23] But if pressed to define exactly what they had written, many might have replied in the words of John of Saint-Victor later, that they had adopted a mixed type.[24] They might begin by imitating past models, or adding continuations to existing chronicles; but as their material accumulated they could easily find themselves imitating several different models in the same work, or continuing an earlier chronicle or dynastic history in a way that transformed its character. Some of the continuators of William of Jumièges's popular history of the Norman dukes emphasized the legitimization of a particular ruler; others interpolated items of local interest that slanted it towards the history of their own monastery.[25] John of Salisbury added to the universal chronicle of Jerome-Prosper-Sigebert a detailed

[21] Orderic, iii. 8-9, 212-15.
[22] See B. Guenée, *Histoire et culture historique dans l'Occident médiéval*, for an introduction to this subject and an extensive bibliography.
[23] Otto of Freising's title, *The Two Cities*, taken from Augustine, was intended to indicate a theme rather than a genre.
[24] John wrote his still unpublished *Memoriale historiarum* in the fourteenth century: his reference to a *modum mixtum* is cited by B. Guenée, 'Histoires, annales, chroniques. Essai sur les genres historiques au Moyen Âge', *Annales: Économies, Sociétés, Civilisations*, xxviii (1973), 1008.
[25] For a discussion of the various continuations of William of Jumièges, see Van Houts, *Gesta Normannorum Ducum*, pp. 157-80, 308.

description of events in the papal court, which was so firmly focused on the papacy that it placed the true centre of the whole of western Christendom there, and in this way twisted the chronicle into a papal history.[26]

Orderic consciously imitated Bede and Eusebius; but whereas in the works of both these historians chronicle and ecclesiastical history were kept in separate volumes, Orderic finally decided to combine them under one title. Besides this he incorporated saints' lives, monastic history, the deeds of the Normans, and a justification of the reign of Henry I, in a single work. To find a definition might well have defeated Isidore. To call it Cluniac history, as Hans Wolter does, is going too far.[27] No Norman monastery was purely Cluniac in allegiance or culture, but an abbey such as Saint-Evroult was indeed a cloister for nobles and knights, and in its priory at Maule, in the Île de France, as Orderic himself wrote from personal knowledge, the knights frequented the cloister with the monks, giving lands and tithes, seeking spiritual enlightenment, finally coming there in the hour of their death. Their interest was in their patrimony and their lineage, their favoured literary expression the *chanson de geste*. Their legends, based on *chansons* and vernacular histories, were as much a part of Orderic's historical outlook as the legends of the saints in the liturgy, and the Latin histories he read and copied in the cloister. None of these things could be expelled from his memory as he added to the earlier history of the church from the birth of Christ the records of his own day. It was in applying his training in a monastic school where history was cherished to recording the miscellaneous stories of his many informants, and in his own observation of contemporary society, that he showed the originality of his approach to the history of his own time.

The result of this diversity was a period of relative neglect after his death, until he was rediscovered in the sixteenth century. The highly individual structure of his work may have limited its circulation. It mirrored an epoch from a particular viewpoint in vivid detail. Written with the immediate

---

[26] *Historia Pontificalis*, ed. Chibnall, *passim*.
[27] Hans Wolter, *Ordericus Vitalis: Ein Beitrag zur Kluniazensischen Geschichtsschreibung* (Wiesbaden, 1955).

purpose of being read aloud in choir, cloister, and refectory for the instruction and enjoyment of his fellow monks, or used as the basis of homilies and moral instruction for the laity, it made its immediate appeal to the monks and knights he knew. But monastic life and society were being transformed, and the political shape of the region where he lived was radically restructured in the years after his death. One result of the spread of the Cistercian and other new orders was to encourage stricter enclosure even in the older monasteries. Vernacular culture was developing apace in royal and baronial courts. Towards the end of Orderic's life Gaimar produced, in his *Estoire des Engleis*, the kind of vernacular rhymed history that was to supply the magnates with an alternative form of historical fare, more solid than the *chansons*, but still popular.[28] The Norman clerk, Wace, who had used parts of Orderic's history, caught the ear of the Angevin court in the 1160s.[29] And when political order was restored under Henry II after the civil wars of Stephen's reign, the pattern was different. The bonds between England and Normandy, which Henry I had struggled all his life to preserve, remained. But the 'Norman empire' which Orderic portrayed so vividly had been subsumed in the wider 'Angevin empire'.[30] His work, much as it eulogized Henry I, could scarcely have commended itself to Henry's half-Angevin grandson, after all the bitter things he had written about the Angevins and his reluctance to acknowledge the victory of Geoffrey of Anjou. Robert of Torigny, a more arid writer but a consistent and careful supporter of the Angevins, became the favoured historian of the new age in Normandy.[31] Orderic's work could not even have appealed to the powerful Beaumont earls of Leicester and counts of Meulan, who had stepped into the Grandmesnil inheritance and become the lay patrons of Saint-Evroult, for Orderic was loyal to

[28] G. Gaimar, *L'Estoire des Engleis*, ed. A. Bell (Anglo-Norman Text Society, xiv-xvi, 1960).
[29] *Le Roman de Rou de Wace*, ed. A. J. Holden (3 vols. in 2. Société des anciens textes français, Paris, 1970-3). Wace was born in Jersey and began his studies at Caen.
[30] For the use of these terms and the contrast between the two 'empires' see Le Patourel, *The Norman Empire*, pp. 116-17.
[31] R. Foreville, 'Robert de Torigni et Clio', *Mont Saint-Michel*, ii. 141-53.

the original benefactors of the abbey and showed his sympathy for the intermittently disloyal Giroie and the (perhaps deservedly) unfortunate Grandmesnil. He was careful and correct, never more, in writing of the descendants of Roger of Beaumont, whose talent for survival with ever-increasing wealth and power through every change of lordship and turn of the wheel of fortune was unrivalled.

Parts of Orderic's history had special interest for one or two particular monasteries, and were copied there. Of surviving manuscripts other than his own holograph from Saint-Evroult, the best come from Saint-Étienne de Caen, though even these are incomplete.[32] Books VII and VIII, which included many of the deeds of William the Conqueror and the magnificent deathbed speech rhetorically attributed to him, as well as the treatise on the new monastic orders, were copied almost in their entirety at Caen in the twelfth century. It was probably this copy that Wace knew. The death of King William had a special interest and value for the abbey founded by the king, and chosen as his burial place. Two-hundred years later another copy of chapters relating to his life was made; beautifully written and lavishly decorated in gold leaf, with William's name inscribed in gold letters wherever it occurred, it was designed to honour a secular patron with all possible revence short of that reserved for a patron saint. In England Crowland Abbey kept and copied the narrative of its own early history and the miracles connected with Waltheof. Robert of Torigny, a Bec-Hellouin, copied the treatise on the new monastic orders. And at Saint-Evroult itself the work had a lasting home. Never greatly thumbed, it still found some readers in each century, as the occasional notes and subject headings inserted in the margin in the handwriting of different periods bear witness. There is surprisingly little sign of use in the first two books, though these contained many lives of apostles, prayers, and hymns that were ideally suitable for use in the church on saints' days; but perhaps the relevant parts were copied into service books and worn out or lost in later centuries. The earliest inserted notes are explanations of unusual or difficult words,

[32] For details of the manuscripts and the later use of Orderic's work see Orderic, i. 112-15, 118-23.

written as interlinear glosses in the chapters that relate the
events of 1100: Robert Curthose's return from the crusade,
the death of William Rufus in the New Forest, and the
coronation of Henry I.[33] They suggest that in describing
political events and highlighting the legitimacy of Henry's
rule Orderic was responding to the wishes of his fellow
monks no less than following his own interests. Nevertheless,
if the surviving fragments other than the holograph give a
true picture, it seems that Orderic's work was too varied, too
individual, and at the same time too much of its own age, to
arouse great interest outside the community for which it
was written until the end of the middle ages.

By contrast, the works of Orderic's contemporary, William
of Malmesbury, enjoyed a much wider circulation.[34] He
wrote a number of shorter works on more limited topics,
including the deeds of the kings of England (*Gesta regum*),
the deeds of the English bishops (*Gesta pontificum*), the
antiquities of Glastonbury, a short general chronicle, and the
history of the most recent times. Each had its receptive
readers, some more than others. The *Gesta regum* was the
most popular; but it might not have circulated so widely if it
had been intermixed with all the other works as well. The
task of copying might have been more daunting, the readers
less numerous. Besides this, Malmesbury wrote in England,
the heartland of the enduring Anglo-Norman realm, not in
Normandy in the centre of a political vortex. Whatever
explanation may be offered for the difference, the *Gesta
regum* was one of the most widely read histories of this period,
and Orderic's *Ecclesiastical History* one of the least copied.

---

[33] Orderic, v. 268-300.

[34] B. Guenée, *Histoire et culture historique*, pp. 250-2, has drawn up a preliminary list of the numbers of surviving medieval manuscripts of some historical
works. This is necessarily provisional and incomplete, as further manuscripts are
already coming to light, and the numbers lost cannot be estimated; but it gives
a useful indication of relative popularity. He notes 35 MSS of William of Malmesbury's *Gesta regum* and 20 of his *Gesta pontificum*. This compares with only
3 for Orderic. Guenée's figures for Bede's *Ecclesiastical History* are 164, and for
William of Jumièges 31 (to which over 10 more have now been added by Van
Houts). For fuller details of the dissemination of Malmesbury's works see Antonia
Gransden, *Historical Writing in England*, pp. 179-80. The early twelfth-century
chronicles with a circulation most nearly comparable to that of the *Gesta regum*
include the chronicles of Sigebert of Gembloux (48), and Hugh of Saint-Victor
(35).

The change in the fortunes of Orderic's work came in a way that would have been gratifying to him, for his intended readership did not end with his fellow monks. He looked beyond twelfth-century Saint-Evroult as Bede had looked beyond eighth-century Jarrow and Wearmouth. Bede quickly found his wider audience, for his work was already very well known when Orderic copied it. But just as Orderic read it 400 years after its composition, and cherished it for the record it preserved of events that would otherwise have been lost, so William Vallin, a sixteenth-century monk of Saint-Evroult perused Orderic's own history with profit and delight. Vallin copied it carefully in his beautiful, humanistic handwriting, and offered his new 'edition' to his abbot, Felix de Brie.[35] He recognized in Orderic a devoted scholar of wide learning: one who had toiled unremittingly to leave a record that was pleasing to read and salutary, both for his contemporaries and for the generations after him. Working in his cloister like a bee in its hive, he had gathered honey from the flowers of knowledge far and wide, finding the work both beautiful and delightful, because it was a worthy task to investigate the works of God's wisdom. Other copies followed in rapid succession; and from the time of the first printing of Orderic's history by Duchesne in 1619 its appeal has never faltered. There can be no doubt that Orderic, in intent and purpose, went far beyond providing useful reading for his monatic brethren, and ultimately achieved the wider aim outlined modestly, but confidently, in his preface to the whole work:

I firmly believe, in accordance with the prognostications of earlier writers, that in time someone will come with greater understanding than myself, and greater capacity for interpreting the multifarious events taking place on earth, who will perhaps derive something from my writings and those of others like me, and will insert it worthily in his chronicle or history for the information of future generations.[36]

Interpretations of the record that he left differ, and will continue to differ as long as it is read; yet it is daunting to think of what we would not know about the twelfth-century Anglo-Norman world if he had never written his *Ecclesiastical History*.

[35] Orderic, i. 115, 122.   [36] Orderic, i. 132-3.

APPENDIX

The Epilogue to Orderic's
Ecclesiastical History[1]

Now indeed, worn out with age and infirmity, I long to bring this book to an end, and it is plain that many good reasons urge me to do so. For I am now in the sixty-seventh year of my life and service to my Lord Jesus Christ, and while I see the princes of this world overwhelmed by misfortunes and disastrous setbacks I myself, strengthened by the grace of God, enjoy the security of obedience and poverty. At this very moment Stephen, king of England, languishes wretchedly in a dungeon; and Louis, king of France, leading an expedition against the Goths and Gascons, is haunted by unremitting cares. Now too, ever since the death of the bishop of Lisieux, his chair has remained empty, and I cannot say when or by what kind of a bishop it will be filled. What more shall I say? Amid such happenings, almighty God, I appeal to thee and humbly implore thee in thy mercy to have pity on me. I give thanks to thee, supreme King, who didst freely create me and ordain my life according to thy gracious will. For thou art my King and my God, and I am thy servant and the son of thine handmaiden, one who from the beginning of my life has served thee as far as I was able. I was baptized on Holy Saturday at Atcham, a village in England on the great river Severn. There thou didst cause me to be reborn of water and the Holy Spirit by the hand of Ordric the priest, and didst impart to me the name of that priest, my godfather. Afterwards when I was five years old I was put to school in the town of Shrewsbury, and performed my first clerical duties for thee in the church of

---

[1] Orderic wrote the epilogue to the *Ecclesiastical History*, containing an account of his own life, in the summer of 1141. See Orderic, vi. 550–7.

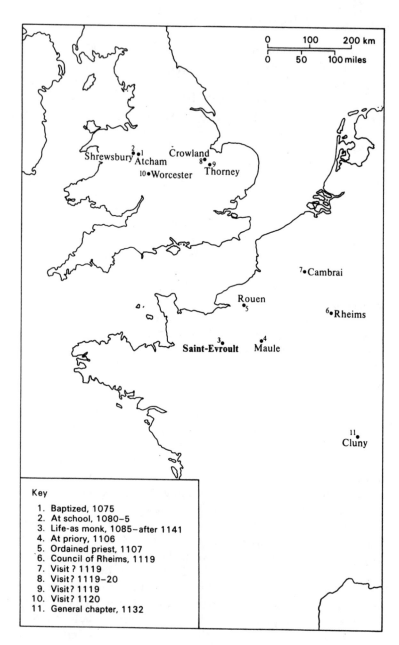

Key

1. Baptized, 1075
2. At school, 1080–5
3. Life-as monk, 1085–after 1141
4. At priory, 1106
5. Ordained priest, 1107
6. Council of Rheims, 1119
7. Visit ? 1119
8. Visit? 1119–20
9. Visit? 1119
10. Visit? 1120
11. General chapter, 1132

III. Places visited by Orderic

St Peter and St Paul the apostles. There Siward, an illustrious priest, taught me my letters for five years, and instructed me in psalms and hymns and other necessary knowledge. Meanwhile thou didst honour this church on the river Meole, which belonged to my father, and didst build a holy monastery there through the piety of Earl Roger. It was not thy will that I should serve thee longer in that place, for fear that I might be distracted among kinsfolk, who are often a burden and a hindrance to thy servants, or might in some way be diverted from obeying thy law through human affection for my family. And so, O glorious God, who didst command Abraham to depart from his country and from his kindred and from his father's house, thou didst inspire my father Odelerius to renounce me utterly, and submit me in all things to thy governance. So, weeping, he gave me, a weeping child, into the care of the monk Reginald, and sent me away into exile for love of thee and never saw me again. And I, a mere boy, did not presume to oppose my father's wishes, but obeyed him willingly in all things, for he promised me in thy name that if I became a monk I should taste of the joys of Paradise with the Innocents after my death. So with this pact freely made between me and thee, for whom my father spoke, I abandoned my country and my kinsfolk, my friends and all with whom I was acquainted, and they, wishing me well, with tears commended me in their kind prayers to thee, O almighty God, Adonai. Receive, I beg thee, the prayers of these people and, O compassionate God of Sabaoth, mercifully grant what they asked for me.

And so, a boy of ten, I crossed the English Channel and came into Normandy as an exile, unknown to all, knowing no one. Like Joseph in Egypt, I heard a language I did not understand. But thou didst suffer me through thy grace to find nothing but kindness and friendship among strangers. I was received as an oblate monk in the abbey of Saint-Evroult by the venerable Abbot Mainer in the eleventh year of my age, and was tonsured as a clerk on Sunday, 21 September. In place of my English name, which sounded harsh to the Normans, the name Vitalis was given me, after one of the companions of St. Maurice the martyr, whose feast was being celebrated at that time. I have lived as a monk in that abbey by thy favour for fifty-six years, and have been loved and honoured by all my fellow monks and companions far more than I deserved. I have laboured among thy servants in the vineyard of the vine of Sorech, bearing heat and cold and the burden of the day, and I have waited knowing that I shall receive the penny that thou hast promised, for thou doest keep faith. I have revered six abbots as my fathers and masters because they were thy vicars: Mainer and Serlo, Roger and Warin, Richard and Ralph. These men have all been lawfully appointed to rule the abbey of Saint-Evroult, they have carefully and diligently guided internal and external affairs, knowing that they must render account for me and all the others, and by thy help and guidance they have provided for all our needs. On 15 March, when I was sixteen years old, at the command of Serlo, abbot elect, Gilbert, bishop of Lisieux, ordained me subdeacon. Then two years later, on 26 March, Serlo, bishop of Sées, laid the stole of the diaconate on my shoulders, and I gladly served thee as a deacon for fifteen years. At length in my thirty-third year William, archbishop of Rouen, laid the burden of priesthood on me on 21 December. On the same day he also blessed two hundred and forty-four deacons and a hundred and twenty priests, with whom I reverently approached thy holy altar, filled with the Holy Spirit; and I have now faithfully performed the sacred offices for thee with a joyful heart for thirty-four years.

Thus, thus, O Lord God, my creator and life-giver, thou hast freely bestowed on me thy gifts through the various orders, and by thy just governance hast appointed all my days to thy service. In all the places where thou has led me since my early days thou hast caused me to be loved by thy servants, not through my own merits but through thy free gift. O kind Father, I give thanks to thee for all thy mercies; I praise and bless thee with my whole heart; weeping, I implore thy mercy for my many offences. Spare me, O Lord, and do not let me be destroyed; look compassionately according to thine inexhaustible goodness on the work of thy hands, and pardon and wash away all my sins. Grant me the will to continue in thy service, and never-failing strength to withstand the malice of deceitful Satan, until I receive by thy gift the inheritance of eternal salvation. And these same gifts, O merciful God, that I ask for myself now and hereafter, I ardently desire for my friends and benefactors, and seek to obtain for all thy faithful people according to thy providence. And since we are unable by our own merits to obtain the everlasting joys on which the desires of the perfect are fixed, grant, O Lord God, Father omnipotent, creator and ruler of the angels, true hope and eternal beatitude of the just, that we may receive help in thy presence through the intercession of the blessed Virgin and Mother, Mary, and all the saints, by the grace of our Lord Jesus Christ, redeemer of all men, who lives and reigns with thee in the unity of the Holy Spirit, God, world without end. Amen.

Genealogical Tables

I. The family of Giroie

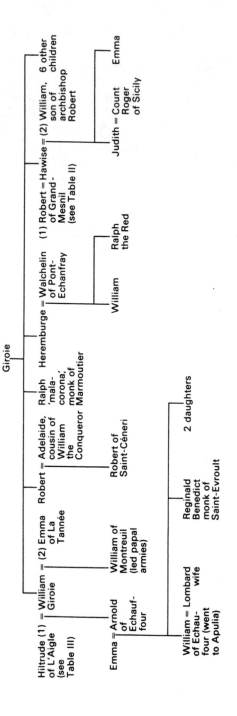

II. The family of Grandmesnil

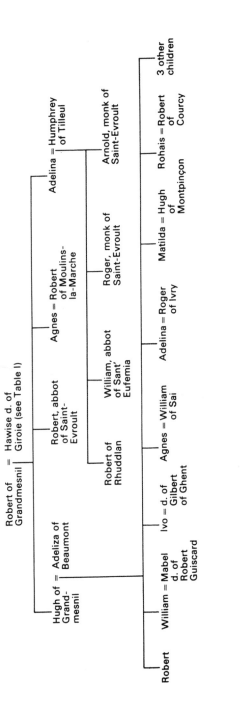

III. The family of L'Aigle

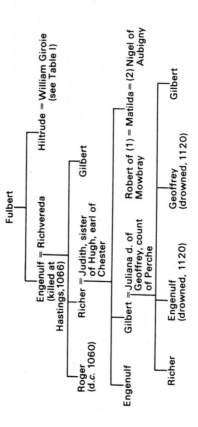

Bibliography of Abbreviated Titles

This bibliography includes only works that are cited more than once in scattered places. Where a reference has been greatly abbreviated and might not be easily recognizable, the shortened form is given before the full reference. Abbreviated references to series and journals are included.

AA SS: Acta Sanctorum ed. J. Bollandus and others (Antwerp and Brussels, 1643-   ).
AA SS OSB: Acta Sanctorum ordinis sancti Benedicti, ed. J. Mabillon (Paris, 1668–1701).
Actus Pontificum cenomannis in urbe degentium, ed. G. Busson and A. Ledru (Société des Archives historiques du Maine, ii. 1902)
Anglo-Norman Studies: Proceedings of the Battle Conference on Anglo-Norman Studies, ed. R. Allen Brown, i–iv (1979–82 for 1978–81), continued as *Anglo-Norman Studies* v–(1983-   ).
Anselm, *Opera: S. Anselmi Opera Omnia*, ed. F. S. Schmitt (6 vols., Edinburgh, 1938–61).
A.S. Chron.: The Anglo-Saxon Chronicle (citations are by year).
Barlow, Frank, *Edward the Confessor* (London, 1970).
Barlow, Frank, *William Rufus* (London, 1983).
Bates, David, *Normandy before 1066* (London, 1982).
Bautier, R.-H., 'La place de l'abbaye de Fleury-sur-Loire dans l'historiographie française du ixe au xiie siècle', *Études ligériennes d'histoire et d'archéologie médiévales*, ed. R. Louis (Auxerre, 1975), pp. 25–33.
Bayeux Tapestry: The Bayeux Tapestry, a Comprehensive Survey ed. Sir Frank Stenton and others (London, 1959).
Bede, *The Ecclesiastical History of the English People*, ed. B. Colgrave and R. A. B. Mynors (Oxford Medieval Texts), Oxford, 1969.
Bligny, Bernard, *L'Église et les ordres religieux dans le royaume de Bourgogne aux xie et xiie siècles* (Paris, 1960).
Brett, M., 'John of Worcester and his contemporaries', in *The Writing of History in the Middle Ages*, ed. R. H. C. Davis and J. M. Wallace-Hadrill (Oxford, 1981), pp. 101–26.
Brundage, J. A., 'Holy war and the medieval lawyers', *The Holy War*, ed. T. P. Murphy, pp. 99–140.
Brut y Tywysogion, or The Chronicle of the Princes (Red Book of Hergest version), ed. Thomas Jones (Cardiff, 1955).
BSAN: Bulletin de la Société des Antiquaires de Normandie.
Calendar of Documents preserved in France, i., ed. J. H. Round (London, 1899).

CCM: *Corpus Consuetudinum Monasticarum* (cura Pontificii Athenaei Sancti Anselmi de Urbe editum moderante Kassio Hallinger OSB).

Chazan, R., *Medieval Jewry in Northern France* (Baltimore and London, 1973), pp. 10–28.

Chibnall, M., 'Ecclesiastical patronage and the growth of feudal estates at the time of the Norman conquest', *Annales de Normandie*, viii (1958), 103–18.

—, 'Feudal Society in Orderic Vitalis', *Anglo-Norman Studies*, i (1979 for 1978), 35–48.

—, 'The Merovingian monastery of Saint-Evroul', *Studies in Church History*, viii. 31–40.

Chron. de Hida: *Chronica de Hida, Liber Monasterii de Hyda*, ed E. Edwards (RS, 1886).

(La) Chronique de Saint-Pierre-le-Vif de Sens, dite de Clarius, ed. R.-H. Bautier and Monique Gilles (Paris, CNRS, 1979).

(The) Chronicle of Battle Abbey, ed. Eleanor Searle (Oxford Medieval Texts), Oxford, 1980.

Clanchy, M. T., *From Memory to Written Record* (London, 1979).

Classen, Peter, '*Res gestae*, Universal History, Apocalypse: Visions of Past and Future', *Renaissance and Renewal*, pp. 387–417.

CNRS: Centre national de la recherche scientifique.

Complete Peerage: *The Complete Peerage of England, Scotland, Ireland, Great Britain and the United Kingdom*, by G. E. C. (new edn., 13 vols in 14, 1910–59).

Constable, Giles, *Cluniac Studies* (London, Variorum reprints, 1978).

—, *Monastic Tithes from their Origins to the Twelfth Century* (Cambridge, 1964).

—, *Religious Life and Thought in the eleventh and twelfth centuries* (London, Variorum reprints, 1979).

Consuetudines Beccenses, ed. Marie Pascal Dickson (*CCM*, vol. iv), Siegburg, 1967.

Contamine, Philippe, *La Guerre au Moyen Âge* (Paris, 1980).

Contamine, Philippe (ed.), *La Noblesse au Moyen Âge: Essais à la mémoire de Robert Boutruche* (Paris, 1976).

Councils and Synods: *Councils and Synods with other Documents relating to the English Church*, Vol. i, ed. D. Whitelock, M. Brett, and C. N. L. Brooke (Oxford, 1981).

Cowdrey, H. E. J., 'The Peace and Truce of God in the eleventh century', *Past and Present*, xlvi (1970), 42–67.

David, C. W., *Robert Curthose, Duke of Normandy* (Harvard Historical Studies, vol. xxv), Cambridge, Mass., 1920.

de Bouard, M., 'Sur les origines de la Trève de Dieu en Normandie', *Annales de Normandie*, ix (1959), 169–89.

de Gaiffier, B., 'L'hagiographe et son public au xie siècle', *Miscellanea Historica in honorem Leonis van der Essen* (2 vols., Brussels and Paris, 1947), i. 135–66.

Delisle, L., 'Manuscrits autographes d'Orderic Vital', *Matériaux pour l'édition de Guillaume de Jumièges*, ed. J. Lair (Paris, 1910).

Dictionary of the Christian Church: The Oxford Dictionary of the Christian Church, revised edn., ed. F. L. Cross and E. A. Livingstone (Oxford, 1983).

Dictionnaire d'archéologie chrétienne et de liturgie, ed. F. Cabrol and H. Leclercq (15 vols., 1907–53).

Douglas, D. C., *William the Conqueror* (London, 1964).

Duby, G., 'Dans la France du Nord-Ouest au xiie siècle: les "jeunes" dans la société aristocratique', *Annales: Économies, Sociétés, Civilsations*, xix (1964), 835–46; trans. *The Chivalrous Society*, pp. 112–22.

—, *Medieval Marriage*, (Baltimore and London, 1978).

—, *The Chivalrous Society*, trans. Cynthia Postan (London, 1977).

Eadmer, *Hist. nov.: Eadmeri historia novorum in Anglia* ed M. Rule (RS, 1884).

—, *Vita Anselmi: The Life of St. Anselm by Eadmer*, ed. R. W. Southern (Oxford Medieval Texts, 1972).

EHR: English Historical Review

Erdmann, Karl, *Die Entstehung der Kreuzzugsgedankens* (Stuttgart, 1935); trans. M. W. Baldwin and W. Goffart, *Carl Erdmann: The Origin of the Idea of Crusade* (Princeton, 1977).

Esmein, A., *Le Mariage en droit canonique* (2 vols., Paris, 1891).

Farmer, H., 'William of Malmesbury's Commentary on Lamentations', *Studia monastica*, iv (1962), 283–311.

Fauroux: *Recueil des actes des ducs de Normandie de 911 à 1066*, ed. Marie Fauroux (*Mémoires de la Société des Antiquaires de Normandie*, xxxvi), Caen, 1961.

Fécamp: L'Abbaye bénédictine de Fécamp (2 vols., Fécamp, 1959–60).

Flint, V. I. J., 'The "School of Laon"; a reconsideration', *RTAM*, xliii (1976), 89–110.

Flori, J., 'Chevalerie et liturgie', *Le Moyen Âge*, lxxxiv (1978), 247–78, 409–42.

—, 'La notion de chevalerie dans les Chansons de Geste du xiie siècle', *Le Moyen Âge*, lxxxi (1975), 211–44, 407–46.

—, 'Les origines de l'adoubement chevaleresque', *Traditio*, xxxv (1979), 209–72.

Foreville, R., 'The synod of the province of Rouen in the eleventh and twelfth century', *Church and Government in the Middle Ages*, ed. Christopher Brooke and others (Cambridge, 1976), 19–40.

Gaimar, G., *L'Estoire des Engleis*, ed. A. Bell (Anglo-Norman Text Society, xiv–xvi, 1960).

Génestal, R., *Rôle des monastères comme établissements de crédit* (Paris, 1901).

Gibson, Margaret, *Lanfranc of Bec* (Oxford, 1978).

Glanvill: *The Treatise on the Laws and Customs of England commonly called Glanvill*, ed. G. D. G. Hall (Nelson's Medieval Texts), London and Edinburgh, 1965.

Gransden, Antonia, *English Historical Writing c.550–c.1307* (London, 1974).

Guenee, B., *Histoire et culture historique dans l'Occident médiévale* (Paris, 1980).

Guibert, *De vita sua* (Benton): *Self and Society in Medieval France: the Memoirs of Abbot Guibert of Nogent*, trans. J. F. Benton (New York and Evanston, 1970).

—, *De vita sua* (Labande): Guibert de Nogent, *Autobiographie*, ed. and trans., E.-R. Labande (Les classiques de l'histoire de France au Moyen Age, xxxiv), Paris, 1981.

Guillou, A. *Le Comte d'Anjou et son entourage au xie siècle* (2 vols., Paris, 1972).

Haskins, C. H., *Norman Institutions* (Harvard Historical Studies, xxiv), Cambridge, Mass., 1925.

H. Huntingdon: Henry of Huntingdon, *Historia Anglorum*, ed. Thomas Arnold (RS, 1879).

Holt, J. C., 'Politics and property in early medieval England' *Past and Present*, lvii (1972), 3–52.

Isidore, *Etymol.*: *Isidori Hispalensis Episcopi Etymologiarum sive Originum libri xx*, ed. W. M. Lindsay (2 vols., Scriptorum classicorum bibliotheca oxoniensis), Oxford, 1911.

Ivo of Chartres, *Correspondance*, ed. and trans. J. Leclercq, i. (Les classiques de l'histoire de France au Moyen Âge, xxii) Paris, 1949.

—, *Epistolae* (Migne, *PL*, clxii).

(The) Jews and the Crusaders, ed. Shlomo Eidelberg (Wisconsin, 1977).

JL: Philip Jaffé, *Regesta pontificum Romanorum*, ed. S. Löwenfeld, F. Kaltenbrunner, P. Ewald (Leipzig, 1885–8).

John of Salisbury, *Historia Pontificalis*, ed. M. Chibnall (Nelson's Medieval Texts), Edinburgh and London, 1956.

—, *Policraticus*, ed. C. C. J. Webb (2 vols., Oxford, 1909).

John of Worcester: *The Chronicle of John of Worcester 1118–1140*, ed. J. R. H. Weaver (Oxford, 1908).

Johnson, P. D., *Prayer, Patronage and Power* (New York and London, 1981).

Jordan Fantosme's Chronicle, ed. and trans. R. C. Johnston (Oxford, 1981).

Jumièges: *Jumièges, Congrès scientifique du xiiie centenaire* (2 vols., Rouen, 1955).

Knowles, M. D., *The Monastic Order in England* (Cambridge, 1962).

Laporte, J., 'Labbaye du Mont Saint-Michel aux xe et xie siècles', *Mont Saint-Michel*, i. 53–80.

—, 'Les origines du monachisme dans la province de Rouen', *Revue Mabillon*, xxxi (1941), 1–13, 25–41, 49–68.

—, 'Tableau des services obituaires assurés par les abbayes de Saint-Evroul et de Jumièges', *Revue Mabillon*, xlvi (1956), 141–88.

Leclercq, J., Predicateurs bénédictins aux xie et xiie siècles', *Revue Mabillon*, xxxiii (1943), 59–65.

Leges Henrici primi, ed. L. J. Downer (Oxford, 1972).

Lemarignier, J.-F., *Étude sur les privilèges d'exemption et de juridic-*

tion ecclésiastique des abbayes normandes (Archives de la France monastique, xliv), Paris, 1937.

Lemarignier, J.-F., *Recherches sur l'hommage en marche et les frontières féodales* (Travaux et Mémoires de l'Université de Lille, N.S., Droit et Lettres, xxiv), Lille, 1945.

Le Patourel, J., *The Norman Empire* (Oxford, 1976).

Le Prévost: *Orderici Vitalis ecclesiasticae historiae libri tredecim*, ed. A. Le Prévost (Société de l'Histoire de France, 5 vols.,), Paris, 1838-55.

(The) Letters and Charters of Gilbert Foliot, ed. A. Morey and C. N. L. Brooke (Cambridge, 1967).

(The) Letters of Lanfranc, ed. H. Clover and M. Gibson (Oxford Medieval Texts), Oxford, 1979.

(The) Letters of Peter the Venerable, ed. G. Constable (2 vols., Harvard Historical Studies, lxxviii), Cambridge, Mass., 1967.

Malaterra: Geoffrey of Malaterra, *De Rebus gestis Rogerii Calabriae et Siciliae comitis*, ed. E. Pontieri (Rerum Italicarum Scriptores, v, pt. i), Bologna, 1928).

Malmesbury, *GP*: *Willelmi Malmesbiriensis de gestis pontificum Anglorum libri quinque*, ed. N. E. S. A. Hamilton (RS, 1870).

Malmesbury, *GR*: William of Malmesbury, *De gestis regum Anglorum* ed. W. Stubbs (2 vols., RS, 1887-9).

Malmesbury, *Hist. Nov.*: *The Historia Novella by William of Malmesbury*, ed. K. R. Potter (Nelson's Medieval Texts), Edinburgh and London, 1955.

Marx: Guillaume de Jumièges, *Gesta Normannorum ducum*, ed. J. Marx (Société de l'histoire de Normandie), Rouen and Paris, 1914.

Memorials of St. Anselm, ed. R. W. Southern and F. S. Schmitt (British Academy; *Auctores Britannici Medii Aevi*, i), London, 1969.

Meyvaert, Paul, *Benedict, Gregory, Bede and Others* (London, Variorum reprints, 1977).

MGH SS: *Monumenta Germaniae historica, Scriptores.*

Migne, *PL*: *Patrologiae cursus completus, series latina*, ed. J. P. Migne (221 vols., Paris, 1844-64).

Momigliano, A. D., *Studies in Historiography* (London, 1969).

(The) Monastic Constitutions of Lanfranc, ed. David Knowles (Nelson's Medieval Texts), Edinburgh and London, 1951.

Mont Saint-Michel: Millénaire monastique du Mont Saint-Michel (4 vols., Paris, 1966-7).

Murphy, T. P., *The Holy War* (Columbus, Ohio, 1976).

Musset, L., *Les actes de Guillaume le Conquérant et de la reine Mathilde pour les abbayes caennaises* (Mémoires de la Société des Antiquaires de Normandie, xxxvii), Caen, 1967.

Northier, G., *Les Bibliothèques des abbayes bénédictines de Normandie* (Paris, 1971).

Orderic: *The Ecclasiastical History of Orderic Vitalis*, ed. and trans. Marjorie Chibnall (Oxford Medieval Texts, 6 vols.), Oxford, 1968-80.

Pfaff, R., 'The *Abbreviatio Amalarii* of William of Malmesbury', *RTAM*, xlvii (1980), 77–113, xlviii (1981), 128–71.

Porée, A. A., *Histoire de l'abbaye du Bec* (2 vols., Évreux, 1901).

Prestwich, J. O., 'The military household of the Norman kings', *EHR*, xcvi (1981), 1–35.

Renaissance and Renewal in the Twelfth Century, ed. R. L. Benson and Giles Constable (Harvard University Press, 1982).

RHC Occ.: Recueil des historiens des croisades, Historiens occidentaux (Paris, 1841–1906).

Robinson, J. Armitage, *Gilbert Crispin, Abbot of Westminster* (Cambridge, 1911).

RS: Rolls Series (Chronicles and Memorials of Great Britain and Ireland during the Middle Ages).

RSB: Rule of St. Benedict (References are to the edition and translation of Abbot Justin McCann (London, 1952)).

RTAM: Recherches de théologie ancienne et médiévale

Smalley, Beryl, *Studies in Medieval Thought and Learning from Abelard to Wyclif* (London, Hambledon Press, 1981).

——, *The Study of the Bible in the Middle Ages* (2nd edn., Oxford, 1952).

Southern, R. W., 'Aspects of the European tradition of historical writing', *TRHS*, 5th ser., xxi (1971), 159–79; xxiii (1973), 243–64.

——, *Medieval Humanism and other Studies* (Oxford, 1970).

——, *St. Anselm and his Biographer* (Cambridge, 1963).

——, *The Making of the Middle Ages* (London, 1953).

Statuta Petri Venerabilis, ed. Giles Constable (*CCM*, vi), Siegburg, 1975, pp. 21–106.

Stock, Brian, *The Implications of Literacy* (Princeton, 1983).

Studies in Church History:

　　Vol. viii, *Popular Belief and Practice*, ed. C. J. Cuming and D. Baker (Cambridge, 1972).

　　Vol. x, *Sanctity and Secularity*, ed. D. Baker (Oxford, 1973).

　　Vol. xi, *The Materials, Sources, and Methods of Ecclesiastical History*, ed. D. Baker (Oxford, 1975).

　　Vol. xii, *Church, Society and Politics*, ed. D. Baker (Oxford, 1975).

　　Vol. xv, *Religious Motivation*, ed. D. Baker (Oxford, 1978).

　　Vol. xx, *The Church and War*, ed. W. J. Sheils (Oxford, 1983).

Suger, *Vita Ludovici*, ed. and trans. H. Waquet (Les classiques de l'histoire de France au Moyen Âge, xi), Paris, 1929.

Torigny, Interpolations: Robert of Torigny's interpolations in the *Gesta Normannorum ducum* of William of Jumièges (see Marx).

TRHS: Transactions of the Royal Historical Society.

van Houts, E. M. C., *Gesta Normannorum ducum* (Groningen, 1982).

VCH: The Victoria History of the Counties of England (references are given in the form *VCH Shropshire*, etc.).

Vernier, J. J., *Chartes de l'abbaye de Jumièges* (Société de l'histoire de Normandie, Rouen and Paris, 1916).

Vita Gauzlini: Vie de Gauzlin, abbé de Fleury, ed. R.-H. Bautier and Gillette Labory (Paris, CNRS, 1969).

Vita Herlewini, ed. J. Armitage Robinson, *Gilbert Crispin, Abbot of Westminster* (Cambridge, 1911).

von Moos, P. *Hildebert von Lavardin* (Pariser historische Studien, iii), Stuttgart, 1965.

Wace: *Le Roman de Rou de Wace*, ed. A. J. Holden (Société des anciens textes français, 3 vols. in 2), Paris, 1970–3.

Walter Map, *De nugis curialium*, ed. and trans. M. R. James, revised C. N. L. Brooke and Roger Mynors (Oxford Medieval Texts), Oxford, 1983.

William of Poitiers: *Guillaume de Poitiers, Histoire de Guillaume le Conquérant*, ed. and trans. R. Foreville (Les classiques de l'histoire de France au Moyen Âge, xxiii), Paris, 1952.

Wiseman, T. P., *Clio's Cosmetics* (Leicester, 1979).

(The) Writing of History in the Middle Ages (Essays presented to Richard William Southern), ed. R. H. C. Davis and J. M. Wallace-Hadrill (Oxford, 1981).

Yver, J., 'Autour de l'absence d'avouerie en Normandie', *BSAN*, lvii (1965 for 1963–4), 189–283.

——, 'Les châteaux-forts en Normandie', *BSAN*, liii (1957 for 1955–6), 28–115.

Index

Abbreviations ab.: abbot; abp.: archbishop; bp.: bishop; ct.: count; d.: duke; kg.: king.

Abbo, ab. of Fleury 172
Abdias, bp. of Babylon 179
Abingdon, abbey
    chronicle of 112-13
Adelais of Le Puiset 14
Adelard, priest of Le Sap 78
Adelina of Warenne 131
Adeline, wife of Rotrou I ct. of Perche 25
Adhémar of Chabannes 96-7, 134
Adrevald, monk of Fleury 172
advocates, lay 48
Agnes of Burgundy, wife of Geoffrey Martel 50
Africa 205, 207
Aigle, L' (Orne) 40
    castle of 211
    lords of 25-6, 228; *and see* Engenulf, Gilbert, Richer
Ailred of Rievaulx
    his *Speculum caritatis* 72
Aimoin of Fleury 172, 173
Albereda, wife of ct. Raoul of Ivry 26
Alberic, ab. of Cîteaux 83
Albert of Aix 154 n.
Alençon (Orne) 5, 22, 24
Alexander II, pope 139, 154 n.
Alexius Comnenus, emperor 127
Alfonso I (the Battler), kg. of Aragón 123, 152, 204-7
Alfred the Giant 101
'Ali ben Yousuf 205, 207
Almoravides 205
Alnwick 140 n.
Alton (Hants.), treaty of 197-9
Alward, son of Edmund 6
Amadeus of Savoy 77
Amalarius of Metz
    his *De officiis* 87-8
Amaury of Montfort 27, 199-200, 203
    his chaplain 199-200
Ambrose, St 61
Amieria, wife of Warin the Bald 5

Anacletus II, rival pope, *see* Peter Pierleonis
Andrew of Fleury 101, 172
    his writings 109
Angelramnus, abbot of Saint-Riquier 93
Angers
    abbey of Saint-Serge 49
Angevins 41, 118
    invade Normandy 196
Anjou 22, 23, 27 *et passim*
    counts of, *see* Fulk, Geoffrey
Ansbert, St 111
Ansegisus, ct. 112
Anselm, St, abp. of Canterbury, ab. of Bec-Hellouin 15, 76-7, 80, 83, 86, 149, 201
    his *Cur Deus homo* 156-7, 160
    his letters 30
    his spiritual discourses 72, 73, 142-3, 146
Anselm of Laon 89-90, 98
    Commentary on Matthew attributed to 91, 95-7
Ansered, monk of Saint-Evroult 78
Ansger, son of Gradeloc 55
Ansold of Maule 35, 67 n., 120, 123
Anthony, St 79
Antioch 123, 127-8, 151
    battle of 209
Apulia 14, 21, 106 n.
archers 13, 140, 143
Argenteuil (Seine-et-Oise), dependency of Saint-Denis 64
Arnold, ab. of Saint-Pierre-le-Vif, Sens 173, 175
Arnold, son of Giroie 132
Arnold, son of William Talvas 22
Arnold of Échauffour 75
Arnold of Le Tilleul, monk of Saint-Evroult 15, 56
Arnulf, bp. of Lisieux 200
Arnulf, precentor of Chartres 102

Arundel (Sussex) 5
Ascelin, son of Arthur 124
Ascelin Goel 26
Atcham, church of St Eata 3, 10, 221
Athelelm of Fly 17 n.
Aubrey, wife of William of Moulins-la-Marche 125
Audoin, bp. of Évreux 199–200
Auffay (Seine-Maritime)
    priory of Saint-Evroult 18; patrons of, 35
Augustine, St
    his writings 91, 97
    his *De concordia evangelistarum* 96, 97
    his *Commentary on the Gospel of John* 96
    on history 170
    on just wars 145
    on spiritual warfare 70
Augustinian rule 83
Avice of Auffay 35
Aymer of Narbonne 205

Babylonian captivity 158
banners, blessed 139, 143
Barbastro 147 n., 152 n.
Bari 106
Bartholomew, St 108
Basil I, emperor 110 n.
Basilia, wife of Gerard de Gournay 80, 81
Battle (Sussex) 6
    abbey 6
        chronicle of 6, 112–13
Baudry, ab. of Bourgueil 17 n., 148, 158, 165
Baudry(?) of Bray 212
Baudry, son of Baudry of Bocquencé 55
Bavent (Calvados) 129
Bayeux (Calvados)
    bp. of, *see* Odo
    dean of 17
    priory of Saint-Vigor 54
    tapestry 185 n.
Beaumont, family of 23, 26
Beauvais 110
Bec-Hellouin, abbey 20, 53
    ab. of 80, 81, *and see* Anselm, Herluin
    monks of 20, 49, 76
    books of 87 n., 176

customs of 65–6
school of 93
its dependent priories 49, 212 n.
Bede 10, 41, 114, 174, 177, 179, 216, 220
    his *Chronicle* 171, 174, 177
    his *Ecclesiastical History of the English People* 34, 177, 213, 219 n.
    his scriptural commentaries 91, 97
Bellême (Orne) 24, 25, 119
    family of 20, 21, 22, 23–5, 50, 52, *and see* Mabel, Robert, William Talvas
Benedict VIII, pope 112
Benedict, St
    Rule of 9, 29 n., 45, 58, 61, 64, 70, 78
        on election of abbot 60
        on child oblates 73
        on manual work 66, 90, 113
        on sacred reading 66, 90–1
        respect for eremitism 80
        adaptability of 82–4, 90–1, 194
    monastic customs of 58, 64, 103
    miracles of 101, 105 n., 172, 174
    relics of 111 n., 172, 174
Benedict, son of Odelerius, monk of Shrewsbury 16, 36
Benedictine monasteries 7, 45, 73, 82–5, 87
Berengar of Tours 164–5
    accused of heresy 162–3
Bernard, monk of Saint-Evroult 75
Bernard, St, ab. of Clairvaux 61, 85, 148
    on the Song of Songs 91–2
    his brother 105 n.
Bernard of Cluny 65
Bernard of Tiron 83
Bernay, abbey 61
Bertha, wife of Philip I 129
Bertrade of Montfort, wife of (1) Fulk le Rechin, (2) Philip I 128–9, 131
Bertrand of Laon, ct. of Carrión 205
Bertrand Rumex 210
Bessin 103
Bible
    historical (literal) interpretation of 94, 158, 181
    allegorical interpretation of 94, 158, 181

tropological (moral) interpretation of 94, 181
glossed 92, 93
Vulgate translation of 9
Gospels, canonical 177, 179; apocryphal 179
gospel harmonies 92, 96-9
psalms 86, 90
commentaries, on the Gospels 91, 95-7, 99; on the Acts of the Apostles 91; on the Pauline epistles 91, 93, 95, 96; on the Apocalypse 91; on the Psalter 92, 93, 95, 96; on Lamentations 94; on the Song of Songs 91, 93; on the Book of Tobit 91
biblical studies
in monasteries 87, 90-9, 113, 157-8
of the Old Testament 156, 187-8
Sentences 92, 95, 98; of Peter Lombard, 93
Billeheld, wife of Baudry of Bocquencé 55
biography
lives of the apostles 177, 179
lives of bishops and abbots 107, 109, 113, 172-3, 174
lives of popes (*Liber pontificalis*) 171, 172-3, 174-5, 177
lives of monarchs 173
Blois 153, 155
blood feud 130, 135
Bobbio, monastery 58
Bocquencé (Orne), bull of 104
Bohemond, prince of Antioch 127-8, 161
Boiano, ct. of
his daughter 142
Bollandists 105, 179
Bourgthéroulde (Eure), battle of 140 n., 142, 143
Brémule (Eure), battle of 137, 140 n., 202
Breteuil, lords of 26
Brian fitz Count 200
Brionne (Eure) 20 n., 24
Brittany 83
Bruno, St, the Carthusian 95
Brut y Tywysogyon (Chronicle of the Princes) 120
Bures-sur-Dive (Calvados) 14

Burgundius of Pisa 96
Burgundy
eremitical movement in 83
monastic reform in 59; *and see* Cluny

Cadwgan ap Bleddyn 120
Caen (Calvados) 27-8
abbey of La Trinité 53, 64, 74 n.
abbey of Saint-Étienne 53, 124, 187, 218
chronicle of 206-7, 208
council at (1047) 134
Calabria 51
Calixtus II, pope 158-9, 198, 199-200
Cambrai 36, 37
abbey of St Sepulchre 36
ritual of 143-4
Cambrésis 62
canons, secular
replaced by monks 18 n., 46, 47-8, 56-7
Canterbury (Kent) 86, 175
abp. of *see* Anselm, Lanfranc, Ralph d'Escures
abbey of St Augustine 103, 107
priory of Christ Church 66
Carenton (Manche) 135
Cassiodorus
his historical work 169
his scriptural commentaries 91
castellans 21, 25, 35, 46
in Normandy 23, 47, 122
in France 23, 46-7
castles 4, 5, 6, 7, 11, 21, 22, 24, 26, 28, 46-7, 68-9, 139, 211
collegiate churches in 47, 57
priories in 25, 47-8, 57
monasteries used as 51, 64 n.
analogy of spiritual castles 146
Cecilia, wife of Tancred, prince of Antioch 142
Centule of Béarn 205
Cérisy (Manche), monastery of Saint-Vigor 101
Chambrais (Eure)
frarria bacalariorum in 68
castle of 68-9
chansons 140, 141 n., 143, 145, 152 n., 175, 204, 207, 212, 216
de Roland 138
d'Antioche 204
de Guillaume 207-8

chansons (cont.)
  de Raoul de Cambrai 132
Chapelle-en-Vexin, La (Oise)
  priory of Saint-Evroult at 27
Charlton (Shropshire) 8, 10
charters 21 n., 49, 50, 63, 101, 107,
  119, 206
  narrative 175
  of Saint-Evroult 29 n., 31, 35, 48,
    55–6
  of Fécamp 61, 112
  of Saint-Étienne de Caen 187
Chartres
  bp. of *see* Fulbert, Ivo
  cathedral church of 128; its lands
    25
  diocese of 35–6, 136
  abbey of Saint-Père 49–50
Chaumont-en-Vexin (Oise) 137
Cheshire 15
Chester
  diocese of 8
  earl of *see* Hugh of Avranches,
    Ranulf, Richard
Childebert II, kg. of the Franks 103
Childebert III, kg. of the Franks 103
chivalry, concept of 138, 139–40, 145
churches
  given to monasteries 63, 78, 83
  proprietary 47, 63
  minster 6, 16
  collegiate 46–7, 56–7
Cicero 145, 196
Cistercians 72, 92, 210, 217
Cîteaux, abbey 77 n.
  ab. of *see* Alberic, Stephen Harding
Clarius, monk of Saint-Pierre-le-Vif
  173 n.
Clement of Lanthony 98, 99
Clermont, council of (1095) 130, 148,
  150, 186
Cluny, abbey 20, 48, 76
  and monastic reform 60–1
  and peace movement 118
  exemption of 60–1
  ab. of *see* Peter the Venerable,
    Pontius
  liturgy of 60, 65, 77, 90
  customs of 37, 60, 65
  general chapter of 37, 48, 60
  statutes of 60, 74
  monks of 46, 146, 164
  abbeys and priories dependent on
    16, 48, 54, 60, 210
  monasteries influenced by 87, *and
    see* Saint-Evroult
Cologne, abp. of 158
Columbanus, St 80, 194
  monastic customs of 58, 61, 103
commemoration
  of benefactors 67, 113
  of patron saints 101
Compostela 149, 210
Conan, son of Gilbert Pilatus 211
Constantinople 123, 137, 161
conversi, adult converts to monastic
  life 15, 16
  in earlier Benedictine monasteries
    73–8, 86
  in Cistercian monasteries 79
Corbet, vassal of Roger of Mont-
    gomery 5
Corbonnais 25
Cordova 205
coronation 121
  of English kings 41, 182–3, 185,
    188–9, 190
corrody 55
Cotentin 50, 125
Coulombs, abbey
  monks of 83–4
councils and synods 8, *and see* Caen,
    Clermont, Lillebonne, Li-
    moges, Lisieux, Mainz,
    Rheims, Rome, Rouen,
    Tours, Vercelli, Winchester
court
  knights trained and invested in 132,
    142, 144
  culture of 203–4, 217
  royal and ducal 75, 120–1, 195;
    English 176; Frankish 104
  feudal 57, 119; at Maule 35, 120;
    of abbots 62
  papal 159, 216
Cronica Adefonsi 206
Crowland, abbey 36, 107–8, 218
  hermits of 80, 107
  ab. of *see* Geoffrey of Orleans
crusade 127–8, 147 n., 150, 154, 161,
  209
  first 24, 31, 32, 151, 152, 158,
    161, 204
  in Spain 25, 154 n., 202
  indulgences for 151
crusaders

attack Jews and heretics 154-5, 161
crusading songs 150
Cuno, cardinal bp. of Palestrina 199
customs, monastic 45, 58, 62, 65-6, 87, *and see* Bec-Hellouin, Benedict, Cluny, Columbanus, Fruttuaria, Hirsau, Lanfranc, Saint-Evroult
Cuthbert, St 41, 101
Cyprus 109

Darb Samada, battle of 142
David, kg. of Scotland 190, 193
De obitu Willelmi 187
demesne land
    monastic 63
    royal 119
Demetrius, St 15
Dijon
    abbey of Saint-Bénigne 46, 49, 60, 65
    ab. of *see* William of Volpiano
Domesday Book 3, 4 n.
Domesday survey 3, 5, 6, 64
Domfront (Orne) 5, 22, 105
Drogo of Commeaux 119
Drogo of Neufmarché, monk of Saint-Evroult 15
Dudo of Saint-Quentin
    his *History of the Normans* 112, 175-6, 214
Durand, ab. of Troarn 162
Durand, monk of Saint-Evroult 77
Durazzo 127, 161
Durham, priory of 101, 175
    hermits of 80

Eadbald, kg. of Kent 10
Eadmer 154, 155
Ebro, valley of 123, 152, 205
Échauffour (Orne) 26, 104
Écouché (Orne) 129
Edessa 151
Edgar Atheling 184
Edric the Wild 4, 12
education, of boys 11, 76, 132-3
Edward the Confessor, kg. of England 3, 4, 6, 12
    his alleged virginity 176
    designates his successor 184, 185
Edwin, earl of Mercia 3-4, 11, 195
Ekkehard of Aura 173

election
    freedom of 29 n., 60-1, 192
    abbatial 28-31, 60, 192
    of bishops 182
Ely, abbey of 107
Emma, daughter of Roger I of Sicily 129
Emma, half-sister of Robert of Grandmesnil 81
Emma, wife of Guitmund of Moulins-la-Marche 49-50
endowments, monastic 175
    in cash and bullion 17, 63
    in estates 20, 21, 23, 63
    possession justified 127
    defended 107, 109, 112-13, 193
    and see churches, tithes
Engenulf of L'Aigle 26
England 23, 27, 40 *et passim*
    conquest of 124, 139 *and see* Normans
    succession to the crown of 131, 182-7
    problem of union with Normandy 182-7
    kings of 26 *and see* Edward the Confessor, Henry I, Henry II, Stephen, William I, William II; their burial places 53-4
Ermenfrid of Sion, papal legate
    his penitential ordinances 127, 139
Ethelwold, St 34
Eusebius, bp. of Caesarea
    his historical writings 169, 170, 174, 177, 178, 216
Eva, wife of William Crispin 80, 81
Everard, son of Odelerius 36
Évreux 198
    bp. of 31, *and see* Audoin
    ct. of 27, 195, *and see* Richard, William
    county of 27
Évroul, St 9, 36, 58
    life and miracles of 38 n., 101-8, 194
excommunication 25, 129, 133, 165, 192
exemption, monastic 60, *and see* Cluny, Fécamp, papacy
Exmes (Orne) 22

Fécamp

Fécamp (*cont.*)
  collegiate church founded 45–6
  abbey of, 46, 49
    customs of 65, 66
    exemption of 61, 112
    books of 87 n.
    monks of 98
    early history of 111–12
    ab. of *see* John of Fécamp, William of Rots, William of Volpiano
Felix, his *Life of St Guthlac* 107
Felix de Brie, ab. of Saint-Evroult 220
Ferrières-Saint-Hilaire (Eure) 68–9
Ferté-Frênel, La (Eure)
  castle of 211
Flanders 4, 137
Flemings 118
  in Wales 13
  monasteries of 66
Fleury-sur-Loire (Saint-Benoît-sur-Loire), abbey 53, 101, 172–3
  ab. of *see* Gauzlin
Fontenelle *see* Saint-Wandrille
Fontevrault, abbey 164 n.
forgery
  of narrative records 107, 109, 111, 194, 208 n.
  of charters 112
Fraga, siege and battle of 152, 204–8, 214
France 8 n., 22, 35 *et passim*
  kings of 26, 35, 123; their burial places 53; *and see* Henry I, Louis VI, Louis VII, Philip I
Frangipani, family of 159
fraternities, monastic 35 n., 67–8, *and see* Saint-Evroult
Friardel (Calvados) 78
Fruttuaria, abbey
  customs of 65
Fulbert, bp. of Chartres
  his pupils 93, 102
Fulcher, bp. of Lisieux 32
Fulda, abbey 73
  ab. of *see* Raban Maur
Fulk IV (le Rechin), ct. of Anjou 128–9
Fulk V, ct. of Anjou 131, 210
Fulk Nerra, ct. of Anjou 50

Gacé (Orne) 129

Gaimar, Geoffroi 213
  his *Estoire des Engleis* 204, 214, 217
Gauzlin, ab. of Fleury
  Life of 109
Genoese 159
Geoffrey, abp. of Rouen 199
Geoffrey, bp. of Vendôme 149–50
Geoffrey, ct. of Anjou, son of Fulk V 40, 149, 189, 217
Geoffrey (Martel), ct. of Anjou, son of Fulk Nerra 50
Geoffrey of Malaterra 129–30, 141–2, 213
Geoffrey of Mayenne 20
Geoffrey II of Mortagne, son of Rotrou ct. of Perche 25–6, 130
Geoffrey of Orleans, ab. of Crowland, monk of Saint-Evroult 36, 75, 107–8
George, St 15
Gerald of Wales 181
Gerard, monk of Cluny 82
Gerard de Brogne, 59, 60
Gerberoy (Oise)
  castle of 142
Gerold of Aurillac, St 133
Gerold of Avranches, chaplain 15, 77
Gesta Francorum, anonymous 158
Ghent 111
  abbey of Saint-Pierre of Mont Blandain 59
  abbey of Saint-Bavon 59
Gilbert, bp. of Poitiers
  his scriptural commentaries 92
Gilbert, monk of Saint-Evroult 75
Gilbert, son of Richer of L'Aigle 26, 31
Gilbert Crispin, ab. of Westminster
  his *Life of Herluin* 119
  his *Disputatio Iudei et Christiani* 156–7, 160
Gilbert Foliot, bp. of Hereford 200–1
Gilbert Maminot, bp. of Lisieux 30–1, 32, 186, 224
  his watchman 186
Gilbert of Brionne, ct.
  his court 119–20
Gilbert of L'Aigle, son of Engenulf 130
gilds, religious 68 n.
Giroie 20
  family of 20–2, 22, 24, 35, 50, 218, 226

his sons *see* Arnold, Hugh, Robert, William
Gisors (Eure) 198, 200
  castle of 211-12
Glanfeuil, abbey 194
Glanvill
  on villeins who become knights 141 n.
Glastonbury, abbey
  chronicle from 112
Gloucester 3
Godebold, clerk 7, 8
Godeschalk 73-4
Goisbert of Chartres, monk of Saint-Evroult 15, 75
Goldcliff, priory of Bec-Hellouin 212 n.
Gomerfontaine (in Trie-la-Ville) 106
Goscelin, monk of Saint-Evroult 75
Goscelin of Saint-Bertin 107
Gradeloc, knight 55
Grandcamp (Eure) 68
Grandmesnil
  family of 20 n., 21, 22, 23, 50, 81, 126, 217-18, 227
  and see Hugh, Pernel, Robert
Gratian 145
Gravençon (Seine-Maritime) 129
Gregory I, pope 91, 93
Grestain, abbey 49
Guibert of Nogent, ab. of Nogent
  his education 11
  monk at Saint-Germer-de-Fly 76, 154
  his memoirs 78
  his scriptural commentaries 94
  his attitude to Jews 154-5, 160
  his treatise on the Incarnation 157
  his mother 11
Guitmund, ab. of La Croix-Saint-Leufroi 184
Guitmund, monk of Saint-Evroult 102
Guitmund of Moulins-la-Marche 25, 49-50
Guthlac, St 34
  Life of 107-8
Guy of Brionne 20 n.
Gyrth, brother of Harold Godwinson 183-4

hagiography *see* saints, lives of
  tastes in 100-1, 105, 172
  of the Bollandists 105
Haimo of Auxerre

  his scriptural commentaries 91
Harold Godwinson, kg. of England (Jan.-Oct. 1066) 11, 126, 135, 183-4, 185, 188, 192
Harvey, son of Gradeloc 55
Haspres (Nord), priory of Jumièges 59
Hastings (Senlac), battle of 3, 5, 26, 126-7, 135, 184
  malfosse episode in 183
  song of Roland at 204
Haughmond (Shropshire), abbey 13
Hauteville, lords of 126 *and see* Tancred
heirs, designated 120, 124-5, 129, 187, 195 n.
  plunder of rightful 126-7
  and see inheritance
Helgaud, monk of Fleury 172
Helias, ct. of Maine 139, 149, 163
Helisende, mother of William ct. of Eu 154
Helwise, wife of William ct. of Évreux 195
Henry IV, emperor 154
Henry V, emperor 209
Henry II, German kg., emperor 146
Henry I (Beauclerc), kg. of England (1100-35) 27, 38, 40, 126, 139, 176, 188
  invested as a knight 144
  holds Domfront 28, 105
  his right of succession 183, 189-90; his coronation 219
  his marriage 200-1, 214
  his rule in Normandy 32-3, 189-90
  pacifies Shropshire 13
  fosters monasteries 13, 196; influences elections 193
  meets Robert Curthose at Alton 197-8; defeats him *see* Tinchebray
  prevents William Clito's marriage 130-1
  visits Saint-Evroult 35
  attacked at the Council of Rheims 198-9
  meets Calixtus II at Gisors 198, 200
  praised by chroniclers *see* Orderic Vitalis, William of Malmesbury
  his court 120-1, 190; his household troops 27, 120, 123, 135, 141-3, 203, 212

Henry I (Beauclerc) (*cont.*)
  his daughter *see* Matilda; his son *see* William; his wife *see* Matilda
Henry II, kg. of England (1154–89) 120, 188, 217
Henry I, kg. of France 195
Henry, son of Bernier 132
Henry, son of David kg. of Scotland, 131
Henry of Lausanne 163–5
herald 120, 121
Herbert Losinga, bp. of Norwich 66
Herbert of Montreuil, monk of Saint-Evroult 75
Herbert the Grammarian, archdeacon of Shropshire 7–8
Hereford
  bp. of *see* Gilbert Foliot, Robert
  earl of *see* Roger, William fitz Osbern
Herefordshire 4
heresy 153, 161–2
  schism as 159, 163
  of the Saracens 161 n.
heretics 160, 161–5
  Arians 162
  Eutychians 162
  Paulicians 161
  Pelagians 162
  and see Berengar of Tours, Henry of Lausanne, Peter of Bruys
Hereward the Wake 12, 212 n.
Herluin, ab. of Bec-Hellouin 76–7, 119–20
hermits 48, 79–80, 90, 104, 107
  attached to monasteries 80, 81
Herodotus 169–70
Hiémois 5, 23, 190
  vicomte of *see* Roger of Montgomery
Hildebert of Lavardin, bp. of Le Mans 17 n., 149, 163–4
Hiltrude, wife of William Giroie 26, 226
Hirsau, customs of 102 n.
history
  of the Church 114, 170, 174, 177–8, 216
  universal 36, 113, 170, 172, 173–4, 215
  chronicles 36, 169, 172, 173, 176, 177, 216
  annals 169, 170, 173, 174, 177

apocalyptic 181
of monasteries 37, 45, 109, 111–12, 177
of peoples 174–6
of families 175, 176, 204
Greek 194 n., 203 *and see* Herodotus, Thucydides
Roman 194 n., 203
vernacular 216, 217
sources of, oral 170, 171, 175, 194, 201, 207–8; written 170–5, 192 *and see* Orderic Vitalis
rhetoric in 196–7
influence of poetry on 203–8
homilies 92, 95, 96, 98, 103, 146, 157, 217
horses 55–6, 137, 140, 207, *and see* knights
hospitals 84
households 57
  chaplains in 7, 15, 120, 121, 133
  of Gilbert Maminot 186
  of Hugh, earl of Chester 15, 77, 119
  of Roger of Montgomery 7, 14
  household troops *see* Henry I, knights, William I, William II
Hubert, monk of Saint-Evroult 102
Hugh, bp. of Lisieux 54
Hugh, ct. of Meulan 76
Hugh, son of Giroie 132
Hugh Bunel 24 n., 151
Hugh l'Asne 4
Hugh de Barzelle 72
Hugh of Avranches, earl of Chester 15
  his court 77, 119
Hugh of Flavigny 172
Hugh of Fleury 172
Hugh of Grandmesnil 21, 23, 77
Hugh of Le Puiset 136
Hugh of St Victor 174, 219 n.
Humphrey de Vieilles 49
hunting 15, 119, 132, 143

Ibn-el-Athir 206
Île de France 24, 35, 62, 118, 120
Ingelmar, knight of Roger I of Sicily 141–2
inheritance
  rights of 121–8, 129, 187, 191, 198; in the kingdom of England 184–5, 187–90
  of churches 8, 10, 29 n.
  of castles 46–7

of fiefs 122
of judicial rights 46-7
by parage 122
of acquisitions 124
and see heir, patrimony
Innocent II, pope 95, 163, 164, 193, 200-1
insignia, royal 53, 186-7
interdict 133, 192
investiture 29, 182, 191
iron-works 70
Isaac, ab. of L'Étoile 98 n.
Isabel of Conches (Tosny) 195
Isabella, wife of Robert of Candos 211-12
Isembard of Fleury 106 n.
Isidore of Seville 97, 169, 170, 171, 191, 213, 216
his scriptural commentaries 91
Italy 137
monastic reform in 59, 61, 80
Normans in 21, 76, 123, 125, 141-2, 176
Ivo, bp. of Chartres 32, 35, 129, 136
his letters 84
Ivo, bp. of Sées, lord of Bellême 22
Ivry, castle of 26

Jacob b. Yekutiel 153
Jarrow, monastery 220
Jerome, St 38-9, 40, 97, 114, 156
his writings 91, 169, 170
Jerusalem 24, 32, 75, 148, 149, 150, 151, 210
kingdom of 41, 123, 151
celestial 150
Jews 146, 152-61, 165
conversion of 153-5
disputations with Christians 155 n., 156-7
their customs 157-8
their laws 82, 156, 158, 184, 187, 188 n.
John, bp. of Lisieux 32-3, 41, 221
John Chrysostom, St 96
John Comnenus, emperor 128
John of Avranches, abp. of Rouen 9
his *De officiis ecclesiasticis* 87
John of Bari 106
John of Fécamp, ab. of Fécamp 61, 91
John of Rheims, monk of Saint-

Evroult 15-16, 34, 38, 75, 78, 176
his studies at Rheims 95
his writings 95, 97, 102
John of Saint-Victor 215
John of Salisbury
his *Policraticus* 144-5
his *Historia Pontificalis* 200-1, 215-16
John of Worcester 36, 37, 175
jongleurs 133, 204, 207, 208, 212
Josephus 169
Joslin of Mareil 120
Jotsaldus, Cluniac monk 146
jousting 137-8
Judith, wife of Richer of L'Aigle 26
Judith, wife of Roger I ct. of Sicily 51, 81
Judoc, St
cult of 106
Juliana, wife of Gilbert of L'Aigle 26
Jumièges, abbey 58, 67 n., 68
prior of 74
monks of 59, 74, 76, 101
its books 87 n., 101
its property 62
priory of *see* Haspres

Kent 17
knighthood 140, 208
influence of church on 121, 143-5, 182
professional and secular 140-2, 144, 145
acquires social significance 141
belt of 132, 133, 142; ceremony of investment with 142-4
knights 4, 5, 50 *et passim*
essential equipment of, horses 55-6, 133, 140, 142-3; arms and armour 133, 143
as fighting 'order' 64, 117
training of 119, 132-3
as a professional class 117, 132-3, 140
attend their lord's court 119-20
as landed vassals 122, 123, 138
dubbed 143
their battle tactics 140-1, 202-3
English 5; French 139, 140, 150; of Maule 203; of Henry Beauclerc 105; of Ivo bp. of

knights (*cont.*)

Chartres 136; of King Stephen 138

household 55, 77, 137 *and see* Henry I, William I, William II

of Mabel of Bellême, 14, 52; of Hugh earl of Chester 15; of Richer of L'Aigle 51

stipendiary 27, 55, 120, 123, 138, 152

form prayer unions 68-9; frequent the cloister 35, 123, 216

become monks 15, 76-7, 133

as sources of news 202, 210-13

Christian 15, 133, 150, 152, *and see milites Christi*

monks as Christ's knights 146

serf knights 141 n.

Lambert, uncle of Lambert of Wattrelos 120

Landry, advocate of Orbec 202

Lanfranc, abp. of Canterbury 9, 29, 30

as a monk of Bec 76

his teaching 93

his monastic customs 66, 84

his scriptural commentaries 93, 99

invests knights 144

crowns William Rufus 185, 187

opposes Berengar of Tours 162

his gifts to Saint-Evroult 17

language

English 10, 11

French 10, 11

Latin 10, 11, 86, 175, 209

Laon, schools at 89-90, 93, 95

Larchamp, battle of 208

law 182, 185, 190

canon 118, 128-32, 133, 136, 191, 192

divine 186

secular 130-2, 133, 137

customary 118, 123, 190, 191

English 126

Norman 122

Roman 191

Jewish 156, 184, 187, 188 n.; of Moses 82, 158

natural 53 n.

lay brothers 55, 79

legates, papal 139

legends 11, 12-13, 18, 45, 104, 105, 212

of saints 38, 45, 100, 102, 204

Le Riche, family of 35 *and see* Ansold, Peter of Maule

Leicester, earls of 23, 217 *and see* Robert

Lesceline, wife of William of Arques 49

lèse majesté 126, 190

Lessay, abbey of 49

Leudegard, St 112

liberal arts

schools of 75, 78, 81, 92

grammar 93, 171, 202

dialectic (logic) 92, 93

rhetoric 92, 93, 171, 196-7, 201, 202, 203

libraries, monastic 18, 33, 86, 89, 91, 94, 99, 172-3

Lillebonne (Seine-Maritime), council of (1080) 134, 192

Limoges, council of (994) 133-4

abbey of Saint-Martial 150

Lincoln

battle of 41, 138, 141 n., 189

castle of 211

Lire, abbey of 92

Lisieux

abbey of Saint-Pierre 49

abbey of Saint-Désir (Notre-Dame-du-Pré) 54

bp. of 28, 32, 221 *and see* Arnulf, Fulcher, Gilbert Maminot, Hugh, John

canons of *see* Osbern

council of (1064) 8-9

diocese of 33

literacy 30,144-5

Livy 169

London 184

tower of 32

Jews in 156, 161

Lotharingia 209

monastic reform in 59, 65

Louis VI, kg. of France 35, 129, 140 n., 192

at the council of Rheims 198, 199

Louis VII, kg. of France 150, 220

Lucé-le-Grand (Sarthe) 136

Luke of La Barre 126, 190

Mabel of Bellême, wife of Roger of

Montgomery 5, 16, 22–3, 52, 125
murdered 14, 24
magic 160
Maine 5, 14, 20, 27, 136, 139, 149, 165 *and see* Normans
eremitical movement in 83
ct. of 153 *and see* Helias
Mainer of Échauffour, ab. of Saint-Evroult 15, 17, 18, 27, 28, 45, 75, 124, 223, 224
Mainz
abp. of 154, 209
council of (829) 73
Jews in 146, 156
Malmesbury 175
Mans, Le (Sarthe)
bp. of *see* Hildebert
citadel of 138–9; Norman garrison of 138–9, 163, 211
canons of 163–4
cathedral of 163–4
Jews in 153
manual work
in Benedictine monasteries 66–7, 90, 98 n., 113, 194
revived by new orders 83
Marianus Scotus 172, 173, 174, 175, 209
marriage 128–32
church influence on 128–32, 144, 182
in secular law 130–2
inheritance secured by 10, 124, 130
status raised by 141–2
annulment of 130–1
consent in 128 n., 131
of clergy 7, 8–9, 78
of Joseph and Mary 158
Martial, St 96–7
Mary, the Blessed Virgin 95, 158
miracles of 157, 160, 165
Matilda, wife of William son of Henry I 131
Matilda, daughter of Henry I, wife of (1) Emperor Henry V, (2) Geoffrey of Anjou 41, 53–4, 131, 209
her claim to the English crown 188, 190, 193, 200–1
Matilda, queen, wife of Henry I 200–1, 214
Matilda, queen, wife of William the

Conqueror 5, 17, 53
Matilda of L'Aigle, wife of Roger Mowbray 124
Maule (Seine-et-Oise), priory of Saint-Evroult at 18, 35, 123, 216
monks of 129
Maurice, St 15, 133, 223
Maurilius, abp. of Rouen 9, 93
Maynard, ab. of Mont Saint-Michel 59
Meole, river 223
mercenaries 141–2 *and see* knights, stipendiary
Mercia, earls of 5 *and see* Edwin
merchants 121, 134, 160
Merlerault, Le (Orne) 17, 37
métayage 64
Meulan, ct. of 23, 26, 217 *and see* Hugh, Waleran
Michael, St 73, 110
milites Christi 146, 148, 150–1, 161
miller 202
mills 56 n., 63
mints, in England 6
miracles *see* Mary, saints
at Cana 157–8
monasteries
Benedictine 7, 45, 73, 82–5, 87; Columbanian 58, 61; Gallo-Roman 58, 61
interests of patrons in 21–3, 45, 48–57, 109
as providers of credit 54–6
hospitality owed by 18, 51–2
as lords of great estates 62–4
monastic life
as a form of martyrdom 70–3
prayer 86, 101, 178, 218; as a form of manual work 66; intercessory duty of monks 53, 54, 64, 67–8, 71–2, 113, 146; prayer unions 67–9, 210 *and see* commemoration, fraternities
almsgiving 67, 71
poverty, corporate 62; personal 62, 71–2
elements of eremitism in 80–3
liturgy 31, 33, 38, 66, 86–9, 139, 165, 194; saints' lives in 100, 101–2, 109; choral offices 100 n., 102; participation of *famuli* in 79; hymns 102, 218; *and see* Cluny, customs

monastic life (*cont.*)
  horarium 64–5, 90
  postulants 9, 15, 58, 72 *and see conversi*, oblates
  monastic officials, duties of 65; assisted by *famuli* 79; oblates excluded 74–6; almoner 67; cellarer 67; librarian (*armarius*) 33, (*bibliothecarius*) 33, 106 n.
  work in scriptorium 34, 90–1, 94, 113, 171 *and see* libraries
  monastic reading, sacred 66, 90–1; public in chapter, cloister, and refectory 90, 100, 113, 217
money fiefs 55, 123
money rents 63, 64
Mont Saint-Michel, abbey 55, 68, 93
  ab. of *see* Maynard
  customs of 65
  books of 87 n., 92
  Sacramentary of 65, 71
  dependent cell at Tombelaine 80
Monte Cassino, abbey 94
Montgomery-Bellême, family of 14, 25, 50, *and see* Mabel, Roger
Moors, in Spain 25, 123, 204, 205
Morcar, earl of Northumbria 11, 195
Mortagne 25, 152
  ct. of 22
mortgage 56
Morville (Shropshire) 37
Mosarabs 151, 152
Moses, law of 82, 158
Moulins-la-Marche (Orne)
  castle of 25
  priory of Saint-Evroult at 25
  lords of *see* Guitmund, William
Mowbray, Roger 124
Myra
  relics of St Nicholas at 106, 110 n.

Neufmarché (Seine-Inférieure) 23
  priory of Saint-Evroult at 23, 27, 157
Nicholas, St
  translation of 106
  relics of 106, 110 n.
  miracles of 107
Nigel of Aubigny 124
Norfolk, earl of *see* Ralph of Gael
Normandy 11 *et passim*

frontiers of 5, 14, 16, 21, 27, 28, 40, 50, 52
monastic reform in 58–62
succession to the duchy 182–3
dukes of *see* Richard I, Richard II, Richard III, Robert I, Robert II, William Longsword, William the Conqueror; their control of castles 47–8; their powers of jurisdiction 47, 134; their relations with the church 29–31, 35–6, 45–7, 48, 61; their burial places 53–4
exchequer in 32
trade and markets in 63, 211–12
Normans
  gens Normannorum 213–14
  their turbulence 118
  in England 5–7, 10–11, 65–6 *et passim*
  in Maine 27, 136, 138–9, 163, 211
  in Spain 152, 207–8
  in Wales 4, 5, 7, 12–13
  and see Italy
Noron (Calvados), priory of Saint-Evroult at 14, 18, 106
Norwich
  bp. of *see* Herbert Losinga
  cathedral priory of 66
Noyon-sur-Andelle (now Charleval) (Eure) 129
  priory of Saint-Evroult at 27

obituary rolls 68, 210
oblates (*nutriti*) 3, 14, 16, 72–6, 86, 132, 223
Odelerius of Orleans, son of Constantius 3, 7–11, 14, 16, 36, 70–1, 223
  his sons *see* Benedict, Everard, Orderic Vitalis
Odo, ab. of Marmoutier 150
Odo, bp. of Bayeux 30, 54, 192
Odo, bp. of Cambrai 157
Odo Borleng 203, 210
Odorannus of Sens 173, 175
Olbertus, ab. of Gembloux 93
Oliver 197, 214
ordeal, of hot iron 15
Orderic Vitalis
  his name 3 n., 221, 222

his early life and education 3, 9–16, 221–2

his life at Saint-Evroult 28–9, 31–41, 178, 222–5

his journeys 13, 36–7, 76, 107, 222

his contacts with Cluny 37, 164

his studies 95, 187–8

his work in the scriptorium 31–4, 95, 97, 179

his handwriting 157 n.

his death 41

his father, *see* Odelerius; his English mother 3, 9–10

his historical work 34–41

his interpolations in the *Gesta Normannorum ducum* of William of Jumièges 34, 176–7

his *Ecclesiastical History* 3, 34, 37, 97, 177–8 *et passim*; copied, 218–20

his *Life of Christ* 97, 99

writes lives of saints 38, 102–8

writes history of Crowland 107

his treatise on the new orders 83, 85, 194

composes verses 34

his oral sources 103, 104, 105, 108, 186, 194, 199, 202, 208

his written sources 103, 148, 158, 174, 179, 194

his use of invented speeches 197–9

on the monastic ideal 70–2

admires English saints 34, 107–8

defends William I 195–6; criticizes him 185–6, 195

admires Henry I 188–90, 196, 198–200, 217, 219

his interest in France 119

his ignorance of German history 209

his accounts of battles 202–8

on the morality of war 137–8

on the Council of Rheims 158–60, 198–200

on legitimate rule 183–93; on tyranny 191–3

on Jews 156–61

on heretics 161–5

orders in society 64, 88–9, 117, 149, 165

Ordric, priest of Atcham 10, 221

Origen 38–9

scriptural commentaries of 91

Orleans 8, 110, 153

Osbern (the steward) 101

Osbern, ab. of Saint-Evroult 67, 75, 102

previously canon of Lisieux 75

Otto of Freising 174, 215

Ouche, forest of 18, 20, 58, 104

Ouen, St 58, 101

outlaws 12, 13, 151

Pain of Gisors 211

Palermo 54

papacy

appeals to 31, 130–1, 153, 193

and exempt monasteries 60, 112

curia (court) 159, 216

papal legates 139

papal army 21

and see Alexander II, Benedict VIII, Calixtus II, Gregory I, Innocent II, Paschal II, Urban II

Paris

schools at 93, 201

Jews in 153

Parnes (Oise), priory of Saint-Evroult at 18, 27

cult of St Judoc at 106

Paschal II, pope 32, 193

Paschasius Radbertus

his commentary on Lamentations 94

patrimony 10, 20, 47, 50, 55, 122, 124–5, 152, 216 *and see* inheritance

of monasteries 62, 63, 101

of saints 111

Paul, St apostle 70

Paul the Deacon

his *History of the Lombards* 171

Pays de Caux 75

peace, king's 12, 27, 118–19

peace movement 118–19, 132, 133–40 *and see* Cluny, William I

in Normandy 118

Peace of God 118, 134

Truce of God 118, 134–6

monasteries as centres of, 51, 136

peasants 56, 105, 211

as labouring order 64, 117, 125 n.

protected by Truce of God 134–5

penitence 126–7, 134, 148, 186 *and see* Ermenfrid of Sion

Perche, ct. of 25-6, 152 *and see* Geoffrey, Rotrou
Pernel of Grandmesnil, wife of Robert II earl of Leicester 23 n.
Peter, ab. of Saint-Rémi, Rheims 201
Peter, St, apostle 73, 101, 110
Peter Leonis 158-9
    his son at the Council of Rheims 158-60
Peter Lombard
    his *Sentences* 93
Peter of Bruys 161, 164
Peter II of Maule 35, 120
Peter of Poitiers, Cluniac monk 82
Peter Pierleonis, son of Peter Leonis, rival pope Anacletus II 159, 163
Peter the Deacon
    his exegetical treatises 94
    on the tomb of St Benedict 111 n.
Peter the Venerable, ab. of Cluny 37, 87
    his statutes 74, 87 n.
    his views on eremitism 82
    his letter to St Bernard 85
    his treatises against Jews, Saracens, and heretics 161
Pharisees 158
Philbert, St 58
Philip I, kg. of France 28, 129, 131, 136, 195
Picardy 110
Picot of Sai 5, 119
Piedmont 61
Pierleoni, family of 159
pilgrimage
    to Rome 15, 16, 210
    to Jerusalem 75, 109, 148-9, 150, 210
    to Compostela 149, 210
    to Monte Gargano and Saint-Gilles 210
    to local centres 106, 108, 210
pilgrims 18, 84, 102, 104, 106, 134, 150, 210
    crusaders as 148, 154 n.
Pisa, council of (1135) 163, 164
Poitou 62, 164
Pont-Audemer (Eure) 139
Pont-Échanfray (now Notre-Dame du Hamel) (Eure) 27
    castle of 211
Pontius, ab. of Cluny 210

Préaux
    abbey of Saint-Pierre 49
Priscian 86
professions of obedience
    of abbots to diocesan bishops 29-31
    of monks 30 n.
Prosper of Aquitaine 170, 215
provostships, monastic 64
Pseudo-Abdias 179
Pseudo-Clement 179
Puiset, Le (Eure-et-Loir) 140 n.
purgatorial punishment 99, 202

quarries 17

Raban Maur, ab. of Fulda 73
    his scriptural commentaries 92
Rainald, ct. of Toul 209
Rainald of Bailleul 152
Ralph, ab. of Saint-Evroult 40, 224
Ralph, monk of Saint-Evroult 75, 102
Ralph d'Escures, abp. of Canterbury 102
Ralph fitz Gilbert 204
Ralph 'Ill-tonsured', son of Giroie 81
Ralph Mortimer 4
Ralph of Conches, *see* Ralph of Tosny
Ralph of Gael, earl of Norfolk 108, 192
Ralph of Laon 89
Ralph of Tosny (Conches), son of Roger of Tosny 31
Ralph Tête d'Âne, 129
Ralph the Red of Pont-Échanfray 26-7, 123, 127
Ramsey, abbey 107
ransoms 24, 137
Ranulf, earl of Chester 211
Ranulf Flambard, bp. of Durham 28, 32
Raoul of Ivry, ct. 26
Rashi, Jewish commentator 156 n.
Ravenna 61
Raymond, prince of Antioch 128
Reading abbey
    burial place of Henry I 54
Rebais (Seine-et-Marne), abbey 38 n., 98, 101, 102
reform
    ecclesiastical 8-10, 29 n., 33, 35-6, 47, 63, 90, 96-8, 114, 182
    monastic 51 *and see* Burgundy,

Cluny, Italy, Lotharingia, Normandy

Reginald Benedict, monk of Saint-Evroult 75-6

Reginald the Bald, monk of Saint-Evroult 102

Regularis concordia 66

relics of saints 59, 100, 102-3, 104, 106, 109, 175

  moved for safety 101, 106, 110

  discovered 110-11

  oaths sworn on 134, 205, 206

Rheims

  council of (1119) 36, 76, 158-60, 198-200, 201, 214

  abbey of Saint-Rémi 201

  schools at 95

  Jews in 153

Richard, ct. of Évreux 131

Richard I, d. of Normandy 45-6, 111, 175

Richard II, d. of Normandy 20, 131, 153, 155

Richard III, d. of Normandy 182

Richard, earl of Chester 12

Richard, son of William the Conqueror 132

Richard Goz, vicomte of the Avranchin 26

Richard of Heudicourt, monk of Saint-Evroult 76-7

Richard of Leicester, ab. of Saint-Evroult 40, 224

  previously canon of Leicester 75

Richard's Castle (Herefordshire) 4

Richer of L'Aigle 26, 51, 135

ritual 18, 60, 77, 79, 88-9

  of coronation 121, 139, 143, 144

  of knighthood 132, 143-4

Robert, deposed ab. of Saint-Pierre-sur-Dive 64

Robert, abp. of Rouen 131

Robert, bp. of Hereford 174

Robert, bp. of Langres 95

Robert, ct. of Eu 54

Robert I (the Magnificent), d. of Normandy 131, 182, 195

Robert II (Curthose), d. of Normandy 21, 24 n., 26, 27, 28, 31, 32, 34, 124, 128, 131, 139, 191, 192

  defended by Louis VI 199

  exiled 142

  a skilled archer 143

  his crusade 155, 189, 219

  his right of succession 176, 183, 184-5, 188-90

  at Alton 197-8

Robert I, earl of Leicester 23 n.

Robert, friend of William of Malmesbury 88

Robert, son of Baudry of Bocquencé 55

Robert, son of Giroie 21-2

Robert II, son of Robert I earl of Leicester 23 n.

Robert Bordet, lord of Tarragona 152, 205, 207-8

  his wife Sibyl 152

Robert Guiscard, d. of Apulia 51, 126

Robert of Arbrissel 83, 164

Robert of Bellême, son of Roger of Montgomery 24, 26, 28, 192

  punished by Henry I 191

  judgement in his court 119

Robert of Candos 211-12

Robert II of Grandmesnil, ab. of Saint-Evroult, later ab. of Sant' Eufemia 21, 51, 81, 102, 125

  trained for arms 75, 77

  at Cluny as a novice 61, 77

  as prior of Saint-Evroult 181

Robert III of Grandmesnil 31

Robert of Molesme 83

Robert of Prunelai, ab. of Thorney 36

  his noble birth 142

Robert of Saint-Céneri, son of Robert son of Giroie 21, 35

Robert of Rhuddlan 12

Robert of Tombelaine 80

  his commentary on the Song of Songs 93

Robert of Torigny 53, 174, 176, 217

  his treatise on the new orders 85, 218

Robert the Monk, monk of Saint-Rémi of Rheims 150

Robin Hood 212 n.

Roger I, ct. of Sicily 81, 142, 213

  opposes conversion of his Saracen troops 154, 155

  his daughter Emma 129

Roger, earl of Hereford 108, 192

Roger, son of Ralph of Tosny 195 n.

Roger de Lacy 4

Roger of Beaumont 26, 218

Roger of Le Sap, ab. of Saint-Evroult 17, 29–31, 36, 37, 55 n., 56, 75, 224
his retirement 86–7

Roger of Montgomery, earl of Shrewsbury, vicomte of the Hiémois (Exmes) 4, 5, 9 n., 16, 21, 22–3, 70, 127, 223
his household clerks 7–8

Roger of Warenne, monk of Saint-Evroult 15, 67

Roland 197, 204, 214 *and see chansons*

Rollo, Norman leader 45, 53 175

Rome 153
pilgrimage to 15, 16, 210
second Lateran Council (1139) at 40, 200–1
synods at (1050 and 1059) 162
Matilda said to have been crowned empress at 53

Romuald, St 61

Roncevaux 138

Rotrou I, ct. of Perche 25
his son *see* Geoffrey
his wife Adeline 25

Rotrou II, ct. of Perche, son of Geoffrey 25, 152

Rouen (Seine-Maritime) 28, 53
abp. of 31, 112 *and see* Geoffrey, John of Avranches, Maurilius, Robert, William Bonne-Âme
council of (1072) 130; (1096) 134–5; synod of (1119) 99
abbey of La Trinité-du-Mont 49, 75
abbey of St Ouen 58, 101, 176
cathedral 53, 54
province 58
Jews in 153, 154–6, 161
citizen of 211

Ruald, vassal of Saint-Evroult 105

Rupert of Deutz
on the monastic life 71–2
his *Commentary on St John* 96, 99

St Albans, abbey 80

Saint-Benoît-sur-Loire *see* Fleury

Saint-Bertin, abbey 100 n., 111

Saint-Céneri-le-Gérei (Orne)
castle of 21–2
Merovingian monastery at 22 n., 62
priory of Saint-Evroult at, 22

Saint-Denis, abbey 53, 64, 173

Saint-Evroult, Benedictine abbey 3, 9, 14 *et passim*
foundation and building 17–18, 21
its endowments 22–5, 34–5, 62–3, 136
its patrons and benefactors 152, 196, 202, 217–18 *and see* Giroie, Grandmesnil
its vassals 55–6, 105
abbey church dedicated 31–2, 186
chapel of St Évroul restored 81
liturgy of 87; customs of 67–8
Cluniac influence 61, 74, 85, 165 n.
prayer unions and fraternities 23 n., 34–5, 67–70, 211
cult of St Évroul at 101–6
its calendar 41
music composed at 100 n., 102
its school 75, 86 n.
its books 91, 157, 176, 179
biblical studies at 94–8
annals of 34
abbatial elections in 28–31
abbots of 126 *and see* Felix de Brie, Mainer, Osbern, Ralph, Richard of Leicester, Robert of Grandmesnil, Roger of Le Sap, Serlo of Orgères, Thierry of Mathonville, Warin of Les Essarts
monks of 35, 36, 38, 51, 74–8, 104 *et passim*
priories dependent on 49, 119 *and see* Auffay, Chapelle-en-Vexin, Maule, Moulins-la-Marche, Neufmarché, Noron, Noyon-sur-Andelle, Parnes, Saint-Céneri-le-Gerei, Ware

Saint-Evroult-Notre-Dame-du-Bois (Orne)
church of Notre-Dame-du-Bois 18
church of St Peter 18, 20
Merovingian monastery at 62, 63, 81, 101
township (rural *bourg*) of 18, 26, 40

Saint-Florent-près Saumur, abbey 50

Saint-Georges de Boscherville, priory 104

Saint-Germain-des-Prés, abbey 62

Saint-Germer de Fly, abbey 154, 157
monks of, 76, 78 *and see* Athelelm, Guibert of Nogent, William

Saint-Josse-sur-Mer, abbey 106
Saint-Pierre-sur-Dive, abbey
   ab. of 76 *and see* Robert
Saint-Valéry-sur-Somme (Somme) 183
Saint-Wandrille (Fontenelle), abbey 58,
   111
   monks of 49, 59
   multiple sanctuaries in 80
saints
   patron 9, 101, 110
   lives and miracles of 38, 77, 90, 99–
      109, 110, 172–5, 179, 204
      and see legends
Sallust 169, 171, 213
Samson of Cullei 56
Sant'Eufemia, abbey 51
   ab. of *see* Robert of Grandmesnil
Sarabites 84
Saracens 24, 146–52, 158, 161, 165,
   205–7
   in army of Count Roger 154, 155
Sarthe, river 20, 21
schism 159, 163, 165 *and see* heresy
schools
   monastic 18, 33, 56–7, 86, 90, 92,
      99, 171, 216 *and see* Bec-
      Hellouin, Saint-Evroult
   secular 90, 92, 96, 99, 171; in
      France and Normandy 8, 75,
      78, 81, 99, 175; in Italy 81,
      93; *see also* Laon, Liège,
      Rheims, Paris
Scotland 123, 152, 210
   kg. of *see* David, William the Lion
Sées 23, 52
   abbey of St Martin 16, 52
   archdeacon of 32
   bp. of *see* Ivo, Serlo
Sens 153
   abbey of Saint-Pierre-le-Vif 173;
      ab. of *see* Arnold
Serlo, son of Tancred of Hauteville 125
Serlo of Orgères, ab. of Saint-Evroult,
      bp. of Sées 28–9, 30–1, 75,
      224
Severn, river 10, 221
Sherborne, abbey 80
Shrewsbury 3–7, 11–13, 36, 221–2
   abbey of St Peter 6, 9 n., 10, 16,
      36, 70, 127, 223
   castle of 11
   earl of *see* Roger of Montgomery
   church of St Alkmund 6, 7

   church of St Chad 6
   church of St Peter 8, 10, 16, 222–
      3
   royal chapel of St. Mary 6
Shropshire 3, 4, 7, 12–16
Sibyl, daughter of Fulk ct. of Anjou
   130–1
Sicily 51, 54, 210
   ct. of *see* Roger
Sigebert of Gembloux
   his chronicle 36, 37, 172, 173, 174,
      209, 215, 219 n.
Simon of Montfort 131
   his wife Agnes 131
simony 7, 29 n., 64 n.; as heresy 163
Siward, lord of Frodesley 6
Siward, priest of St Peter's, Shrews-
      bury 10–11, 176, 223
slaves 12, 125 n.
Soissons, John ct. of 160
Spain, 25, 151–2, 210 *and see* crusade,
   Normans
Spirtes, priest 6
Squillace 51
squires 75, 119, 132, 140, 142
Staffordshire 14
Standard, battle of the 141 n.
Stephen, converted Jew 155
Stephen, kg. of England (1135–54)
      25, 26, 34, 41, 217, 221
   his claim to the throne 188–90,
      193, 200
Stephen, St, protomartyr 110, 155,
   158
Stephen Harding, ab. of Cîteaux 83
Suger, ab. of Saint-Denis 196 n.

Tancred of Hauteville 51, 125
Tarragona 152, 207
Theban legion 133
Theobald IV, count of Blois and Cham-
      pagne 189, 190
Theodechilde, queen 173, 175
theology, monastic 89, 94
Thierry of Mathonville, ab. of Saint-
      Evroult 52, 74–5, 78, 149,
      150, 181
   his colloquies 98
   Orderic's account of his life 109
Thomas, son of Ranulf Flambard 32
Thomas of Marle 24, 192
Thorney, abbey 36
   ab. of *see* Robert of Prunelai

Thucydides 169, 170, 178
Thurstan, ab. of Glastonbury 192
Thurstan Haldup 49
Tinchebray (Orne), battle of (1106)
140 n., 189, 190
tithes, given to monasteries 55, 63, 78,
84, 216; renounced by new
orders 83
Tombelaine, cell of Mont Saint-Michel
80
Toret of Wroxeter 6
Tosny, lords of 195 *and see* Ralph,
Roger
tournaments 133
Tours, synod at (1054) 162
Troarn, ab. of 30
Trogus Pompeius 169
Trojans 203
Troyes 153
Truce of God *see* peace

Ulger, bp. of Angers 201
Ulrich of Cluny 65
Urban II, pope 32, 148, 150
usurers 56, 104, 158
usury 84, 159, 202

Val-ès-Dunes, battle 118
Vaninge, St 111
Vendôme
abbey of La Trinité 50
county of 50
Venetians 106 n.
Venosa, abbey of La Trinità 107
Vercelli, synod at (1050) 162
Vergil 86, 203
Vexin 195
French 23, 27, 62, 77, 106, 118,
136
Vikings 45, 59, 109, 111, 118
visions 99, 108, 146, 155, 202
Vitalis, companion of St Maurice 223
Vitalis, founder and ab. of Savigny 83,
164
vivum gagum, form of loan 56

Wace 213, 217
his *Roman de Rou* 204
Walchelin, priest of Saint-Aubin de
Bonneval 99, 202
Waleran, ct. of Meulan 142, 203
Wales, Normans in 4, 5, 7, 12-13
Walter Map 120-1

Walter Tirel 143
Waltheof, earl of Northampton
his rebellion and execution 3, 108,
195
his cult at Crowland 108, 218
Wandrille, St 58, 111
miracles of 111
war *passim*
just 145, 147, 149, 166, 182
holy 139-40, 145, 147-8, 152,
165-6
as spiritual combat 15, 70, 71, 76,
132, 148, 150, 151, 165,
182
Ware (Herts.), priory of Saint-Evroult
at 23
Warin of Bellême 25
Warin of Les Essarts, ab. of Saint-
Evroult 23 n., 29, 37, 40,
75, 102, 224
his teaching 98
Warin of Sées, monk of Saint-Evroult
95, 98-9
Warin the Bald, sheriff of Shropshire 5
Wearmouth, monastery of 220
Wenlock, priory 13, 16
Wenlock Edge 13
Westminster
abbey 80
royal court at 144
White Ship 12, 183
Wibert of Ravenna, antipope 163
William, ct. of Eu 155
William, ct. of Évreux 128-9
William I, d. of Aquitaine 60
William IX, d. of Aquitaine 204
William Longsword, d. of Normandy 53
William I (the Conqueror), kg. of
England (1066-87), d. of
Normandy (1035-87) 4, 21,
23, 26, 50, 131, 176, 213
his control of Norman castles 47
his protection of Norman monasteries 20, 48
his wars on the Norman frontiers
22, 23, 25
his conquest of Maine 27
invades the Vexin 195
enforces the peace movement 118
his relations with Norman bishops
118
his influence on church elctions 61,
192

his claim to the English crown 183
his conquest of England 126-7, 139
results of his coronation 182-5
deliberate ravaging by 135, 185, 186, 195
his court 75, 195
his household knights 47
makes his sons knights 144
death-bed speech attributed to 184-6, 218
his death 24
his funeral 124
his sons *see* Henry I, Richard, Robert Curthose, William II
his wife *see* Matilda
William II (Rufus), kg. of England (1087-1100) 34, 124, 143, 149, 190
 invested as a knight 44 n.
 crowned king 185, 187
 his wars in Normandy 28, 195
 governs Normandy during the absence of Robert Curthose 31, 189
 protects Jews in Rouen 153-4
 holds Le Mans 138-9
 acts tyrannically 192
 his household knights 135-6
 his death 193, 219
William, monk of Saint-Evroult 75
William, monk of Saint-Germer 154
William, son of Arnold of Échauffour, grandson of William Giroie 21
William, son of Henry I 131, 183
William Bonne-Âme, abp. of Rouen 33, 224
William Clito, son of Robert Curthose, ct. of Flanders 38, 183, 188; his marriage prevented 130-1
William fitz Osbern, earl of Hereford 4
William Giroie, son of Giroie 20-1, 26 becomes a monk at Bec-Hellouin 76
William Gregory, monk of Saint-Evroult 75
William I of Bellême 25
William of Breteuil 26, 31, 129, 195 n.
 his steward 56 n., 202
William of Gellone, St 15, 66, 208
William of Glos, steward of William of Breteuil 56 n., 202
William of Jumièges

his *Gesta Normannorum Ducum* 176, 213-14, 219 n.; continuations of 215; interpolated by Orderic Vitalis 34, 176-7; interpolated by Robert of Torigny 176
William of Malmesbury 129, 138, 144, 179, 204; oblate monk 76
 his *Gesta regum* 39, 170-1, 219
 his *Gesta pontificum* 108, 219
 his *Historia novella* 40
 his *Abbreviatio Amalarii* 88-9, 94
 his *Miracles of the Virgin* 160
 his *History of Glastonbury* 219
 his Commentary on Lamentations 94
 his theological work 40
 on the English church 7
 on Robert of Bellême 24
 admires Henry I 196 n.
 on the new monastic orders 83
 on the Vexin war 195
 his attitude to the Jews 155
 on the witch of Berkeley 201
William of Merlerault, monk of Saint-Evroult 95, 106
 his homilies 157-8
William of Montreuil, son of William Giroie 21
William of Moulins-la-Marche 25
 his wife Aubrey 125
William of Poitiers 183, 184, 185
William of Rots, dean of Bayeux, ab. of Fécamp 17
William of Roumare 211
William of Volpiano, ab. of Dijon, ab. of Fécamp 46, 49, 60-1, 112
William Pantulf 5, 14-15, 106
William Talvas of Bellême 20, 22
 his son Arnold 22
William the Lion, kg. of Scotland 140 n.
William Vallin, monk of Saint-Evroult 220
Winchester 189
 council of (1076) 9
Worcester 36-7
 cathedral priory of 13, 36, 80; chronicle written in 36, 174, 175
Wrockwardine (Shropshire) 8
Wulfram, St 111

Yorkshire 185